Language and gender

Language and gender:
Interdisciplinary perspectives

Edited by Sara Mills

LONGMAN
LONDON AND NEW YORK

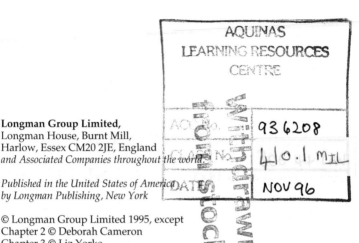
Longman Group Limited,
Longman House, Burnt Mill,
Harlow, Essex CM20 2JE, England
and Associated Companies throughout the world

Published in the United States of America
by Longman Publishing, New York

© Longman Group Limited 1995, except
Chapter 2 © Deborah Cameron
Chapter 3 © Liz Yorke
Chapter 4 © Margaret Williamson

First published 1995

ISBN 0 582 226317 PPR

British Library Cataloguing-in-Publication Data
A catalogue record for this book is available from the British Library

Library of Congress Cataloging-in-Publication Data
Language and gender : interdisciplinary perspectives / edited by
    Sara Mills.
        p.   cm.
    Includes bibliographical references and index.
    ISBN 0–582–22631–7 (ppr)
    1. Language and languages—Sex differences.   I. Mills, Sara.
1954–
P120.S48L34   1995   95–12460
306.4'4—dc20   CIP

Set by 8 in 10/12pt Palatino
Produced through Longman Malaysia, PP

To Tony and Gabriel

Contents

List of Contributors

Farida Abu-Haidar is a sociolinguist specialising in gender and language and feminist literature. She has written extensively on Arabic linguistics: *A Study of the Spoken Arabic of Baskinta (Lebanon)* (1979) and *Christian Arabic of Baghdad* (1991). She has lectured on Arabic sociolinguistics at various institutions. She is currently working on language maintenance and shift among native speakers of Arabic in Britain and France.

Cleopatra Altani gained her PhD from the University of Lancaster in 1992. Her research interests are the construction of gender in classroom interaction and gender issues in the Greek education system.

Carmen Rosa Caldas-Coulthard is Professor of English Language and Linguistics in the Graduate School of English at the Federal University of Santa Caterina, Brazil. She has a PhD from the University of Birmingham. She is interested in the connection between language and social practice and is currently researching Brazilian women's magazines. Her most recent publications are: the edited collection *Traducao: Teoria e Pratica* and contributions to *Techniques of Description* and *Advances in Written Text Analysis*. She is currently working on an edited book, *Texts and Practices: Readings in Critical Discourse Analysis*.

Deborah Cameron is Senior Lecturer in the Programme in Literary Linguistics at Strathclyde University, Glasgow. She has researched and published widely in the fields of language and gender studies and sociolinguistics. Her recent work includes *Feminism and Linguistic Theory* (2nd edition, 1992) and *Researching Language* (with E. Frazer, P. Harvey, M. Rampton and K. Richardson, 1992). She is co-editor, with Jennifer Coates, of the collection *Women in their Speech Communities* (1989).

Jennifer Coates is Professor of English Language and Linguistics at Roehampton Institute, London. Her published work includes

Women, Men and Language (2nd edition, 1993) and *Women in their Speech Communities* (1989) (co-edited with Deborah Cameron). She is currently working on a new book, *Women Talking to Women*, which is an account of her long-term research project on the talk of single-sex friendship groups.

Barbara Crowther lectures in media and cultural studies, communication, and women's writing in the Women's Studies Department at the University of Wolverhampton. Her essay, written with Dick Leith, is part of a larger project on gender representation in popular science. She is also working on a study of girls' diary-writing.

David Graddol is a lecturer in the Centre for Language and Communications at the Open University, where his work includes the production of multi-media in-service materials for teachers as well as distance-learning materials in linguistics. He has co-authored with Joan Swann *Gender Voices* (1989) and *Evaluating Language* (1994), and with Jenny Cheshire, *Describing Language* (2nd edition, 1994), and he has co-edited with Boyd-Barret, *Media Texts: Authors and Readers* (1994), and with Maybin and Stierer, *Researching Language and Literacy in Social Context* (1994), and with Thompson and Byram, *Language and Culture* (1993).

Nigel Hewlett is a lecturer in the Department of Speech and Language Sciences, Queen Margaret College, Edinburgh. He has published articles and reviews on disorders of speech production and is currently researching speech development in children and models of speech production and development.

Helen Hills, disillusioned by the inadequate resources for funding Art History in most British universities, left her post as Lecturer in Art History at Keele University in 1993 and moved to the Department of Art at the University of North Carolina at Chapel Hill, where she is Assistant Professor of Art History. In all ways she has found the move to be extremely stimulating. She has published on iconography and ideology in 17th-century Palermo, and her book on marble decoration in 17th-century Sicilian churches, *Marmi Mischi Siciliani*, is to be published in 1995.

Alison Lee qualified with a BSc MCSLT from Queen Margaret College, Edinburgh, in 1991. She now works in the Dryburn Hospital in Durham, where she specializes in neurological disorders; she has a special interest in dysphagia [swallowing disorders].

Dick Leith taught linguistics at Birmingham Polytechnic until 1990. Since then he has been a freelance academic and is presently working as a consultant at the Open University. He has co-written (with

George Myerson) *The Power of Address: Explorations in Rhetoric* (1989) and is currently revising and enlarging his *Social History of English*. He is also working on a book about the language of orally narrated Scottish folktales.

Elisabeth Mahoney is a Fellow of the Department of English at Aberdeen University. She has written a doctoral thesis on the feminist dystopia, focussing on contemporary texts and feminist theory. Her current research is for an interdisciplinary project on gender and city representations in the 20th century. She has edited Austen's *Northanger Abbey* (1994), and is engaged in work on an edition of Hardy's *A Pair of Blue Eyes* (forthcoming).

Sara Mills is Research Professor in English at Sheffield Hallam University. She has co-written: *Feminist Readings/Feminists Reading* (Harvester, 1989) and *Ways of Reading* (Routledge, 1992); and she has written: *Discourses of Difference: Women's Travel Writing and Colonialism* (Routledge, 1992). She has edited: *Gendering the Reader* (1994) and she is currently working on *Feminist Stylistics* (forthcoming) and *Discourse Theory* (forthcoming).

Moray Nairn is a research student in the Department of Speech and Language Sciences, Queen Margaret College, Edinburgh. His research interests are gender differences and practical and instrumental phonetics and he has published articles on the effect of context on the transcription of vowel quality.

Jane Sunderland is currently researching a PhD on 'Learner gender in the modern foreign language classroom' in the Linguistics Department, Lancaster University. She also teaches on language and gender and other courses at Lancaster. Her most recent publication is *Exploring Gender: Questions and Implications for English Language Education* (1994).

Joan Swann is a lecturer in the Centre for Language and Communications at the Open University. Her work involves the production of distance-learning materials as well as in-service courses and packs for teachers. Books co-authored with David Gradoll include *Gender Voices* (1989), *Evaluating Language* (1994); with Jenny Cheshire: *Describing Language* (2nd edition 1994). Other books include: *Girls, Boys and Language* (1992) and, with Claire and Maybin (eds.): *Equality Matters: Case Studies from the Primary School* (1993).

Debs Tyler-Bennett works in the Department of English, Sheffield Hallam University, where she lectures in 19th- and 20th-century literature and contemporary writing. She has published both critical works and poetry. Her most recent publication is an article on Djuna Barnes, in G. Griffin (ed.), *Women and Modernism: Difference in View* (1994). She has published poems in *Writing Women*, *Feminist Review*, *Scarlet Women* and *Poets '94*. She is currently researching the poetic career of Edith Sitwell.

Margaret Williamson is Senior Lecturer in Classical Studies at St Mary's College, University of Surrey. She has written on various aspects of Greek literature and has assisted with translations of Greek tragedy for the stage. She is author of *Sappho's Immortal Daughters* (forthcoming from Virago Press, 1995).

Jenny Wolmark is Senior Lecturer in Theoretical Studies in the School of Art and Design at the University of Humberside. She is author of *Aliens and Others: Science Fiction, Feminism and Postmodernism* (Harvester Wheatsheaf, 1994) and articles on feminism and science fiction.

Liz Yorke is a Counsellor at Nottingham Trent University. Before that, she taught women's writing in the Department of English and History at Manchester Metropolitan University, where she worked for her doctorate. She is the author of *Impertinent Voices: Subversive Strategies in Contemporary Women's Poetry* (1991), and is currently working on a study of the poetry and prose of Adrienne Rich.

Acknowledgements

We are grateful to the following for permission to reproduce copyright material:

William L. Rukeyser for 'Despisals' and 'The Poem as Mask' by Muriel Rukeyser from *A Muriel Rukeyser Reader*, 1994, W.W. Norton, NY, NY, © William L. Rukeyser, 'What do I Give You' from *Collected Poems*, 1973, McGraw-Hill, NY, NY, © Muriel Rukeyser, by permission of William L. Rukeyser; Carcanet and New Directions Publishing Corporation for 'Hymen' from H.D., *Collected Poems 1912–1944* © 1982 by the Estate of Hilda doolittle. International Thomson Publishing Services (Routledge) for the essay by Liz Yorke entitled 'Constructing a Lesbian Poetic for Survival: Lorde, Rich, Rukeyser, H.D., Broumas' published in *Sexual Sameness: Textual Difference in Lesbian and Gay Writing*, 1992; The Authors League Fund as executors of the Estate of Djuna Barnes, 330 W. 42nd Street, NY, NY for lines from *Ladies Almanack*; Manchester University Press for extracts from Maggie Humm's *Border Traffic*; Harvester Wheatsheaf, Hemel Hempstead, for chapter 6 'Cyborgs and cyberpunk: rewriting the feminine in popular fiction', being an earlier version of 'Cyberpunk, cyborgs and femanist science fiction' in Jenny Wolmark (1993) *Aliens and Others, Science Fiction, Feminism and postmodernism*, Hemel Hempstead, Harvester Wheatsheaf; Ydessa Hendeles Collection for Figure 15.1; the Artist Barbara Kruger and the Mary Boone Gallery, New York for Figure 15.2 "Untitled" (You are not yourself) 55" by 48" photograph 1983 Collection; Edward R. Downe, Jr., New York, Courtesy: Mary Boone Gallery, New York, also Figure 15.3 "Untitled" (We have received orders not to move) 72" by 48" photograph 1983 Collection: Private Collection, Courtesy: Mary Boone Gallery, New York and Figure 15.4 "Untitled" (Your gaze hits the side of my face) 55" by 41" photograph 1982 Collection: Vijak Mahdavi and

Bernardo Nadal-Ginard, Boston, Courtesy: Mary Boone Gallery, New York; Barbara Gladstone Gallery, New York for the image Kassell Wall, Times Square Sign by Jenny Holzer. Selections from *Greek Lyric I* from the Loeb Classical Library reprinted by permission of the publishers and the Loeb Classical Library from Sappho Nos. 16, 22, 31 and 96 *Greek Lyric I* translated by D.A. Campbell, Cambridge, Mass.: Harvard University Press, 1982 and selection from *Greek Lyric II* from the Loeb Classical Library reprinted by permission of the publishers and the Loeb Classical Library from Anackeon No. 358 *Greek Lyric II* translated by D.A. Campbell, Cambridge, Mass.: Harvard University Press, 1988.

Whilst every effort has been made to trace the owners of copyright material, in a few cases this has proved impossible and we take this opportunity to offer our apologies to any copyright holders whose rights we may have unwittingly infringed.

Introduction

Sara Mills

This book developed from debates and discussions arising from papers which were originally presented at the Language and Gender conference held at Loughborough University in May 1992. The essays in this edition are a selection of the papers which were presented at the conference: they have been significantly revised in the light of recent research and also in the light of debates at the conference and since. The essays reflect some of the diverse facets of the complex interrelationship of the terms 'language' and 'gender'.

The conference itself was structured around a number of themes which were considered to be crucial to the analysis of the relationship between gender and language in current theoretical debates across disciplines, and this is reflected in the structure of this book. The first section is concerned with the theoretical distinction between difference and dominance theorists; the essays in the section on lesbian poetics consider the way that lesbian writers structure their texts in relation to the mainstream; the section on gender/genre examines the relationship between language and the production of texts within specific generic boundaries; the sections on gender, language and education and on gender, language and children both consider the ways in which gender identities are constructed and negotiated through an intense process of socialisation; and the final section on language, media/visual analysis and gender considers the analysis of non-literary texts and gender. Thus, rather than simply structuring the conference and the book on disciplinary lines, it was felt to be more productive to traverse boundaries by using themes as the principal form of organisation. The resulting essays are necessarily diverse and in many ways that is their strength. Some of the essays draw explicitly on empirical work and others are focussed on textual/visual analysis. This diversity of focus and methodology leads to a defamiliarisation of the ways that research is undertaken in language and gender studies. The conference was interdisciplinary, drawing on work within literary studies, linguistics (especially sociolinguistics and EFL), cultural/media studies, art history, education and psychology. The essays in this book are interventions into current theoretical debates within these subject areas, but each of the essays attempts to speak across those disciplinary barriers. One of the most important features of feminist work is the fact that it has always attempted to be interdisciplinary, since feminists have had to research outside their field in trying to answer questions which could not be, or were not being, addressed within the mainstream. Cooperation with feminist colleagues from other departments and disciplines has always been an integral part of women's studies courses, but this cooperation and sharing has not always been easy. At the conference itself it was clear that many participants had a feeling of speaking different languages to those of the speakers and much of the debate focussed on this sense of defining and redefining what we meant. This book aims to consolidate those dialogues, arguments and debates across disciplines, following in the tradition of this type of work in earlier books on feminism and language (McConnell-Ginet *et al.* 1980).

LANGUAGE AND GENDER

The two terms of the title of this book are equally problematic in isolation and even more so when they are brought into conjunction. Language is a problematic term, especially in interdisciplinary contexts such as this, since within each discipline the object of analysis is necessarily different – language for a psychologist is very different from language for a psychoanalyst. It is clear from many of the essays in this book that the term 'language' is being used in very different ways. For example, Alison Lee *et al.*, in their essay on children's speech, see language as a series of sounds which may disclose gender identity: language here is more like an arena where 'symptoms' can be disclosed. For Liz Yorke, in her essay on lesbian poets, language is a series of institutionalised constraints within which women writers negotiate their meanings. For Helen Hills, in her essay on language used by experimental women artists, language is a site of contestation and necessary ambiguity. For Joan Swann and David Graddol, in their essay on the feminisation of language in the classroom, language is seen as an array of speech styles, some of which are valorised. This book is an attempt to achieve some form of translation of the term 'language' across disciplinary boundaries, however difficult that task. Translation does not entail a dulling of the precision of the meanings of the term 'language' within their disciplinary contexts; it is not the intention of this collection to develop a unitary definition of 'language'. Rather, it is hoped that each of the meanings of 'language' will interact with each other when juxtaposed and indicate other possible areas of research.

'Gender' is also a term which these essays approach from different perspectives. In recent years there has been intense debate about the possible definitions of the term 'gender'. Early feminist work on language focussed almost exclusively on analysis of women's language (Spender 1980; Lakoff 1975). Some feminists have argued that 'gender' is a term which erases the political edge of feminism, and indeed this has been the case in some work in this area, most notably Elaine Showalter's collection, *Speaking of Gender* (1989). Feminists such as Tanya Modleski have been anxious that using the term 'gender' entails treating males and females as if they had the same political power, rights, upbringing, access to education and so on (Modleski 1991). Rather than focussing on women as objects of analysis, as has been the case in women's studies courses, it is feared that this move towards the analysis of gender will bring about a return to the status quo, where women are treated as a marginal group once more. Modleski states that a focus on gender almost inevitably leads to a focus on men and heterosexuality, even when the debates seem to be about a male identity 'in crisis'. She says: 'however much a male subjectivity may currently be in crisis ... we need to consider the extent to which male power is actually consolidated through cycles of crisis and resolution, whereby men ultimately deal with the threat of female power by incorporating it' (Modleski 1991: 7). For such feminists, the term 'gender' simply allows for all of the gains brought about through feminist work, which have demonstrated the ways in which women and men have been treated differently and oppressively, to be lost. However, other feminists have argued that 'gender' is an enabling term which allows for the analysis of difference – by this I mean that sexual difference is not considered as a given whereby all males are classified as sharing certain characteristics which are opposed to the characteristics supposedly shared by all women. Instead, women are viewed less as a fixed, homogeneous caste than as a grouping of people intersected and acted upon by other variables and elements, such as class, race, age, sexual orientations, education and so on. Thus, these factors of difference within sexual difference can be analysed, without having to prioritise them over sexual difference and without having to erase them, as frequently happened in early feminist work. The *Journal of Gender Studies* contains examples of some of the work which has been undertaken on gender which does not entail a prioritisation of focus on males. Sexual difference is considered relationally rather than essentially; so that, when discussing the nature of femininity, it is only possible to do so in relation to other forms of sexual identity, such as masculinity. Similarly, this view of gender attempts to be specific about factors such as sexual orientation (for straights, gays and bisexuals), race (for both black, white and mixed race) and class (for all class positions). The essays in this book argue that the term 'gender' can be usefully employed so that the differences within sexual groupings can be considered, at the same time as retaining the categories male, female, gay, straight and so on as indicators of distinctive oppressions and resistances within language.

Much of this new work on gender has been informed by the work of Judith Butler and Diana Fuss (Butler 1990; Fuss 1989). This challenging work has questioned the seemingly self-evident nature of sexual difference, and has thrown into disarray work by both constructionists (those who think that sexual difference is constructed by society and culture) and essentialists (those who think that sexual difference is based on biological difference). Fuss states for example that 'what is risky is giving up the security – and the fantasy – of occupying a single subject position' (Fuss 1989: 19). Fuss attempts to destabilise the category 'woman', arguing that it is impossible to justify the category's boundaries as we cannot base it on essence (not all women share the same characteristics), nor on experience (women do not share a single experience). As she states: 'Can we ever speak . . . simply of the female . . . or the male . . . as if these categories were not transgressed already, not already constituted by other axes of difference (class, culture, nationality, ethnicity . . .)?' (Fuss 1989: 28). Modleski cautions against the move towards emptying the terms 'male' and 'female' of their meaning; she states that this move 'can mean the triumph either of a male feminist perspective that excludes women or of a feminist anti-essentialism so radical that every use of the term "woman" however "provisionally" it is adopted is disallowed' (Modleski 1991: 15). This is not the aim of this collection of essays. Changing the focus from feminist analysis of women's language to feminist analysis of gender and language does not in any way mean that the feminist nature of our research is tempered or muted; work on gender is obviously and necessarily informed by an awareness of the power differences involved in gender differences. The contributors to this collection will be using the term 'gender' to refer to an analysis which is concerned with the interactions of power, the process of production, consolidation and resistance to sexual identity – a process in which language is of prime importance. The contributors to this collection are female and male and all of them locate their work within a feminist framework; some of them focus on women's language and some of them on men's language, but it is with a focus on the relation between those terms, 'male–female', and on the difficulty of coming to a definition of either of the terms, that each of these essays has been written.

The first section of essays consists of interventions by Jennifer Coates and Deborah Cameron. These two essays embody different approaches to the analysis of gender and language and aim to survey the state of current research from these different perspectives. Coates' essay, 'Language, gender and career', situates itself largely within theoretical work focussing on difference, that is, within a concern with the way that females and males grow up within gendered subcultures (Maltz and Borker 1982). She argues that women and men speak differently, tending to use cooperative and competitive speech styles respectively. She goes on to argue that women and men are still largely segregated into the private and the public sphere and that this division results in language differences, and differences in attitude to women's and men's speech. Coates argues for a revision of the so-called 'weak' characteristics of women's cooperative strategies in speech and analyses the way that women are judged if they use competitive strategies in their work in the public sphere. Deborah Cameron's essay, 'Rethinking language and gender studies: feminism into the nineties', surveys the current popularisation of feminist linguistics, primarily with the publication of Deborah Tannen's book *You Just Don't Understand* (1990). Cameron surveys the main models of feminist linguistics work: difference, deficit and dominance, and she argues that the difference model of feminist linguistics, that is, one that argues that men and women simply speak differently because of their different upbringing, is at present the most popular. She questions the use of such a model when there are power differences which inform sexual difference, but she does not suggest that the dominance model is one that should be adopted instead. Rather she argues that these theories entail a view of gendered subjectivity as achieved. Instead of this reified view of sexual difference, she argues that we need to see subjectivity as a process which is always being negotiated.

In Section 2, the essays consider the difference that sexual orientation makes – here focussing on lesbianism, but by implication, forcing the reader to consider heterosexuality as a choice in sexual orientation. The essays foreground the fact that most of the discourses within which we write are primarily male, white and heterosexual; in order to claim a space for lesbians it is necessary firstly to demarcate the space as one which silences or denigrates lesbians. The essays consider the *difference* of lesbian writing and its implications for gender ascription and expression of desire, together with the difficult and also productive relation lesbian writing has to 'mainstream writing'. Liz Yorke, in her essay 'Constructing a lesbian poetic for survival', considers the choices that writers who are lesbian have to make, when they are faced with silence and silencing within dominant discourses. She examines the work of Broumas, Ruykeyser, H.D., Rich and Lorde in order to analyse the different strategies that lesbian poets adopt in order to negotiate a lesbian poetic, a lesbian language. She argues that the lesbian can and does challenge patriarchal definitions of herself, within language, in transformed terms. In this essay she argues that these lesbian poets use the language of poetry to re-present lesbian libidinal difference, sexual identity and lifestyle – in their own terms. Margaret Williamson, in her essay 'Sappho and the other woman', compares Sappho with a male poet, Anacreon, in order to attempt to map out the difference of being a woman writer. She argues that within Sappho's fragmentary verse, there is a shifting of speaking voices and subject position which is not found within contemporary male-authored verse. The range of voices, speaking positions and self–other relationships in the expression of desire is far wider and more subtly modulated, in contrast to the repeated and clear-cut pattern of erotic domination found in male-authored verse. Instead of the sharply demarcated subject–object positions found in Anacreon, there is a circulation of desire through constantly shifting and eliding subject positions. Sappho's poetry shares some elements with Luce Irigaray's 'parler femme', raising questions about whether and how French feminist thought can be used to elucidate writing from this early period. Debs Tyler-Bennett's essay, '"Her wench of bliss": gender and the language of Djuna Barnes' *The Ladies Almanac'* does not represent a close linguistic study of Barnes' work, but rather considers the way in which the text engages with verbal stereotypes and subverts and explores older verbal forms, such as ballads, almanacs and chapbooks. In engaging with the almanac form, Barnes both reworked and rewrote that form. By doing so, Tyler-Bennett argues, she was writing into the past and writing a lesbian past, through the use of pastiche. These essays thus attempt to consider the way that lesbian women writers negotiate with the language constraints in literary writing.

In Section 3, 'Gender/genre', the essays focus on the way that genre categorisation and the rules of the genres themselves tend to correlate with gender difference. Some genres are especially masculinist, for example, science fiction, where focalisation and subject matter are frequently from a masculine, heterosexual perspective. Language used in science fiction thus has to be transgressed by women writers, and as Jenny Wolmark shows in her essay 'Cyborgs and cyberpunk: rewriting the feminine in popular fiction', science fiction written by women makes explicit cross-references to other genres and is characterised by unresolvable narrative dilemmas. Wolmark shows that feminist writers have had a significant influence on male writing in the use of the cyborg – a form of interface between human and machine, one which can replace the opposition between nature and culture and other binary oppositions. Cybernetics and cyberpunk provide a radical context in which feminist writers can explore the potentialities of the disintegration of the unitary self. In Elisabeth Mahoney's essay 'Claiming the speakwrite: linguistic subversion in the feminist dystopia', there is a focus on those texts by women, particularly Suzette Haden Elgin's *Native Tongue*, which specifically suggest linguistic subversion as a means of ending women's oppression. In these feminist texts, there is a concentration on language, to the extent of including dictionaries and texts in newly formulated women's languages. These texts suggest that it is through fundamental changes in language and narration that women can gain control over their lives and bodies. Mahoney attempts to view these efforts to formulate women's languages as not simple idealism, as has often been claimed, but in fact as a problematising of the notion of a sharing of a common women's language.

The essays in Section 4 consider the relation between the terms 'gender', 'language' and 'education'. These essays consider the way that gender identity is negotiated and consolidated within the school context. Each essay questions the characterisation of gender as a simple category; the essays focus instead on the process whereby gender identity and certain valorised styles of speech and behaviour are imbricated. Joan Swann and David Graddol, in their essay 'Feminising classroom talk?', examine the shift towards the examination of oracy in schools, which may favour girls. They argue that boys have been favoured in the public domain of speech, but that this new focus of attention on oracy and collaborative talk may lead to a 'feminisation' of classroom talk, where the styles of speech more normally associated with girls may be valued highly. However, although this move towards feminisation of classroom discourse may seem to indicate that girls' language skills will be valorised, Swann and Graddol note that girls may not be accorded the same level of positive evaluation as boys when using collaborative speech. Cleopatra Altani, in her essay 'Primary school teachers' explanations of boys' disruptiveness in the classroom', considers the way that some teachers try to justify their own sex-preferential behaviour. Taking as given the fact that teachers do favour boys and concentrate more on responding to them than to girls, Altani compares the types of ideological frameworks which inform teachers' explanations of their concentration on dealing with boys in classrooms. Jane Sunderland, in her essay '"We're boys miss!" Finding gendered identities and looking for gendering of identities', examines the way that in the foreign-language classroom, female students may be prepared to play with gender identity, whereas boys are more rigidly located within their own masculine identity role. This focus on the flexibility of girls' gender identity forces us to recognise that gender identity is a very different process for girls and boys.

Continuing this concern with the processes whereby children assume gendered identity through language, in Section Five, 'Gender, language and children', Farida Abu-Haidar examines the way that children in rural Lebanese communities produce sex-differentiated language behaviour. Drawing on social-network theory, she examines the way that boys display dominance in mixed-sex communication in marked contrast to the girls' behaviour. Abu-Haidar also notes that this display of dominance seems to entail a lack of communicative competence on the part of the boys. Rather than focussing on the needs of their interlocutors, the boys direct the topic of the conversations to themselves and their own needs. Abu-Haidar considers some of the factors which have led to the development of this speech style. Alison Lee, Nigel Hewlett and Moray Nairn investigate whether it is possible to distinguish between pre-adolescent boys and girls from hearing their voices. They describe a study which they undertook to test out whether a perceptual difference exists between boys' and girls' voices and whether this difference is based in speech production.

The essays in Section 6, 'Language, media/visual analysis and gender', focus on non-literary texts and visual texts for the analysis of language and gender. Barbara Crowther and Dick Leith, in their essay 'Feminism, language and the rhetoric of TV wildlife programmes', investigate the way that both visual and verbal discursive practices can be analysed when examining the rhetoric of television wildlife programmes. In this way it is possible to investigate the gendering of the television audience and the way that this is achieved through specific verbal and visual choices. They also examine the way that gender makes an effect on choices at the level of narration. Carmen Rosa Caldas-Coulthard, in 'Man in the news: the misrepresentation of women speaking in news-as-narrative discourse' examines the notion of accessed voices, that is, who is given voice within the news. She notices that women's voices are generally not represented both at the level of what is represented and at the level of whose speech is represented. This linguistic choice has profound effects on the audience and the evaluation of women in the public sphere. In 'Commonplaces: the woman in the street: text and image in the work of Jenny Holzer and Barbara Kruger', Helen Hills examines the way that the artists Kruger and Holzer play with representation practices in order to mount a critique of gender identity. Like the essays in the section on lesbian identity, Hills investigates the way that through irony and parody, women artists can attempt to undermine the representational practices within which they work. Both artists work explicitly with gender identity and both of them play with the juxtaposition of texts and images. Hills questions the assumption that their work is necessarily a simple and easy critique and considers the potential dangers of ambiguity.

These intersecting and interrogating approaches to the analysis of gender and language constitute an attempt to see the issue from outwith our disciplinary boundaries and to inform our theoretical perspectives with insights from other disciplines. In the process of reading this collection, it is hoped that the seemingly self-evident and unitary meanings of both terms 'language' and 'gender' will be destabilised, so that we have available to us a range of meanings and a range of areas of future research.

POSITION PAPERS: DIFFERENCE OR DOMINANCE

ONE

Language, gender and career[1]

Jennifer Coates

1 INTRODUCTION

In this paper, I want to argue that gender-differentiated language use may play a significant role in the continued marginalisation of women in the professions, particularly in terms of career progess and development. It is now widely accepted that women and men talk differently, that is, that women and men make differential use of the linguistic resources available to them (Thorne and Henley 1975; Thorne, Kramarae and Henley 1983; Coates 1986; Graddol and Swann 1989). There is a great deal of evidence to suggest that male speakers are socialised into a competitive style of discourse, while women are socialised into a more cooperative style of speech (Kalcik 1975; Aries 1976; Coates 1989, 1991, forthcoming). Maltz and Borker (1982), using an ethnographic approach, argue that same-sex play in childhood leads to girls and boys internalising different conversational rules, with boys developing adversarial speech, and girls developing a style characterised by collaboration and affiliation. Support for such a distinction comes from more psychologically oriented research on gender identity and moral development (Gilligan 1982; Gilligan et al. 1988) and on gender differences in epistemological development (Belenky et al. 1988), which characterises the feminine orientation as focussing on the relationship, on connection, and the masculine orientation as focussing on the self, on separateness.

In public life, it is the discourse patterns of male speakers, the dominant group in public life, which have become the established norm. The isomorphism of male discourse patterns and public discourse patterns is the result of the split between public and private spheres; it was at the beginning of the last century that the division between public and private became highly demarcated in Britain. This demarcation involved the exclusion of women from the public world. In other worlds, in the early nineteenth-century, patterns of gender division changed: 'men were firmly placed in the newly defined public world of business, commerce and politics; women were placed in the private world of home and family' (Hall 1985: 12).

One significant consequence of the gendered nature of the pub-lic–private divide is that the discourse styles typical of, and considered appropriate for, activities in the public domain have been established by men. Thus women are linguistically at a double disadvantage when entering the public domain: first, they are (nor-mally) less skilful at using the adversarial, information-focused style expected in such contexts; second, the (more cooperative) dis-course styles which they *are* fluent in are negatively valued in such contexts.

As women start to enter the professions in greater numbers, there are calls for women to adapt to the linguistic norms of the public domain. A commentator writing in the *Independent* (20 December 1990) criticises women for not 'fighting back' in public debate; she argues: 'If women genuinely want to succeed in these [public] spheres, they can learn to hold their own. And learn they must if they wish to have a voice' (Daley 1990). The possibility that adver-sarial talk might not always be the most appropriate or effective does not cross this writer's mind; if women want to succeed in the public domain, then women will have to change. This view is endorsed by women who have themselves been successful in the public domain. In a forceful article in the *Daily Telegraph*, Mary Warnock (Mistress of Girton College and ex-chair of the Warnock Committee) is highly critical of women's behaviour on committees. 'I wonder whether women themselves realise quite how bad they can be as members of boards' (Warnock 1987). She lists what she sees as women's shortcomings, such as their proneness 'to think they are entitled to make fey, irrelevant, "concerned" interventions' and 'to disregard economic considerations for "human" ones'. She goes on:

> If I were the chairman [*sic*] of a great company, I should be very chary indeed of having one of these old-style wreckers, non-conformists, exponents of the free flow of ideas, on my board. The days of the whimsical and the wayward are over. Addressing the chair is not a

stuffy man's rule to be disregarded by the charming lady-member, but part of the disciplined professionalism that makes the board or committee workable.

She urges women 'to adapt to what is required', implicitly accepting the male-dominated discourse patterns of conventional committee meetings.

Women who succeed in adopting a more competitive discourse style in public meet other problems. Jeanne Kirkpatrick, former US ambassador to the UN, describes the dilemma faced by women in high positions, where there is a clash between gender and work identities. 'There is a certain level of office the very occupancy of which constitutes a confrontation with conventional expectations . . . Terms like "tough" and "confrontational" express a certain general surprise and disapproval at the presence of a woman in arenas in which it is necessary to be – what for males would be considered – normally assertive' (Kirkpatrick, quoted in Campbell and Jerry 1988). In other words, women are in a double-bind: they are urged to adopt more assertive, more masculine styles of discourse in the public sphere, but when they do so, they are perceived as aggressive and confrontational.

In contrast with this, a different point of view is now starting to be heard, a point of view which emphasises the *positive* aspects of women's communicative style. There is space here for only three examples. A female environmental engineer working for the Bonneville Power Administration of Portland, Oregon, claims: 'As a woman, you can communicate in a different way which is helpful in a sphere usually analytical' (quoted in Barker 1988). Carol Tongue, talking about her work as MEP for London East, contrasts 'the friendly and supportive meetings of the women's committee' of the European Parliament with 'the all-male environment of industrial affairs', another committee she serves on (quoted in Lovenduski 1989). The writer Jill Hyems, interviewed for Channel 4 (*Ordinary People*, 6 February 1990) expressed a preference for working with female producers and directors 'because there are a lot of short cuts, one's speaking the same language'.

These conflicting views are indicative of the lack of consensus and the social confusion about women's role in the public arena. The long struggle to give women equal access to professions and to careers is now giving way to the struggle over whether women have to adapt to androcentric working practices. Victory in terms of equal opportunities may turn out to be pyrrhic as we come to recognise that the price demanded by the dominant group is acceptance of dominant-group norms.

2 THE LANGUAGE OF THE PROFESSIONS

In this section, I want to examine in greater detail the language used in the public domain. The talk which takes place between professionals and clients, such as doctor–patient talk or teacher–pupil talk, can be seen as prototypical professional discourse. The distinguishing feature of such encounters is that they are *asymmetrical*: the professional uses language not only to carry out particular professional tasks, such as giving clients medical or legal advice or instructing pupils, but also to construct and maintain power relations.

So what is this discourse like? What are the linguistic features which characterise professional talk? In this paper, I shall focus on three features – questions, directives and interruptions – in order to illustrate the language used by professionals in their work. Examples will be drawn from the domains of law, medicine and education.

2.1 Questions

In the discourse of the public sphere, questions function as *information-seeking* devices. This is illustrated in examples 1 and 2 below. The first is an extract from symmetrical talk between colleagues, the second comes from an asymmetrical encounter between magistrate and defendant. (Questions in these examples are underlined.)

(1) [Two academics talk in college]
     A: How big is the program, is it a very long one?
     B: I don't think it's all that long, there's a lot of iterative stuff in it
                                                      (Coates MK01: A399)
(2) [Magistrates' court dealing with arrears and maintenance]
     Magistrate: Are you paying anything at all?
     Defendant: No I haven't been able to at all sir

                                                      (Harris 1984: 15)

In both examples, one of the participants asks a question in order to gain information. But questions don't just seek information; they are also used to establish power and status. Discourse analysts have identified questions as potentially powerful forms, as they oblige the addressee to produce an answer, and to produce an answer which is conversationally relevant (see Grice 1975). The following extract, taken from doctor–patient interaction, shows how the doctor's questions constrain what the patient can say.

(3) Doctor: <u>What brings you here today?</u>
     Patient: My head is killing me
     Doctor: <u>Have you had headaches before?</u>
     Patient: No

(Beckman and Frankel 1984: 693)

The doctor's second question here – 'Have you had headaches before?' – is close-ended, and effectively narrows the focus of the consultation from the outset.

Not surprisingly, questions are asymmetrically distributed in asymmetrical discourse: powerful participants typically ask many more questions than less powerful participants, as Table 1.1 demonstrates.

Table 1.1   Distribution of questions in professional discourse

		% of questions asked	
Field	Research	Professionals	Laypeople
Medicine	Todd 1983	85%	15%
Medicine	West 1984b	91%	9%
Medicine	Frankel, in press	99%	1%
Law	Harris 1984	97%	3%
Education	Barnes 1971	97%	3%

In some contexts, such as the law court, the asking of questions by less powerful participants is explicitly disallowed:

(4) Magistrate: I'm putting it to you again – <u>are you going to make an offer – wh – wh – to discharge this debt?</u>
     Defendant: <u>Would you in my position?</u>
     Magistrate: I – I'm not here to answer questions – you answer *my* question

(Harris 1984: 5)

Through the use of questions, powerful participants are able to control the topic of discourse. Recent analysis of doctor–patient interviews (Mishler 1984; Fisher 1991) shows how the structure of such interviews constrains patients' ability to tell their stories coherently. Doctors' choice of questions does ideological work, promoting the values of medicine and the status quo, and silencing the alternative values of the patients' life experience.

2.2 Directives

A directive can be defined as a speech act which tries to get someone to do something. Directives can range from the bluntness of imperative forms (e.g. 'Shut the door') to more mitigated forms (such as 'Could you possibly shut the door?'). Typically, powerful participants will demonstrate their power (i.e. their ability to ignore the face needs of their addressees) by using direct commands. Those given in example (5) below are from the classroom; those in example (6) are from the doctor's surgery (imperatives underlined).

(5) (a) <u>Raise</u> your hand, any children whose name begins with this letter

(Mehan 1979: 163)

   (b) Now <u>don't start</u> now, just <u>listen</u>

(Stubbs 1983: 51)

(6) (a) <u>Lie down</u>
   (b) <u>Take off</u> your shoes and socks
   (c) <u>Pull off</u> a shirt [taps patient on knee] for me
   (d) <u>Sit</u> for me right there

(West 1990: 92)

To show how directives are embedded in discourse, here's a more extended example from the medical domain:

(7) Doctor: . . . if you don't flow, <u>call me</u>, then I will give you an injection, <u>don't take</u> any more tablets then
   Patient: Uh huh
   Doctor: I'll give you an injection and I'll, uh, get you started with your menstruation and I'll give you a different type of pill
   Patient: Okay
   Doctor: Okay?

Patient:	All right
Doctor:	But meanwhile <u>stay</u> on the pills. <u>Don't you get</u> into trouble.
Patient:	Right.

(Todd 1983: 169)

The doctor's use of unmitigated forms here emphasises the power asymmetry of the situation. He clearly feels that since what he is saying to the patient is 'for her own good', there is no need for him to protect her face needs.

Doctors also tell patients what they *need* to do, or what they *ought* to do:

(8)   I think you need to try to get out

(West 1990: 192)

(9)   I think you ought to knock that off for a while

(West 1990: 193)

Sometimes less aggravated forms are chosen, as the following examples from classroom discourse illustrate:

(10)   Teacher: I could do with a bit of silence

(Stubbs 1983: 51)

(11)   Teacher: Can you come up and find San Diego on the map?
       Pupil: [goes to board and points]

(Mehan 1979: 54)

Covert imperatives such as (10) and (11) constitute a more subtle exercise of power; but like bare imperatives, they assume a universe where the speaker ('I') is all-powerful, and the addressee ('you') has no power. The use of more aggravated directives helps maintain a universe where professionals are constructed as repositories of wisdom, and clients are viewed as objects to be helped, rather than as subjects in their own right.

2.3 Turn-taking and interruptions

The Sacks, Schegloff and Jefferson (1974) model of turn-taking in conversation views simultaneous speech by two or more participants as an aberration. Their rules for turn-taking are designed to ensure that (i) one speaker speaks at a time and (ii) speaker change recurs. In terms of this model, interruptions are seen as 'a violation of a current speaker's right to complete a turn' (Zimmerman and West 1975: 123), while overlaps are merely cases of slight mistiming or over-eagerness on the part of the next speaker. So example (12) below would be viewed as an overlap:

```
(12)  J:   because they've only got to win two seats   =
      R:                                        two   =   yes I know
                                                      (Coates 1991: 299)
```

However, if speaker R had begun to speak any earlier, this would have constituted an illegitimate bid for the floor, that is, an interruption.

The Sacks, Schegloff and Jefferson model of turn-taking works well for language in the public domain. Normally, one speaker speaks at a time and speaker change recurs. Simultaneous speech represents a breakdown in the system, and is nearly always the result of the more powerful participant in asymmetrical discourse interrupting the less powerful, as the following examples illustrate. (A double slash // indicates the start of an interruption.) The first comes from doctor–patient interaction:

```
(13)   Doctor:   Swelling or anything like that that you've noticed?
       Patient:  No, not th//at I've noti
       Doctor:               //tender to the touch? pressing any?
       Patient:  no, just when it's – sitting
       Doctor:   OK =
       Patient:     =er lying on it
       Doctor:   Even lying. Standing up? walking around [singsong]
       Patient:  No //just
       Doctor:       //not so much, just – lying on it . . . .
                                                     (West 1984: 61–2)
```

The next example comes from a legal context, and demonstrates what happens when a defendant attempts to provide more than a brief response to the magistrate's questions:

(14) Defendant: I realise entirely that it's up to me to
    ⌈Magistrate: //are you paying anything
    ⌊Defendant: counterbalance that by paying//you know I know (xx)
    ⌈Magistrate: at all   //are
    ⌊Defendant   no I haven't been able to – at all sir – //no I
    ⌈Magistrate: you supporting anyone else
    ⌊Defendant: get (xx)   not at all, no – I live on
    ⌈Magistrate: and how much do you receive then
    ⌊Defendant: my own sir   fourteen
    ⌈Magistrate: well can't you spare something of
    ⌊Defendant: pounds thirty-five
    ⌈Magistrate: that for your children – um   //when did you last
    ⌊Defendant: yes – I would do (xx)
    Magistrate: pay anything
                                            (Harris 1984: 15–16)

Interruption is used as a strategy by powerful participants in discourse to gain the floor and to control the topic of conversation. Speakers who interrupt others infringe others' right to speak and in effect demonstrate their power. Interruptions have been described as 'a way of "doing" power in face-to-face interaction' (West and Zimmerman 1983).

Research on doctor–patient interaction (Frankel 1983; Beckman and Frankel 1984; West 1984a and 1984b) has revealed how physicians regularly intrude into patients' turns at talk. At first sight, such intrusions may seem warranted by the external constraints of medical examination and treatment. 'But when these inquiries cut off the patient's utterance-in-progress, particularly when that utterance-in-progress is the presumed necessary response to a prior necessary question, then the physician is not only violating the patient's right to speak, but is also systematically cutting off potentially valuable information that is necessary to achieve a diagnosis' (West and Frankel 1991: 186). This comment is presumably equally applicable to other professional contexts where the professionals' interruptions cut off the client's response. Example (14), from law rather than medicine, is a case in point. Professionals need to learn to listen, otherwise they, as well as their clients, have much to lose.

3 WOMEN'S DISCOURSE PATTERNS

As we saw in the previous section, the language of the professions, like all-male discourse, tends to be information-focused and adversarial in style, favouring linguistic strategies which foreground status differences between participants. Women's talk in the private sphere, by contrast, is interaction-focused, favouring linguistic strategies which emphasise solidarity rather than status. This dichotomy is in part functional: the chief goal of discourse in the public domain is the efficient exchange of information; that of discourse in the private domain is the creation and maintenance of good social relations. However, those working in the professions need to be sensitive to the interpersonal function of language: interaction in any context involves more than the exchange of information.

Analysis of all-female discourse patterns is beginning to establish which linguistic features have a significant role in the construction of cooperative discourse (see Coates 1989, 1991, forthcoming). I shall summarise here findings related to questions, directives and turn-taking.

Questions

As we have seen in 2.1, questions often function as information-seeking devices. In conversation, a speaker can take on the role of 'expert', while other participants ask the 'expert' questions. Women avoid the role of expert in friendly conversation (since this would disturb the symmetry of the group); information-seeking questions are consequently rare in all-female discourse. Instead, interrogative forms are used to invite others to participate, and to check that what is being said is acceptable to everyone present. They are also used as part of a general strategy for conversational maintenance: questions are speech acts which require a subsequent speech act (an answer), so using questions is a way of ensuring that conversation continues.

Directives

The most important study of the use of directives in same-sex talk is that carried out by Marjorie Goodwin (1980, 1988, 1992). She observed the group play of girls and boys in a Philadelphia street, and noticed that the two groups used different directive forms. The boys used 'aggravated' directives, that is, directives which explicitly establish status differences between participants, such as 'Get outa here sucker' or 'You shut up you big lips'. By contrast, the girls typically used directives which minimised status differences. They frequently used 'let's' as in 'Let's use these first' and 'Let's ask her "Do you have any bottles?"'. The form *let's*, which was hardly ever used by the boys, explicitly includes the speaker as well as the addressee in the proposed action. The girls preferred to use directives which were phrased as suggestions for joint action: 'We gonna paint 'em and stuff'; 'We could go round looking for more bottles'. As Goodwin (1992: 147) concludes: 'boys' directives display distinctions between participants and stress individual rights [while] girls' directives stress the connectedness of girls to each other and their caretaking concerns'.

Turn-taking and simultaneous speech

Turn-taking strategies in all-female discourse do not always correspond to those assumed by current models of turn-taking (e.g. Sacks, Schegloff and Jefferson 1974). Simultaneous speech (that is, two or more people speaking at the same time) is common in all-female discourse, yet it is rarely a sign of conversational malfunction. It seems that female speakers use a turn-taking model where the rule of one-person-at-a-time does not apply. Co-conversationalists ask questions or make comments *while another participant is speaking*; these questions and comments are, like minimal responses, signals of active listernership, but they contribute more substantially to the production of joint text. Simultaneous speech also occurs when speakers complete each others' utterances, or repeat or rephrase each others' words. Finally, overlapping speech is found when two or more speakers pursue a theme simultaneously; this does not threaten comprehension, but on the contrary permits a more multi-layered development of topics.

The talk of single-sex groups is still under-researched, and there is a need to re-assess those linguistic features characteristic of all-female discourse which were previously described as 'weak'. Where the chief goal of talk is the maintenance of good social relationships, then cooperative discourse strategies are highly functional. There are situations where a more competitive style of interaction may be more appropriate; but it would be foolish to claim that either style is 'better' than the other. Ideally, speakers should be competent in a range of styles.

4 WOMEN IN THE PROFESSIONS

I now want to look at the language used by women in the professions, that is, women's language in the public domain. In the public sphere, there is evidence to suggest that some women have resisted adapting to the androcentric discourse norms which prevail there. Instead, they are employing their own more cooperative speech style. In this section I shall examine a few examples of this phenomenon: Fisher's (1991) work on the questions used by nurse practitioners; West's (1990) analysis of directive–response sequences in doctor–patient talk; Atkinson's (in press) exploration of simultaneous speech in the talk of home-helps with elderly clients; and Nelson's (1988) description of the collaborative interactive patterns adopted by teams working in a university writing centre.

4.1 Nurse practitioners and the use of questions (Fisher 1991)

Sue Fisher compares how nurse practitioners and doctors communicate with women patients during medical encounters. The nurse practitioner is a relatively new health care professional in the United States, who claims to provide care differently from doctors, by adding caring to curing. Fisher describes two cases, comparable in all respects except that one patient is seen by a doctor, while the other is seen by a nurse practitioner. The patients were both young women in their 20s who had vague, non-specific complaints. Fisher focuses on the role of questions in structuring the discourse. The (male) doctor uses questions 'which pay little linguistic attention to the life context of patients' symptoms, with an emphasis on technical information and a technical fix even when the medical complaint is marked as social' (Fisher 1991: 161). The (female) nurse practitioner, on the other hand, 'probes for the life context of the patient's symptoms and emphasizes the social rather than the technical' (*ibid.*). The doctor's questions are narrowly focused in such a way as to constrain the range of answers possible and to keep control of the discourse (see 2.1 above). The nurse practitioner, on the other hand, uses questions to open up the discourse, to get the patient to explore her feelings and to give a full picture of the situation. When the patient describes how she got a job to get her out of the home, the nurse practitioner comments:

(15)   You know that's a real growth step for you, to realise those needs and then to go take some action, to do something about them. Do you see that as a growth step?

(Fisher 1991: 169)

Notice how the question that this utterance ends with ('Do you see that as a growth step?') allows the patient to accept or reject the professional's assessment. The nurse practitioner constantly encourages the patient to talk about her symptoms in the context of her emotional and social life, through the use of sensitive questions. The professional is inevitably the dominant interactional partner, and questions are used as a way of controlling topics. But professionals can use this control in very different ways. Throughout the encounter, the nurse practitioner accepts the patient's definition of the situation and validates her opinion. The doctor is committed to a traditional discourse, in which motherhood is seen as a full-time job, while the nurse practitioner supports an alternative discourse in which women take control of their lives. The nurse practitioner's use of questions arises directly from her different conception of her role.

4.2 Women doctors' use of directives (West 1990)

Candace West analysed directive–response speech sequences between doctor and patient, drawing on Marjorie Goodwin's (1980, 1988, 1992) work on gender differences in children's use of directives. West discovered that women and men doctors issued directives in very different ways. Moreover, women doctors are more likely than men to use directive forms which elicit a compliant response from the patient. While male doctors preferred to use imperative forms, or statements in which they told patients what they 'needed' to do, or what they 'had to' do, female doctors preferred to use more mitigated forms. For example, women doctors often made directives in the form of proposals for joint action, using the form *let's*:

(16) Okay! well let's make that our plan.
(17) So let's stay on uh what we're doing right now, OK?

They also used the pronoun *we* rather than *you* in their directives:

(18) Maybe what we ought to do is, is stay with the dose of di(avameez) you're on

Where a woman doctor did use *you*, she typically mitigated the directive by the use of modal forms such as *can* or *could*, as well as *maybe*:

(19) one thing you could do is to eat the meat first
(20) and then maybe you can stay away from the desserts and stay away from the food in between meals

West measured the compliance rates for different types of directives for male and female doctors. Male doctors' bare imperatives (e.g. 'lie down!') elicited compliant responses in 47% of cases in which they were used, while their statements of patients' needs elicited only 38% compliant responses. As West puts it, 'the more aggravated the directive, the less likely it was to elicit a compliant response' (West 1990: 108). Female doctors' proposals for joint action (using *let's*) elicited compliant responses in 67% of the cases in which *let's* were used. Suggestions for action ('you could try taking two every four hours') had a 75% success rate. Overall, the women doctors used far fewer aggravated directives than the male doctors, and their overall rate of compliant responses was 67%, compared with the male doctors' 50%.

This study shows women using more collaborative interactive strategies in the medical profession. The women doctors used more mitigated directive forms, thus minimising status distinctions between themselves and their patients. The more egalitarian relationships they established with their patients emphasised doctors' obligations as well as patients' rights. The evidence from this study is that such an approach has better outcomes for patients than more traditional approaches which emphasise asymmetry in doctor–patient relationships.

4.3 Simultaneous speech in talk between home-helps and elderly clients (Atkinson, in press)

Karen Atkinson (in press) has carried out long-term participant observation of the interaction between young home-helps and elderly clients. The majority of carers who look after the elderly are female, as are most of the elderly population. Thus, the inter-generational talk occurring in home-help–elderly person dyads tends to be all-female. Despite the asymmetry of both age and status, Atkinson has observed a significant amount of simultaneous speech in such dyads, similar in kind to that found in the talk of female friends. The following is an example from her data (words in double bracket are indistinct; / = end of unit type):

(21) elderly client (EC) talks to home-help (HH) about new gadget for arthritis

```
1   ⎰ EC:    now if my knee [b], got bad again /
    ⎱ HH:                            yeah     yeah now that'd
2   ⎰ EC:        that might be worth it/ .  ((your))  knee
    ⎱ HH:    be lovely ((there)/        yes      yeah     where
3   ⎰ EC:    you would use it on yourself/            yes/
    ⎱ HH:    you can use it   .    yourself/      that's it, yeah/
```

This short extract from one of Atkinson's sixty audio-recorded conversations between young female home-helps and their elderly female clients illustrates the way overlapping speech is used in these interactions. Speakers perform as a single voice, saying the same thing in different words ('now that'd be lovely'/'that might be worth it', line 2) and even saying the same thing at the same time, ('yourself', line 3). Speakers use minimal responses ('yes', 'yeah', 'that's it') to confirm that what one has said has the support of the other. In terms of the conventional norms of turn-taking (where one-speaker-at-a-time is the rule, see 2.3), virtually all the simultaneous speech occurring here should be labelled 'interruption', since the overlapping segment involves more than the last syllable of a speaker's turn. But in all-female conversation, as this

example demonstrates, such categories are inappropriate: participants do not view conversation as a battle to hold the floor; the
floor can be (and often is) jointly held. When EC says 'you would
use it on yourself' in line 3, she is not trying to seize the floor from
HH, but is agreeing with HH and saying the same thing in her own
words. These 'conversational duets' (Falk 1980; Coates 1991) are a
central feature of all-female discourse.

It seems that young female home-helps are bringing to their job
as carers the collaborative speech styles typical of symmetrical
all-female talk. This suggests that gender solidarity may be overriding age and status differentials. While this may be good
professional practice, we should note that professions which are
female-dominated (such as nursing, certain kinds of social work,
nursery and infant teaching, caring for the elderly), and which are
therefore capable of supporting more cooperative speech styles,
have lower status and prestige than those which are male-
dominated (such as medicine, law, university teaching).

4.4   Interactive patterns in teacher-research teams (Nelson 1988)

Nelson observed and recorded the interactive patterns of five suc-
cessive teacher-research teams, working in a university writing
centre in Washington, DC. These teams were made up of graduate
Teaching Assistants (TAs), who were mostly female. Nelson's
research shows how the women successfully used the interactive
patterns familiar to them, while the occasional male TAs adapted to
these interactive patterns and were positive about the experience.
The members of the team enjoyed the trust and closeness engen-
dered by close collaborative work. One of the rare male TAs
commented:

> I just love being in here with all you women. You make it such a nice
> place to work. You're so warm and supportive that I never feel stupid
> when I make a mistake. It's different in here from how I've seen people
> do things before. Most graduate students are so competitive.
>
> (Nelson 1988: 202)

Transcripts of team discussion sessions confirm the claim that
women's interactions are rooted in emotional openness and
reciprocity, and are cooperative rather than competitive. They

show what Miller (1976) calls 'productive conflict', that is, conflict which is beneficial to all participants, as opposed to conflict which results in one winner and many losers.

The success of this collaborative venture is borne out both in the achievement of the teams in helping students to write better, and in the comments of participants on how much they had gained from the experience. One graduate TA, who subsequently worked for a large corporation, described the contrast between the competitive ethos of the large corporation, and the collaborative ethos of the university research teams: 'The corporation emphasises only negative aspects of performance, but we female teachers have been used to stressing the positive first. Our emphasis has always been on what students do right – to help students build on what they do well instead of discouraging them. In addition, we've all been used to using collaborative methods' (Nelson 1988: 220). Nelson discusses the problems women face in trying to maintain their collaborative style in more competitive environments, and argues that we must try to overcome these problems since the interactive patterns into which women are socialised 'offer substantial benefits to academic and professional teams' (Nelson 1988: 203).

5 CONCLUSION: WOMEN, LANGUAGE AND CAREER

The studies described in section 4 above are only a few of a growing number of research projects which demonstrate the positive aspects of incorporating cooperative discourse styles typical of women into the public domain. Troemel-Ploetz (1985) compares male and female TV interviewers and shows how female interviewers encourage more open and more equal discussion through their interactive strategies. Graddol and Swann (1989: 178–81) describe how some firms are trying to encourage the promotion of women and to introduce more 'feminine' styles into management. Campbell (1988) argues that women's presence on high-powered committees has had beneficial effects. She quotes Tessa Blackstone, Master (sic) of Birkbeck College, who said of her experience as a member of the Central Policy Review Staff: 'Women are less competitive for a start and there's less confrontation in a group that's got women in it . . . I just think that organisations that have women are more in touch with the society in which they work' (Campbell 1988). We should also note that in professions such as psycho-therapy and counselling, where more 'female' interactive patterns are highly valued, women are a significant presence.

On the other hand, women attempting to pursue careers in the public domain will continue to encounter problems. If they adopt a more adversarial, more 'male', interactive style, they are in danger of being labelled 'unfeminine'. If they attempt to retain a more cooperative style of interaction, they risk being viewed as ineffectual. Moreover, in mixed interaction male speakers will use their competitive discourse skills to dominate female speakers (see, for example: Edelsky 1981; Troemel-Ploetz 1985; Woods 1989). Men dominate mixed interaction even when a woman has higher status: West's study of doctor–patient interaction has been referred to extensively in this paper; her analysis of interruption makes depressing reading. While male doctors were rarely interrupted by patients, and used interruptions to control the progress of the medical interview, women doctors *were* interrupted, especially by white male patients (West 1984b).

As women enter the workforce in greater numbers and with higher expectations, it remains to be seen whether the more cooperative discourse style which women are skilful in will be welcomed in the public sphere as a new resource, or whether it will be challenged. More overt forms of discrimination against women are slowly being eradicated. But the continuing marginalisation of women in the professions, and the fact that women are still having difficulty progressing in their chosen career, suggests that other, covert means of discrimination are still at work. The androcentric norms of public discourse are alien to most women. This discourse is extremely powerful in promoting and maintaining the competitive ethos of the world of work. If the dominant elite insist that women must acquire a public 'voice' in order to take their place in the public sphere, then society as a whole will be the loser. As the studies described above in section 4 demonstrate, the professions already benefit from the use of more collaborative discourse styles. It is time the value of such discourse patterns was acknowledged.

NOTE

1. This paper arises from work I carried out as a member of the Women and Career research group based at the Sociology Department, University of Nottingham. A shorter version of the paper will appear in *Women and Career: Themes and Issues* ed. J. Evetts (Longman, in press).

TWO

Rethinking language and gender studies: some issues for the 1990s

Deborah Cameron

These remarks are prompted in the first instance by some interesting recent events. There has been a serious breakdown of sisterly solidarity in the field of feminist linguistics, with a recent issue of the journal *Discourse and Society* featuring a defensive piece by Deborah Tannen, responding to a hostile review of her book, *You Just Don't Understand*, by Senta Troemel-Ploetz.

I find the occasion for this public quarrel more than a little ironic. When I began to do feminist linguistics there was, in Britain anyway, no field more generally obscure and lacking in credibility – an interviewer once commented, about my own book *Feminism and Linguistic Theory*, 'But isn't that like writing a book on linguistics and organic gardening?'. Yet today feminist linguistics are being polarised by an issue that seems to turn precisely on the popularisation of our research. Once our credibility was threatened by obscurity; now it seems a little more obscurity would enhance it.

Yet perhaps this disagreement, overtly over popularisation, has the virtue of bringing to light other disagreements that were already lurking in the shadows, and forcing us to confront them. I believe the new popular linguistic advice literature, of which Deborah Tannen's book is only one example, salient to us because it happens to have been written by one of our own, raises both ethical and theoretical problems that might lead us to rethink some aspects of what we do. Certainly it has led me to clarify my own position, and here I want to present both the position I have reached and the steps by which I reached it.

I began by thinking about popular texts, then and now. At either end of the 1980s, a book about language and gender was published which seemed to contribute to the current state of the art, and at the same time was able to reach a sizeable popular audience. In 1980 the book was Dale Spender's *Man Made Language*: written by a radical feminist, uncompromising in its politics and broad in its scope; the book was a feminist bestseller, and the object of considerable media attention. In 1990 by contrast we had Deborah Tannen's *You Just Don't Understand*. Written by a linguist with impeccable scholarly credentials, politically more ambiguous and more modest in its aims, this much-hyped book was a trade blockbuster of astounding proportions, spending more than a year on the *New York Times* bestseller list.

What happened in the ten intervening years? Perhaps feminist linguistics simply came of age intellectually, and was therefore able to speak with more authority in 1990 than in 1980. Or perhaps feminist linguistics sold out – Deborah Tannen succeeded by compromising the political principles of Dale Spender. Or perhaps, since this story is set in the 'decade of greed', it is simply about feminism's increasing commodification: Deborah Tannen's book reached a wider market than Dale Spender's because it was better packaged and more aggressively marketed. I will argue that none of these accounts is wholly without merit; but none is wholly satisfactory either.

As a preliminary, let me mention a few things that are not at issue here. First, and contrary to Tannen's own beliefs, the issue is not popularisation *per se*. Traditional academic snootiness about popular writing has never sat well with feminist politics, and feminist linguists from the beginning have tended to write accessibly for a non-specialist audience. Where Dale Spender, a non-linguist, was often taxed with doing this out of ignorance, Deborah Tannen, a well-respected linguist, has been charged instead with calculation: with setting out cynically to write a lucrative bestseller. But the motives of individual scholars are not the issue either. What's important is that Spender and Tannen each succeeded because they were skilful in capturing the mood of the moment. It is the change in mood from 1980 to 1990 that is really the issue.

I have come to believe that my initial understanding of this change was too simple. Nevertheless, I will start by putting it the way it originally appeared to me. When I first came across *You Just Don't Understand*, my reaction was to feel, as Senta Troemel-Ploetz obviously did, that feminist linguistics was being turned into a branch of the self-improvement industry. Tannen's text is actually sold in bookshops in the section labelled 'psychology', 'self-help' or 'personal growth'; it reproduces all the features of the popular advice genre; and the considerable attention it got from the media focused primarily on its potential for helping men and women to solve their problems (the US paperback edition's back cover proclaims, for instance, 'People are telling Tannen that the book is saving their marriages').

I think it will be obvious why this development might give cause for concern. Many feminists have criticised the self-help genre for glossing over systemic problems of gender inequality, and urging that those problems be addressed through individual adjustment rather than collective political action. Saving a woman's marriage is a far cry from producing a critique of marriage itself. What troubles me even more, though, is that in producing a self-help book about language and gender, Deborah Tannen is not just harnessing linguistics to reactionary trends outside the academy: she is carrying recent trends in feminist linguistics to what is arguably their logical conclusion.

A crude historical-typological account of feminist linguistic approaches since 1973 would probably distinguish between three models of language and gender. One is a *deficit* model in which women are seen as disadvantaged speakers because of their early sex-role socialisation: the obvious example is Robin Lakoff's *Language and Woman's Place* (Lakoff 1975). The second is a *dominance* model in which women are seen, often through an ethnomethodological frame, as negotiating their relatively powerless position in interacting with men: male social privilege is made manifest in recurrent patterns of language use. This model could be exemplified by the work of Candace West on interrruptions (Zimmerman and West 1975; West 1984) or by Pamela Fishman's studies of heterosexual couples' talk (1983; 1990). Finally, there is a *cultural difference* model in which analogies are made between gender and other social divisions such as ethnicity; segregation of the sexes during childhood and adolescence produces marked differences in their conversational goals and styles. A major reference point for this model is the work of Gumperz and his associates (e.g. Maltz and Borker 1982); the work of Deborah Tannen also exemplifies it.

Chronologically speaking there has been considerable overlap between the three models, but during the 1980s I think it is fair to say that the difference model gained ground while the dominance and deficit approaches lost it. This development, I think, goes some way to explain why a self-help approach has recently become an option for feminist linguists. The dominance approach emphasises inequality as the root of any problems in cross-sex interaction, and suggests therefore that to solve the problems we must eliminate the underlying inequality. The difference approach, on the other hand, reinterprets the same problems as misunderstandings. Women and men are positioned not unequally, but *symmetrically*, as outsiders to each other's verbal culture. In such a situation, given good intentions on both sides, the problems can conceivably be solved by exposing the roots of misunderstanding and acting upon our new awareness of what causes it.

This is exactly the project of Deborah Tannen's *You Just Don't Understand*: to explain to women and men why they so often seem to be at odds when they talk. Starting from the postulate of separate cultures, the problem Tannen identifies is that each sex interprets the other's verbal strategies through the lens of their own. This gives a distorted picture: what your husband means by saying something may not be the same as what your girlfriend would mean if she said exactly the same thing.

For example, a much excerpted portion of Tannen's book deals with 'Eve', just out of hospital after a lumpectomy and worried that the scarring has made her unattractive. Eve's husband suggests that if it's really bothering Eve she could have plastic surgery. Eve is upset: not only does he seem to be confirming her suspicion that she is unattractive, but after all she's been through he wants her to have more surgery. Yet when she taxes him with this, he is hurt and puzzled, protesting that she has totally misunderstood what he said.

What's going on here, Tannen explains, is a clash of male and female norms for doing 'trouble talk'. Women bring up troubles wanting sympathy and reassurance. The commonest female response to someone's mentioning a problem is to produce 'matching troubles' – the 'I-know-just-what-you-mean-I've-had-the-same-thing-myself' syndrome. Men bring up troubles in the expectation that someone will suggest a solution – which is what Eve's husband does. Since Eve expected reassurance, however, this response strikes her as uncaring. Neither Eve nor her husband is consciously aware of violating the other's norms, and as a consequence they quarrel.

This is one example of a much more general difference. Men, Tannen claims, see the world as a hierarchy in which any individual may be 'one-up' or 'one-down'; the interactive task they set themselves is to gain or maintain status. They expect women to do likewise, but women have other goals. What women value is connection and intimacy, and in talking they are likely to insist on the commonality of their experience, not its uniqueness. This is one reason why men boast and women gossip. Each sex engages in the sort of talk which secures the rewards they prefer – status for men, connection for women.

The overall message of *You Just Don't Understand* is that both styles are valid, they are simply different. If women and men had a more explicit knowledge of the differences in question, they would not misunderstand each other so frequently and disastrously. Tannen argues that we should acknowledge gender differences without making value judgements on their content.

Has this line of argument been successful because of intellectual considerations, or political ones? Probably, both. The difference approach is no doubt attractive to certain people because it does not cast men as villains and feminists as anti-male. But it's only fair to point out that the difference approach gained ground among scholars for other reasons too.

One of these was a desire to get away from Lakoff's rather negative evaluation of women's language. In characterising women as speakers who lacked authority, Lakoff had seemed to many feminists to be accepting at face value men's own biased judgements. Another difficulty (which Tannen discusses) arose in relation to ethnicity, race and class. If men were to be criticised for their insensitive dominant behaviour, couldn't the same arguments be used against other groups with similarly combative styles, such as Jewish people and people of African descent?

But I think there is a deeper logic here. The gradual ascendancy of difference over dominance was almost inevitable given the ideology of twentieth-century linguistics, especially its anthropological and sociological variants. Difference, and not inequality, is what the framework of structural linguistics is designed to deal with. Indeed, for the linguist, inequality is conceived as resulting not from difference itself but from intolerance of difference. Thus linguists have insisted it is wrong to label languages 'primitive' or dialects 'substandard'; it is wrong to force people to abandon their ways of speaking, or to judge them by the yardstick of your own linguistic habits. Throughout this century, the norm in linguistics has been linguistic and cultural relativism – 'all varieties are equal'. It has always been an honorable position, and sometimes an outright radical one. In applying it to the case of male–female differences, Deborah Tannen and her colleagues have only reasserted the historical logic of the discipline they were trained in.

The question, of course, is whether relativism has any virtue in the case of gender difference. Applied to the speech styles of women and men in the same society, is 'all varieties are equal' a radical position? I am not persuaded that men and women are a parallel case to historically distinct nations or ethnic groups, and this is a point we must return to later on. In any event, the notion of gender as a quasi-cultural difference has caused questions of power which were fundamental to feminism to disappear almost entirely; and it is arguably because of this that the difference paradigm has been easily co-opted to the interests of self-help in its most politically questionable form.

Let me try to demonstrate how relativism becomes reactionary. Deborah Tannen may say that she is trying to promote mutual understanding and tolerance between the sexes; like the women in her book, she prefers reassurance to advice. But since men and women are *not* in fact symmetrically positioned, in practice her book undermines its own aims.

To see this, it is only necessary to ask who the book is really addressed to. It purports to be addressing both women and men, but in reality the market for books about male–female relationships is overwhelmingly a female market (the UK rights were bought by Virago). Tannen herself argues that women care more about interpersonal relationships and invest more energy in them than men do. Avoiding or resolving cross-sex misunderstandings thus becomes women's responsibility.

That women do feel a need to act on what they read is borne out strongly in the reception given to Tannen's book. Over and over again, reviewers and subeditors have used the metaphor of the phrasebook: 'a fine Berlitz guide', in the words of one reviewer; or as American *Cosmopolitan* put it with exemplary crassness, 'Here, the secrets of mantalk, and how to decode it'. One does not buy a phrasebook out of abstract interest in the language: one buys a phrasebook for the immediate purposes of basic communication. And the point is, this is not a two-way street. To be fair to Deborah Tannen, she says in her introduction that for women to do all the adjusting is 'repugnant', and she registers some objections to the selective presentation of her thesis by the media. Yet the terms of the book's reception were surely depressingly predictable.

Women's magazine features based on *You Just Don't Understand* have been both very numerous and extremely prescriptive. *Glamour* ran a piece, unusual for focusing on workplace relations rather than domestic ones, which translated Tannen's arguments into a set of handy hints – for example, to avoid indirect requests to male colleagues because 'women shy away from giving blatant orders, but men find the indirect approach manipulative and confusing'. The piece repeats Tannen's view that there is nothing inherently wrong with making indirect requests; but it immediately undercuts this message by saying, in essence, that if you don't want to be misinterpreted you will do better to adopt the male norm.

One could argue, then, that *You Just Don't Understand* is in practice a rather reactionary self-help book which does not serve feminist ends; and that its problematic aspects arise from the shift in feminist linguistics to a difference approach. But as I warned earlier, this argument, while it is not wholly false, needs to be complicated. For it turns out that Deborah Tannen's brand of linguistic self-help is not the only one on the market. There is also a tradition based on work not in the difference framework.

The alternative genre of advice is mainly oriented to professional career women, and is to be found in manuals used in corporate training. A typical one is titled *Leadership Skills for Women: Achieving Impact as a Manager* (Manning and Haddock 1989). This title does not mention language explicitly, but it is full of material clearly if selectively derived from the scholarly literature on gender differences in speech. An important reference point through this genre is the work of Robin Lakoff, with its thesis that women speakers 'lack authority'; well-known findings from the dominance perspective are also invoked, though in conformity with the tenets of self-help they are often recuperated to a deficit model. The substance of the advice is to emulate men: not simply in order to be understood by them, but because the male way is the best way. *Leadership Skills for Women* explains that 'men typically use less body language than women', and urges: 'Watch their body language to see how they do it'. It also admonishes, in a remarkable display of victim-blaming:

> Speak directly and stand firm when you are interrupted. Statistics show that women allow themselves to be interrupted 50% more often than

men. Don't contribute to those statistics.

(Manning and Haddock 1989: 15)

The same sort of thing turns up in women's magazines. US *Cosmopolitan* for instance ran an article in 1990 headed 'Why not talk like an adult?', though it should have been called 'Why not talk like a man?'. This piece informed readers that women often fail to gain respect in the workplace because of the way they talk. Certain characteristics of female speech – tag questions, rising intonation, whiny, breathy or high-pitched voices – must be scrupulously avoided. Obviously, this laundry list of alleged female linguistic offences comes straight from Robin Lakoff, whose negative inter-pretation of them is presented as fact. *Options* magazine in 1992 included 'tentative language' – again defined in terms drawn from Lakoff – as one of the 'Ten classic career mistakes women always make'.

Though more overt in its sexism than *You Just Don't Understand*, this type of advice has a similar outcome, i.e. women are advised to adjust to masculine norms. Both types underline the essential limi-tation of self-help: by definition, it is about changing one's own behaviour, but in some cases it is other people's behaviour that really needs to change. However, 'Don't allow your husband/ boyfriend/boss to contribute to those statistics' would be an idle suggestion at best.

I think I have said enough to make clear what I find disturbing in the prescriptive application of linguistic research on gender differ-ence. It is worth pointing out, though, just how ironic the transformation is. No discipline has been more insistent than lin-guistics on the descriptive/prescriptive distinction, the absolute line between 'is' and 'ought'. And feminist linguists in earlier years consistently took aim at the very tendencies that are now embodied in some of their work: at massive generalisations about male and female speech, at assumptions of all-pervading difference, at stereo-typical explanations and myths of origin, at the stultifying and restrictive advice with which women were bombarded. Scholars laboured long in the archives of conduct books and guides for brides, producing scathing critiques of the mythical creature they found there: a nurturing good listener, smoothing gently over con-flict and deferring to others' opinions in the interests of domestic harmony. Now this same woman steps forth from women's maga-zines, and peeps coyly from the pages of scholarly journals. And the question that has to be asked is how the field of language and gender studies, a field historically created by feminists in the hope that their research would empower women, has been so domesticated and depoliticised in the space of only fifteen years.

No doubt any research which is on a topic of public interest and reasonably accessible will sometimes get distorted and misused. But when findings on a particular subject are regularly giving rise to intellectually and politically objectionable consequences, we might begin to suspect some very basic flaw in the paradigm researchers are using. This is just what I suspect about current language and gender studies.

Although I find the difference approach particularly problematic, I do not think we can simply return to the good old days of the dominance approach. Both dominance and difference represented particular moments in feminism: dominance was the moment of feminist outrage, of bearing witness to oppression in all aspects of women's lives, while difference was the moment of feminist celebration, reclaiming and revaluing women's distinctive cultural traditions. It would be foolish to suggest that these responses are no longer necessary. But I do think the theories which underpinned them are no longer sufficient. Their moments have passed. And if feminist scholarship does not develop new theoretical positions in response to new conditions, it risks falling into obsolescence or hardening into reaction. That is what has happened to feminist linguistics: the monolithic notion of (male) power that informed early dominance work is now more or less obsolete, while the blithe assertion of women's difference now seems either so essentialist or else so depoliticised as to be reactionary.

It is not a coincidence that feminist *linguistics* finds itself in this impasse when other disciplines have managed to move on. In the study of language and gender – again, following the practice established in sociolinguistics more generally – it is *language* that is taken as the phenomenon to be explained, and gender which constitutes the explanation. Gender itself remains untheorised: it is a given, the bottom line. A linguist may seek to explain the effects of gender on language by talking about the differential socialisation of the sexes, the inequality between the sexes, the segregation of the sexes. What she cannot do is interrogate this crucial construct 'the sexes'.

It is hardly surprising if such an approach produces overgeneralisation (men do this, women do that) and stereotyping (men are competitive, women are cooperative). What else could it produce?

In this static commonsensical worldview, there are men and there are women, bearers of the attribute we call gender: our task becomes one of simply cataloguing the ways they mark this attribute in their linguistic behaviour. Men do this, women do that – must feminist linguistics be an endless repetition of this formulaic cliché? Or can we somehow reconceptualise the terms of the debate about language and gender?

I would like to propose that feminist linguistics take a long hard look at two problems in particular. One is the problem of linguistic and cultural relativism; the second is the problem of conceiving gender itself.

Let me begin with the relativism question. What I mean by this is the assumption, traditional in linguistics, that difference itself is neutral, while inequality results from the suppression or stigmatisation of difference. Thus there is nothing 'wrong' with non-standard dialects, only with the prejudice against them. Linguistic diversity is good: only the suppression of diversity is bad.

This approach works well enough when the difference in question is a relatively superficial matter of linguistic form. *Aint, isn't, tomayto, tomahto*, let's call the whole thing off. But when we are dealing with the sort of global discourse strategy that interests many language and gender researchers today, the questions become more complicated, because they relate not just to the forms but also to the functions of language.

Different discourse strategies arise in distinct social contexts, and they are used to accomplish different verbal tasks, rather than to do the same task in a different way. Deborah Tannen's version of this, unexceptionable as far as it goes, is that girls and boys are not engaged in the same activities, nor motivated by the same goals: therefore they evolve different norms of interaction. Another way of looking at it is to say that girls and boys already occupy different positions in the social formation, to which different activities and goals, and consequently different interactional patterns, are relevant. The question arises, then, of whether those who typically use a particular style of discourse are being excluded from (or conversely, are monopolising) not only certain verbal practices but more significantly, a range of *social* practices. If so, the issue is not so much whether X's way of speaking is as good as Y's, as whether the division of labour has significant political consequences, empowering some groups at the expense of others.

In the case of gender, a very good argument can be made that it does. To be sure, it makes little sense to argue about whether 'status' is better than 'intimacy', or vice versa. The position that these are both valid goals has much to recommend it, particularly if we define status as having to do with personal autonomy rather than competition for supremacy. Nevertheless, the gender specialisation whereby girls seek intimacy and boys seek status is hardly arbitrary in terms of the larger social structure. It could be characterised as a training of boys for public and girls for private life; or as a training for boys in the exercise of power and for girls in the abdication of autonomy.

This is not a neutral difference. The fact that it appears in single-sex peer groups in no way detracts from the important point that *this difference arises in the first place out of unequal gender relations*. To suppose that the 'problem' is intolerance of difference, and that if only we valued women's styles as highly as men's there would be no problem, is reminiscent of that brand of right-wing pseudo-feminism which enjoins us to honour the housewife and mother, glossing over the fact that her gendered occupation is itself a product of inequality and exploitation. Feminism is not about giving housewives their due, it is about changing the conditions of domestic labour altogether. Similarly, feminism cannot stop at validating the linguistic strategies typical of women; it must also ask why women find some communicative practices more relevant than others to their circumstances: a question of their social positioning, of the social practices in which they are allowed to participate.

This argument depends on accepting that inequality can give rise to difference, rather than vice versa. The conventional view is to see subordinated groups as oppressed *because* they are different; I am suggesting rather that many of the differences invoked to justify oppression, to the extent that they exist at all, have actually arisen historically because of it. In the case of these differences, there can be no place for cultural relativism.

One of the problems with *You Just Don't Understand* is that Deborah Tannen reifies gender differences. I do not accuse her of biological essentialism, but she does practise what you might call 'social essentialism', i.e. she invokes a socially produced difference as a simple fact of life, without ever asking what it is socially produced by or socially produced for. If in fact it is produced by inequality and functions to maintain unequal relations, to accept it as a fact of life is not only theoretically naive, it is politically damaging.

Let me give an example. In an opinion piece for the US *Chronicle of Higher Education*, Tannen noted the discomfort many women feel with adversarial teaching methods such as requiring students to defend a position in debate. She suggested that teachers employ more single-sex small-group discussions so that women are not forced to participate (at a disadvantage) in a verbal practice for which their peer group norms do not prepare them.

Granted, small-group discussion has many virtues, and granted, there is a real question whether effective public discourse always needs to be adversarial. But the fact remains, there are many contexts where individuals gain autonomy and power by being able to debate and argue a case. Debate and argument are 'languages of power' in our culture. If, as Tannen claims, women experience them in the classroom as 'public humiliation', this is surely bound up with the conflicting pressures women face in that setting: for women, intellectual autonomy and academic success conflict with social and sexual acceptability to a greater degree than is true for most men.

A feminist solution to this very real problem involves not removing women from the context that causes discomfort, but going to the roots of their positioning as 'outsiders' to powerful language and trying to change the conditions (including male behaviour) that keep them outside. Deborah Tannen's relativism perpetuates women's exclusion from languages of power, while failing to challenge any of the masculine behaviours which reinforce that exclusion.

This brings me to the other question I raised: theorising gender. As I said earlier, I believe linguists can learn from scholars in other disciplines. The most important insight we need to take account of is that *gender is a problem, not a solution*. 'Men do this, women do that' is not only overgeneralised and stereotypical, it fails utterly to address the question of where 'men' and 'women' come from. Feminists must take it as axiomatic that this is indeed a question worth asking. As Simone de Beauvoir said, 'One is not born, but rather becomes a woman'. The question is, how?

Not only the difference theorists of language and gender but also those working in the tradition of Robin Lakoff are dependent on a view of 'becoming a woman' as something accomplished once and for all at an early stage of life – either in the pre-school years within the nuclear family or slightly later in the peer group. Thereafter, an already fixed gender identity becomes the solution to the problem of why women and men behave as they do.

Recent feminist theory emphasises, by contrast, that one is never finished becoming a woman, or a man. Each individual subject must constantly negotiate the norms, behaviours, discourses, that define masculinity and femininity for a particular community at a particular point in history. From this point of view, it would be desirable to reformulate notions such as 'women's language' or 'men's style'. Instead of saying simply that these styles are produced by women and men as markers of their gender affiliation, we could say that the styles themselves are produced as masculine and feminine, and that individuals make varying accommodations to those styles in the process of producing *themselves* as gendered subjects. In other words, if I talk like a woman this is not just the inevitable outcome of the fact that I am a woman; it is one way I have of becoming a woman, producing myself *as* one. There is no such thing as 'being a woman' outside the various practices that define womanhood for my culture – practices ranging from the sort of work I do to my sexual preferences, to the clothes I wear, to the way I interact verbally.

Let us be clear that this way of talking about gender does not make it into something consciously and freely chosen. On the contrary, many aspects of becoming a woman (working in a suitable occupation or having certain kinds of sexual relationships) are heavily coerced, and where choice becomes possible (say I apprentice myself to a plumber, refuse to wear skirts, have affairs with women), there are real social costs. What this way of talking does, though, is problematise gender identity and leave open the possibility of challenge and change. Cooperation and competition need not be forever mutually exclusive, feminine and masculine principles of speech. We can intervene in the discourse that defines them thus. And this also allows us to account for the exceptions that exist already, the women and men who – in spite of early experiences virtually identical to what Lakoff and Tannen describe – end up outside the gender norms proposed by feminist linguists.

In our time and place, social science is a powerful discourse: what followers of Foucault call a 'regime of truth'. Feminist linguistics has produced a 'truth', a version of what it means to be a gendered speaker, that defines many women as deviant, while treating women's continued exclusion from important

communicative practices as normal. Whereas what we need is a linguistics that can empower women – not by glossing over crucial
issues about language, as Dale Spender did, and not by ignoring
issues of power, as Deborah Tannen does, but by combining a more
sophisticated theoretical approach with a clearer view of what's
actually at stake. It is by these criteria, rather than by generic
oppositions such as 'scholarly' versus 'popular' writing, that our
intellectual and political credibility should be measured.

LESBIAN POETICS

THREE

Constructing a lesbian poetic for survival [1]

Liz Yorke

Growing up during the fifties and sixties in a conventional work-ing-class family, I did not have any words to enable me to know about women-loving women – the much censored word *lesbian* had virtually disappeared from the public discourses around me, and certainly did not enter into my consciousness. In the discourses of poetry, lesbian voices have also been subjected to extensive public or personal censorship. Indeed, this artificial silencing underlies the feminist critic's difficulty in locating lesbian voices within poetic forms. In her introduction to *Lesbian Poetry: An Anthology*, Elly Bulkin suggested that 'it was easy, a few years ago, to think that lesbian poetry didn't exist' (Bulkin and Larkin 1981: xxi). It did, of course, but it was neglected, 'lost' altered by others – or repre-sented in coded forms by the poets themselves. Bulkin points to the 'impossibility of identifying [lesbian poets] unless they were repre-sented by poems about subjects connected directly and explicitly to lesbian oppression and/or sexuality'.

Historically speaking, it is hardly news to say that lesbians have been excluded from the cultural symbolic order. They have found themselves situated at the margins of acceptability and have been virtually eradicated from many public discourses – including the male-dominated discourses of poetry. Lesbian voices have literally been silenced, lesbian experience and identity have been erased and, for centuries, lesbians have been systematically dispossessed of their heritage. Yet as poets, writers, and academics, we are not bound to accept such silencing, invisibility, and erasure. In our work we may be attentive to the silences, may identify, theorise and explore what Diana Collecott has called the 'gap between experience and repre-sentation', that is, the gap between lesbian lives and those dominant discourses which problematically avoid, distort, suppress or condemn the actualities of lesbian existence (Collecott 1990: 94). The necessity is to challenge and oppose these discourses as a matter of urgency, for our survival within cultural forms depends on it.

When a lesbian writer begins to tell her own story in her own words, she also begins to redefine herself and her community – in her own terms – within public discourses. Her disruptive words, traditionally barred from the consciousness of conventional discursive practice, blatantly exceed the limits of what is linguistically permissible within patriarchal representation. It is the task of this essay to examine how lesbian poets have negotiated the difficult gap between silence and speech in their attempts to construct within the symbolic, a language adequate to lesbian experience. The lesbian writer has long been 'conscious of herself as an absence from discourse' and, in the face of censure, has traditionally adopted strategies of concealment involving a 'necessary obliquity' (Collecott, 1990: 94). Above all, the struggle to articulate a poetic for survival has meant a struggle with fear, with internalised homophobia, with the otherness and difference of being lesbian.

As Adrienne Rich has commented, 'women writers are now beginning to dare to enter that particular chamber of the "unspeakable" and to breathe word of what we are finding there' (Rich 1978: 201). In so doing, the lesbian writer may well bring to language the distress, anger and fear of *being the other*. She may also, much more disturbingly, celebrate and claim the *joy* of lesbian existence within language. In refusing to collaborate with the mechanisms of silencing, the lesbian writer brings to articulation the suppressed alternatives to the conventional male/female heterosexual relation. In that the lesbian can and does challenge patriarchal definitions of herself, she defiantly identifies herself for herself: she makes herself, her sexuality and her body visible – in spite of repressive discursive practices. Here, Olga Broumas' lines lovingly transform the terms of lesbian sexuality: the woman's patriarchally named 'cunt' is considered to be 'miraculous' and a 'seething / of holiness'. Symbolised as a 'small cathedral', her body's interior becomes a 'light-filled temple' in which worshippers light many candles to mark their profound respect. In addressing her lover, Broumas suggests that

A woman-made language would
have as many synonyms for pink/light-filled/holy as
the Eskimo does

for snow . . .
   You too, my darling, are
folded, clean
round a light-filled temple, complete
with miraculous icon, shedding
her perfect tears

(Broumas, in Bulkin 1981: 12)

Clearly, Broumas has defiantly brought to language a lesbian interpretation of her lover's body, in a poetry that affirms the ecstatic
sensuality of lesbian sexual love. Lesbian poets, however tyranni-
cally they have been marginalised within discourse, may devise
strategies of writing that can be set against definitions assailing
them from homophobic culture. In this essay, I explore how poems
by Olga Broumas, Muriel Rukeyser, H.D. (Hilda Doolittle),
Adrienne Rich and Audre Lorde work to re-present lesbian
libidinal difference, sexual identity and cultural identity – in their
own terms.
   The task for the lesbian poet is, I should say at the outset, not one
of searching for the repressed 'authentic' lesbian voice. Rather, it
involves identifying and powerfully articulating the repressed
representations, practices, and discourses which construct lesbians as
intelligible, sexually complex beings able to make a critical challenge to the regulatory practices of patriarchal discursive systems.
For lesbian writers this involves deconstructing the heterosexual
matrix which stabilises phallogocentrism. For example, the tran-
scendent 'I' of lyric poetry presents itself as a free subjectivity and
at the same time denies/conceals its heterosexual masculinist bias.
The western lyric tradition has long presented itself through a universal 'I' voice. Diana Collecott has spoken of this 'anonymous
tradition of white male lyricism' in which love poems have been
addressed 'from "I" to "you", with the sex of both partners uniden-
tified' (Collecott 1990: 101).[2] Such gender-neutral language acts as a
mask which allows the presumption of heterosexuality to go
unchallenged: 'masculist traditions of interpretation assume that
the poet or speaking subject is male, and the beloved object is
female, unless there is internal evidence to the contrary'. Whilst, as
Collecott suggests, these conventions have allowed homosexual
writers to publish 'with impunity', they have also functioned to
perpetuate the exclusive heterosexual matrix which preserves phallogocentrism in all its inequity. Thus lesbian writing needs to

contest these sites of gender-neutral language for they conceal but-tresses to (heterosexual) masculist authority and power. For the poet, this means re-signifying differences and desires in gender-specific language and re-producing the lesbian sexual body in both its variation *and* its specificity – it means articulating the full diversity and difference of lesbian experience within the public discourses of poetry.

Historically, lesbian poets have too often been driven to hide behind a mask of gender neutrality – to shelter under the veil that myth can draw over the personal – precisely because discursive fictions relating to the personal lives of lesbians have been rigorously excluded from cultural forms. As Adrienne Rich comments: 'Along with persecution, we have met with utter, suffocating silence and denial: the attempt to wipe us out of history and culture altogether. This silence is part of the totality of silence about women's lives' (Rich 1978: 224).

For lesbians living within a hostile patriarchy, survival has depended on secrecy, on deviousness and the deliberate exclusion of specific aspects of our private sexual and emotional lives. In her introduction Elly Bulkin also pointed to the impossibility of identifying lesbian contributions to culture as such, and the 'potential for erroneous (or at best, incomplete) reading' of lesbian work (Bulkin 1981: xxv). For a poet to be able to speak out in celebration of a lesbian relationship directly and openly, she has to have reached an acceptance, intellectually and emotionally, of lesbian sexual difference. Here is Muriel Rukeyser, writing in 1973:

> Yes, our eyes saw each other's eyes
> Yes, our mouths saw each other's mouth
> Yes, our breasts saw each other's breasts
> Yes, our bodies entire saw each other
> Yes, it was beginning in each
> Yes, it threw waves across our lives
> Yes, the pulses were becoming very strong
> Yes, the beating became very delicate
> Yes, the calling   the arousal
> Yes, the arriving   the coming
> Yes, it was there for both entire
> Yes, we were looking at each other

(Rukeyser 1982: 493)

What is the sexual difference to be celebrated here? The 'difference'

lies in the sameness of the different women's bodies, the reciprocity
of their desires for each other, the delicacy of their lovemaking. It
can be seen in the concern of the speaker as she notes whether each
moment of recognition and further arousal has been reached by the
other – through each noticing and responding to the other's 'look'.
The body that 'looks' is the same sex as the body that is looked at,
and the women's sexual rhythms and responses have the same
form. These particular lovers take care that both partners are orgas-
mically satisfied – 'Yes, it was there for both entire'. Rukeyser's use
of chiasmus as a structuring figure for lesbian desire is intriguing:
the contrasting parallel phrases 'the calling', 'the coming', 'the
arousal', 'the arriving' may be considered as a kind of spatial
metaphor. The Greek root of the term chiasmus is chiasma, a cross-
shaped mark. Here, the figure takes the shape of an intertwining
cross – which conveys a strong sense of the powerfully tender and
erotic bond between women who have said 'Yes' to each other's
desiring sexual bodies.[3] Coming to recognise and use the complexity of difference as a resource for poetry in the struggle against
persecution of lesbians and gay men, requires the poet to abandon
reticence, secrecy, and self-hatred:

> Among our secrecies, not to despise our Jews
> (that is, ourselves) or our darkness, our blacks,
>
> . . . never to despise
> the homosexual who goes building another
> with touch   with touch   (not to despise any touch)
> each like himself, like herself each
> You are this
>
> (Rukeyser 1982: 491)

Again, through the use of similes, the poet explores the sameness-
in-difference, the difference-in-sameness of homosexuality.
Same-sex love between men is clearly different to that between
women and yet it is also 'like'. In this complex word-play the word
'like' becomes very mobile, moving between genders and putting
in parallel the key marks of sexual difference. The poem both
acknowledges differences *and* collapses the key distinctions of class,
race, and sexuality. Blacks, Jews, and homosexuals become 'ourselves', indistinguishable from 'them', no longer the other in their
difference from us, we become them, they become us – 'You are
this'. Damaging projections onto the other are to be reintegrated

into the field of identity, and unconsciously acquired internalisa-
tions examined and held up to question. Constructing a poetic for
survival thus requires the poet courageously to examine the unacknowledged fears, the 'darkness', 'the secrecy' within, and requires
her to refuse to accept the disparagements and discriminations
discursively produced by an anti-Semitic, racist and sexist hetero-
patriarchy.

But before 1973, creating a lesbian voice was far from easy for
Rukeyser. Elly Bulkin describes having 'read through Rukeyser's
work without thinking of her possible lesbianism until *after* I had
heard that she had agreed to participate in the lesbian poetry reading at the 1978 Modern Language Association convention'.
Rukeyser did not make the convention and died in 1980. But Bulkin
was compelled to reassess her approach to Rukeyser's work: 'send-
ing me back to her work, the discovery allowed me to understand
for the first time that the opening poems in *The Speed of Darkness*
(1968) celebrate coming out' (Bulkin 1981: xxiv). Rukeyser's oblique
and ambiguous representation in 'What do I give you?' (one of the
opening poems of that 1968 collection) gives us little indication that
she is a lesbian writer whose lesbianism may not be spoken of and
whose memories could not enter into the language of her poetry:

> What do I give you? This memory
> I cannot give you. Force of a memory
> I cannot give you: it rings my nerves among.
> None of these songs
> Are made in their images.
> Seeds of all memory
> Given me give I you
> My own self.   Voice of my days.
> Blessing;   the seed and pain,
> Green of the praise of growth.
> The sacred body of thirst.

> (Rukeyser 1982: 435)

Following Bulkin's example and reading retrospectively, we can
see that Rukeyser speaks, but only indirectly and in gender-neutral
language, of the effects of repressive censorship on the lesbian poet.
To produce and develop a lesbian practice is vitally necessary if we
are to recognise and understand the poetics of lesbian survival. As
Diana Collecott suggests, this requires 'a revision of reading practices, and especially the New Critical convention that a literary text

contains within itself all the information necessary to its interpretation' (Collecott 1990: 104).

It is clear that, under conditions of censorship, Rukeyser may not draw on her own reminiscences. She may not make poetry out of the substance of her own life's experiences, out of her own emotional complexities, her own cultural attachments: 'None of these songs / Are made in their images'. The poet is driven instead to use symbolic 'seeds' to encode her memories, to give voice to 'my days'; to give 'you' (the reader? who else? her lover?) 'My own self'. She does not speak openly of her pains and blessings, nor of her relationship to imposed or internalised censorship. All is veiled by the movement into symbolic/mythic reference. Without contextual knowledge of Rukeyser's own life and of her lesbianism, it would be easy to miss the point of this poem.

The poem that opens *The Speed of Darkness*, and which is placed immediately preceding the above poem, is 'The poem as mask, Orpheus'. This equally cryptic poem is hardly speaking out about its lesbianism. Yet, given the knowledge that Rukeyser is a lesbian poet, it may be read as a manifesto, as a coded declaration of the necessity for lesbian poets to break through the façade mythopoesis provides and identify themselves for themselves within discourse.[4] Rukeyser clearly indicates her wish to 'sing her own music' and her passionate desire to position herself as no longer utterly fragmented but rather as a 'rescued' subjectivity able to reach towards a sense of her uncompromised integrity as a lesbian:

When I wrote of the women in their dances and wildness, it
was a mask,
on their mountain, gold-hunting, singing, in orgy,
it was a mask; when I wrote of the god,
fragmented, exiled from himself, his life, the love gone down
with song,
it was myself, split open, unable to speak, in exile from myself.

There is no mountain, there is no god, there is memory
of my torn life, myself split open in sleep, the rescued child
beside me among the doctors, and a word
of rescue from the great eyes.

No more masks! No more mythologies!

Now, for the first time, the god lifts his hand,
The fragments join in me with their own music.

(Rukeyser 1982: 435)

The poet states that her writing had previously been masked. Jacob Korg suggests that the use of the poetic mask was developed substantially by Ezra Pound who tried to 'convey character or states of mind through style in poems written through fictional or historical characters'. Pound viewed these poems 'as steps in a search for his own identity which he carried on by first creating and then casting off "complete masks of the self in each poem"' (Korg 1979: 90). Here, masked or personified as Orpheus, the poet is 'in exile' from herself, she is 'unable to speak', is 'split open', fragmented. The male god Orpheus, which had functioned as a masculine projection, is revealed as a masquerade concealing the personal voice of the poet. Rukeyser's use of the personal reflexive pronoun 'me', repeated three times, emphasises her desire to reveal the subject behind this mask – the silenced, torn-apart identity of the lesbian poet. She begins a reconstructive process of re-membering, of reminiscence – and attempts a symbolic reintegration of the 'fragments' of her disintegrated self. She reviews her 'torn life', the 'child' is rescued, the poet's own voice may be heard. Rukeyser seems to be rejecting her earlier poetic strategies. Now 'there is no mountain, there is no god' and there is very evidently an urgent desire to sing her 'own music'. In the wry reversal of the concluding lines when 'the god lifts his hand' we may well ponder – is he waving farewell? is he releasing her? Or is he beckoning her to speak her own words, sing her own song? It is tempting to think that in retaining the figure of Orpheus, Rukeyser is signalling her continuing allegiance to the use of Greek mythology as an alternative cultural resource having especial resonances within homosexual writing. But in fact, very few of her later poems actually do so. When Rukeyser does refer to Greek myth again her usage is ironic. Henceforth, when she speaks – she speaks as herself.

Yet the Greek poet Sappho is an inspirational and very special precursor for a great many lesbian poets. Lesbian and bisexual poets have, despite their ambivalent reactions to Sappho's possible suicide, frequently mythicised the resonances of their lives – in poetry that draws its symbolic imagery from Sapphic sources. Her surviving fragments have enabled modern and contemporary poets to build on them and to invent a classical inheritance where none truly exists. As Susan Gubar has remarked, since so many of the original Greek texts were destroyed, 'the modern woman poet could write "for" or "as" Sappho and thereby invent a classical inheritance of her own', through what Gubar calls a 'fantastic col-laboration' (Gubar 1984: 47). They reach for that 'long-lost ecstatic lyricism that inscribes female desire as the ancient source of song'. Rachel Blau DuPlessis follows Gubar when she claims that 'to need Sappho as a literary woman is to participate in an erotic-textual chain of longing that occurs for several reasons, not the least that Sappho has been left in fragments, and hence can be fleshed out, re-animated by being rewritten (DuPlessis 1986: 23).

DuPlessis argues further that modernist poet H.D. 'inspired her-self repeatedly by engagement with Greek materials, imitated and reproduced them to produce herself as a writer' (*ibid.*: 3–4). This classicising impulse allows the writer to assume both 'real and imagined' personae and revise them in texts that emerge 'aslant to reigning conventions'. These strategies may also be used both to project *and* to veil the self. As DuPlessis points out:

> despite the unstinting Greek contexts and references, it is possible to see (as Norman Holmes Pearson has suggested) the whole set of lyrics only coincidentally Greek: the landscapes are American, the emotions are personal, the 'Greek' then becomes a conventional but protected projection of private feelings into public meanings.
>
> (Du Plessis 1986: 14)

H.D. chose to locate her poetic within the ancient world of Sappho and frequently invoked the gods and goddesses, the religious cere-monial and symbology familiar to us from pagan classical texts. The appropriation of ancient myth has particular value to a twen-tieth-century woman writer engaged in the task of reconstructive re-vision. She may use it to support and sustain an alternative cul-tural perspective; to resymbolise a scene, plot or narrative; to project and re-enact within a transformed setting her personal story; or she may dramatise some moment that has been important to her in her personal life.

H.D. frequently and deliberately echoed Sappho's lyricism, her extreme simplicity of style, her intense sensuality and her fine emo-tional delicacy. Sappho's sparse, short lines, her clarity of image, her personal dramatic narratives – all were vital parts of H.D.'s speaking 'for' or 'as' Sappho, as she displaced and mythicised her experience into poetry. 'From citron-bower', an extract from 'Hymen (1921)', can be read as a semi-ironic 'temple service' of lament which enacts ceremoniously the coming of (heterosexual) love to the bride at the Temple of Hera. 'Hymen' is directly related

to Sappho through its form, its imagery, its trajectory of desire, and
its symbolic reference:

> From citron-bower be her bed,
> Cut from branch of tree a-flower,
> Fashioned for her maidenhead.
>
> From Lydian apples, sweet of hue,
> Cut the width of board and lathe.
> Carve the feet from myrtle-wood.
>
> Let the palings of her bed
> Be quince and box-wood overlaid
> With the scented bark of yew.
>
> That all the wood in blossoming,
> May calm her heart and cool her blood
> For losing of her maidenhood

(H.D. 1984: 108)

This poem echoes the sense of grief in Sappho's 'Fragment 34'. The
song is a lament for a maidenhead, its imagery 'Lydian' – soft,
slow, luxurious, feminine. The Cretan quince-apple, sacred to
Aphrodite, speaks tellingly of erotic connection; it is also the sacred
apple of the tree of life and death in Hera's garden. The sensual
appeal of fragrant wood and fragrant blossom is ambivalently
linked to death; the yew is emblematic of grief in Greek mythology;
the myrtle signifies life in death. The bed may blossom to 'calm her
heart and cool her blood', but as we read the poem, the carved
wood becomes ever more overlaid, box-like, coffin-like, closed in,
as these symbolic references resonate. Sung by a chorus of boys, the
final section tells how the desire of the woman becomes more and
more eclipsed, 'mute and dumb', before the 'fiery need' of the male
'plunderer' (H.D. 1984: 109–10). Ultimately, we are told, 'Where
love is king' there is little need to 'dance and sing'. The consumma-
tion of heterosexual love renders her speechless – it is not quite a
moment to be celebrated:

> Where love is come
> (Ah, love is come indeed!)
> Our limbs are numb
> Before his fiery need;
> With all their glad
> Rapture of speech unsaid,

Before his fiery lips
Our lips are mute and dumb.

(H.D. 1984: 110)

A deathly failure of light, colour and sound signals the end of the service. 'Blinded the torches fail' and 'flicker out', the music 'dies away' and is 'finally cut short', 'the purple curtain hangs black and heavy', the figures 'pass out like shadows'; the service concludes in gloomy darkness and in silence. The over-romanticised 'flame, an exaggerated symbol' of heterosexual love was hardly a figure to be welcomed. Thus it appears that H.D. has encoded the patterns of the heterosexual marriage on the surface but the sorrow and mourning of a lesbian *funeral* underlies the writing. In this liturgy of lament, as in Sappho's poetry, the direction of emotional attention is towards the woman. The emotion underlying this service is the profound sense of loss felt by the 'concealed' lesbian poet, who represents, complexly, her passionate concern and caring for the plundered, wan-faced bride: muteness, numbness and grief appear to overwhelm her as the one she loves (herself or another) is 'taken' into heterosexual alliance.

H.D. surely has played hide and seek with the mask and the myth to find a way of rehearsing creatively situations and experiences drawn from her life. In working within and against a modernist aesthetic, H.D. makes use of the unsatisfactory heterosexual codes that so distort lesbian realities – in order to produce a lesbian encoding of her alternative story. In constructing a performative drama as a way to enact her grief, the poet also contests the socially instituted meaning of the heterosexual encounter. She subverts its power to transfix and fascinate and works to deconstruct its coercive ideological force. Ultimately the poet creates a subversive matrix in which the normative terms given within heterosexual discourses are rendered absurd and ridiculous. The intelligibility of lesbian desire, attachment and loss does not reside in 'joy decreed' or in the 'flamboyant bird, half emerged in the sunset' – images in which the power discourses of heterosexual love are rendered either as seductive or as ridiculous.[5] Rather, it lies with the 'wail of flute and trumpet', the 'black and heavy' signifiers of (concealed) lesbian loss and grieving. It seems important to look more closely at these often tragic experiences of concealed lesbian loss and grieving.

Lesbian loss and grief become literally unmentionable in a world where compulsory heterosexuality rules discourse. The loss or death of a lover, or separation, or an unsatisfiable yearning for an unavailable woman become unrepresentable, unintelligible to a world in which their existence is denied. Lesbian sadness or grief, the unsatisfied longing for tenderness, for an intimacy lost or never found – all the confused strands that constitute the breadth of lesbian experience – need to be made coherent and distinctly lesbian. Fully articulated themes of lesbian grief, separation and loss dominate Adrienne Rich's much later poem, 'Splittings (1974)'. At the same time, however, the poem is a celebration of the freedom to 'choose to love this time for once / with all my intelligence'. A spoken-of loss can be given a matrix of intelligibility, the limits of loss may be ascertained, the pain assuaged.

> I am not with her   I have been waking off and on
> all night to that pain   not simply absence but
> the presence of the past   destructive
> to living here and now   Yet if I could instruct
> myself, if we could learn to learn from pain
> even as it grasps us   if the mind, the mind that lives
> in this body could refuse   to let itself be crushed
> in that grasp   it would loosen

(Rich 1978: 10)

Like H.D., Rich seeks to come to terms with an experience of separation from her lover. In the poem, this profound sense of loss is linked to the infant's experience of the estranging separation from and the ultimate loss of the mother. The poet speaks of her anguish on hearing the inward echo that repeats the 'cry' of 'primordial loneliness', 'the pain of division' that is comparable to the mother–daughter relationship. The poet's words proceed hesitantly, change direction, turn back on themselves, assume multiple tones, positions, and voices. There is no certainty, except that self-division is fundamental to existence: the voice(s) speak(s) out of that pain, become(s) it:

> *We are older now*
> *we have met before   these are my hands before your eyes*
> *my figure blotting out   all that is not mine*
> *I am the pain of division   creator of divisions*
> *it is I who blot your lover from you*
> *and not the time-zones nor the miles*

It is not separation calls me forth   but I
who am separation   And remember
I have no existence   apart from you

('Splittings (1974)")

The destructive 'dark breath' of separation and loss is viewed here as a pain that is a left-over; it is 'not simply absence but / the presence of the past'. Some way must be found to counter or cope with this destructive reminiscence, so as 'not to suffer uselessly   yet still to feel'. The poet dramatises this lesbian's acknowledgement of her present pain, recognises its propensity to carry with it 'configurations of the past'. She seeks to limit the pain of loss to the particularity of the present relationship, the separation of the lovers. Yet, at the same time, paradoxically, the poet fantasises a unity of relation. Just as the baby may 'memorise the body of the mother / and create her in absence', so too does the poet experiment with images that recreate a sense of the lover's presence. In a contradictory movement which involves a degree of disavowal, almost a self-conscious denial of her lover's absence, the poet seeks to contain and limit the pain of separation, division and difference. In this willed fantasy, she invokes the very physical presence – the 'mind and body' – of her lover:

I will not be divided   from her or from myself
by myths of separation
while her mind and body in Manhattan are more with me
than the smell of eucalyptus coolly burning   on these hills

('Splittings (1974)')

The woman speaker is in San Francisco, her lover 'in Manhattan'. Yet the lover is 'more with me', more present to her body's senses than 'the smell of eucalyptus'. This sensuous affirmation plays with traditional heterosexual ideologies of romantic love: the illusion that oneness and completion is possible through the agency of the lover. A phantasmatic relation of body to body underpins this imaginary unity of relation. The metonymy of the (mother's) body, what Jane Gallop emphasises as 'the register of [the mother's] touching, nearness, presence, immediacy, contact', is reiterated many times in Rich's poem.[6] Throughout, there is a tantalising sense of closeness to *and* distance from the body of the mother/lover. Desire plays across the contiguities of feminine *jouissance* and sparks the pleasure of *contact* enjoyed in this fantasised relation, as well as the poignancy of the loss of that connection to the mother's body:

> Does the infant memorise the body of the mother
> and create her in absence?   or simply cry
> primordial loneliness?   does the bed of the stream
> once diverted   mourning   remember wetness?
> ('Splittings (1974)')

I have noted elsewhere the fascinating parallels between the work of Adrienne Rich and Luce Irigaray.[7] Here, Irigaray points to the political strategy necessary for women to survive despite the ravishments of hetero-patriarchal discourses:

> Let's not be ravished by their language again: let's not embody mourning. We must learn how to speak to each other so that we can embrace across distances. Surely when I touch myself, I remember you. But so much is said, and said of us, that separates us.

This restorative fantasy of contiguity – of imaginary contact represented in the poem – is not comparable to the heterosexual fantasy which symbolises woman as the 'stand in' for the lost object. In the final section of 'Splittings (1974)', the woman states:

> I refuse these givens   the splitting
> between love and action   I am choosing
> not to suffer uselessly   and not to use her
> I choose to love   this time   for once
> with all my intelligence

In ultimately repudiating the 'givens' – the imposed choices, the useless sufferings – of conventional heterosexual discourse, the poet refuses either to take refuge from the world in the lover, to give up power for love 'as women have done', or to hide from power in her love, 'like a man'. Instead, the poet accepts the responsibility of a choice *outside* the violating consistencies of gender polarity. Insistently, Rich eschews the 'refuge' of the dualistic world of complementary heterosexual roles, neither abnegating nor hiding from her own power as a woman to choose for herself what she wants. In this poem, written in 1974 and included in her 'coming-out' collection *The Dream of a Common Language*, Rich is able to explore the specificity of lesbian relationship and her experience of loss overtly without recourse to the veil of ancient myth or the devious mask of obliquity.

I want to turn now to the Black lesbian poet Audre Lorde, whose profoundly political writing is dedicated 'to an acceptance, understanding and use of difference in the struggle to change the world' (Lewis 1990: 100). Her personal quest for survival – not separate from her politics – compelled her to speak out about her own heartrending campaign against invasive cancer of the breast. Reading of Lorde's struggle not to die, I want to celebrate her life of resistance – and her life-giving words which, though she herself is now dead, will continue to survive, to do battle against the aggressor – 'those of us who live our battles in the flesh must know ourselves as our strongest weapon in the most gallant struggle of our lives' (Lorde 1988b: 133). Lorde spells out the particular aggressions she faces as a Black lesbian: 'battling racism and battling heterosexism and battling apartheid share the same urgency inside me as battling cancer' (*ibid.*: 116). And for all of these struggles, Lorde requires

> the nourishment of art and spirituality in my life, and they lend strength and insight to all the endeavours that give substance to my living. It is the bread of art and the water of my spiritual life that remind me always to reach for what is highest within my capacities and in my demands of myself and others. Not for what is perfect but for what is the best possible.
>
> (Lorde 1988a: 122–3)

Throughout her work, the spiritual life is inseparable from both personal and political struggle for survival. And cancer, racism, heterosexism and apartheid are intimately related to the forms of her spirituality as it becomes symbolised in her writing. The retrieval and reconstruction of the suppressed voices of marginalised spiritual traditions remains particularly important in the context of Lorde's poetry. Drawing from the rich resources of the folk tales of Black African cultures allows this Black lesbian feminist poet to create sites in which to contest the racist and heterosexist constructs of not only white western patriarchy, but also of white western feminism. The poet draws on these alternative mythologies for inspiration in the struggle to construct a poetic of survival that will not transmit the old colonial message untransformed. This recourse to a fictive matrilineal world does not in my view constitute a regressive nostalgic return to origins. It is, rather, an attempt to fabricate a poetic matrix which is committed to dramatising and re-symbolising sexual ambiguity, creating a confusion of gender categories, and offering a celebration of racial and sexual differences as both challenging and productive – a celebration rather similar to that which we have found in Rich. But Lorde takes this further than Rich, in that she also offers a feminist post-Christian challenge to patriarchal Christianity, the dominant form of faith her community has inherited from the colonising white missionaries.[8]

In her poem 'Dahomey', Audre Lorde reaches back to the Black African culture of Abomey, specifically to the Dahomeyan Amazons, those 'highly prized, well-trained, and ferocious women warriors who guarded, and fought under the direction of, the Panther Kings of Dahomey' (Lorde 1978: 10). Yoruban spirituality informs this complex reworking of the ancient myths of Nigerian communities:

> It was in Abomey that I felt
> the full blood of my fathers' wars
> and where I found my mother
> Seboulisa
> standing with outstretched palms hip high
> one breast eaten away by worms of sorrow
> magic stones resting upon her fingers
> dry as a cough

Rejection of white western feminism's pacifist emphasis leads Lorde to acknowledge and feel 'the full blood of my fathers' wars'. Lorde does not condemn violence as such, but sees its use as valid in the war against racism and apartheid. Where white feminism has a long history of opposing the violence of war, Lorde accepts its necessity. White lesbian feminist Adrienne Rich condemns those men who commit war in this short extract from 'The Phenomenology of Anger (1972)', a poem which relates to the Vietnam War:

> This morning you left the bed
> we still share
> and went out to spread impotence
> upon the world
>
> I hate you.
> I hate the mask you wear, your eyes

assuming a depth
they do not possess . . .

(Rich 1975: 201)

These lines are not about hating men for simply being men, but about hating the mask of indifference and the acts of violence per- petrated by men under conditions of war. In 'Dahomey', Lorde refuses to make that condemnation and thus takes up a very differ- ent position from Rich. However, in identifying with and supporting to the full the urgent projects which lead Black 'fathers' into war, she is not uncritical. Lorde's poem does not sing the praises of the masculine heroic; rather, she ambiguously recognises both the horror of the blood as well as the situation of the anguished Seboulisa, 'one breast eaten away by worms of sorrow'.

Seboulisa, the goddess of Abomey, is, in the Dahomeyan pan- theon, 'the Mother of us all' (Lorde 1978: 121). She is also a local representation of Mawulisa. Mary K. DeShazer sees Lorde as 'pay- ing homage' to Seboulisa: 'Lorde celebrates Seboulisa as a mother of both sorrow and magic, a sorceress who will help her daughter find a language from which to speak' (DeShazer 1986: 183). This link between the mother and the daughter has great importance in Lorde's work overall, yet as we shall see, it is not exclusive.

Lorde comments that 'Mawu is regarded as the Creator of the Universe, and Lisa is either called her first son, or her twin brother' (Lorde 1978: 120). She is thus a composite being combining a pow- erful mother and subordinate son or brother – a mythic figure in which the boundaries between male and female are blurred and in which gender categories collapse in confusion. In this poem, links of kinship and family are important, as are the relationships between women. Yet Seboulisa, 'the Mother of us all' is not 'pure' woman or even biological woman: she is to be understood as a sex- ually ambiguous figure possessing mixed gender attributes.

As this composite figure of Seboulisa suggests, Lorde does not limit her poetic to a reductive matriarchalism, or any other exclu- sionary politics – she will not accede to any politics which fails to negotiate difference: 'difference must be not merely tolerated, but seen as a fund of necessary polarities between which our creativity can spark like a dialectic' (Lorde 1984: 111).

Thus, in refusing to condemn either male or female violence, Lorde also refuses to ally herself with Rich's pacifist position.

Instead, she situates herself alongside the male, like the African Amazon, ready to do battle as a woman who is 'not enjoined from the shedding of blood' (Lorde 1978: 119). She accepts the necessity for the 'brother' and 'nephew' to stitch 'tales of blood'. Are these tales of the past? Or are they ones to be stitched in readiness for future encounters with the white racist oppressor? Again, Lorde's poetry constitutes a radical challenge to the gender assymetries characteristic of the white western patriarchy, which would limit female participation in the culturally constructed forms of militarised power, its defences and hostilities. Lorde fuses an ancient mythic world with what could be a contemporary world of brass-workers and cloth: the mundane world of work is not separate from the spiritual world in Lorde's poetic. There is, however, underlying this poem, a clear-sighted realist recognition of the world of necessity for Black peoples: the need for both male and female to be ready to counter actual, often physically enforced, subjugation; and also the need to empower Black men to respect themselves.

An aside here to mention Lorde's relationship to her own son – and her own necessity to find ways to empower him to respect himself – is perhaps relevant. In caring for Jonathan after he had been bullied, Lorde recounts how she had to check herself from hissing at her son in anger and frustration at his tears – '"the next time you come in here crying . . ." and I suddenly caught myself in horror' (Lorde 1984: 75–6). She had recognised how she, as his mother, was playing her part in perpetuating the 'age-old distortions about what strength and bravery really are. And no, Jonathan didn't have to fight if he didn't want to, but somehow he did have to feel better about not fighting'. Empowerment, self-respect for boys and men growing up in a patriarchal world – Black or white – is not easily found or earned. As caring mother to her son, Lorde finds herself having to acknowledge her own impotent fury – her own pain at watching her son suffer the violence of the street corner – and it is a struggle for her to find ways to empower him, to help him achieve a measure of self-respect.

Despite Lorde's support of the necessity for violent, bloody, militant action, for typically masculine modes of confrontational politics, she does not fully approve of unmuted phallic power. In 'Dahomey', 'Eshu', the male god of language who 'transmits and interprets', is mocked by the women. His 'iron quiver / standing erect and flamingly familiar' is silenced, rendered 'mute as a porcupine in a forest of lead'. His potential for penetrative violence, his phallic weaponry – the 'iron quiver', the 'forest of lead' – is tamed. Eshu is often teased and, according to Lorde's notes, he is even often 'danced by a woman with an attached phallus' (Lorde 1978: 119–20). This figure stands erect, displays a 'huge erect phallus', is potent, virile, and, importantly, is also female. This humorous, probably intentional ambivalence towards masculinity – or the masculine female – is left unresolved within the poem. Indeed, the prankster as an 'unpredictable' and 'mischievous' figure of parody, becomes a site or location in which gender confusion proliferates, in which the attributes of what the white western world has considered masculine and what feminine, become comically denaturalised. It is a site in which differences no longer carry a fixed meaning, in which gender is rendered complex and its intelligibility questioned. The discourses which organise sexuality on the basis of anatomical distinctions are flouted – here biology is not destiny – and so laughter rules.

In contrast, Lorde attributes to the woman a position of serious responsibility toward the men. The 'woman with braided hair' has the awesome power to spell and prophesy over Shango, 'one of Yemanja's best-known and strongest sons, the god of lightning and thunder, war and politics' (Lorde 1978: 121). Women in this culture have spiritual and political power and are prepared to use violence, but, in this instance, it is only the violence of the tongue, of metaphor: 'I speak / whatever language is needed / to sharpen the knives of my tongue' (*ibid.*: 10). The poet's voice dynamically represents its power in the image of the drums whose 'speech' is honoured throughout old Africa. Her dignity, symbolised in the composure and poise of the woman's quiet integrity, is to be respected: 'whether or not / you are against me / I will braid my hair / even / in the seasons of rain'.

Desire for the mother, and for cultural unity, focuses this poem: the woman speaker searches for and finds her mother. Seboulisa, as personal mother and as mythic mother, is filled with sorrow. The mutilation of her breast may, in this context, be seen as signifying the agony inflicted by the white aggressor on generations of black cultures. ('Racism. Cancer. In both cases, to win the aggressor must conquer, but the resisters need only survive' (Lorde 1988a: 111). As I write, Lorde's current life fuses with the myth of Seboulisa, as she courageously resisted not only racism, but also cancer: a foremother herself.) The absent breast has not been purposefully removed in order to hold the Amazonian bow in battle but, rather, has been 'eaten away by worms of sorrow'. Seboulisa's 'outstretched palms hip high' suggest her mute appeal to end her suffering, the suffering of the Black mother responsible for her peoples. She is ready with her magic stones, her poetry. She continues to carry out her responsibilities towards her people in working her word-magic for the future.

As Lorde's poetry all too clearly reveals, a vital necessity for Afra-American women, alienated from their ancient matrilineal cultural roots by the ideological supremacy of white European forms of thought, is the retrieval of the hidden knowledges of non-European cultures. The persistence of racist and colonialist oppression requires a strategy of resistance. In Lorde's terms, such a strategy emerges out of the desires for/of the 'Black mother, the poet' whispering her subversive charter for the future:

> The Black mother within each of us – the poet – whispers in our dreams:
> I feel, therefore I can be free. Poetry coins the language to express and
> charter this revolutionary demand, the implementation of that freedom.
> (Lorde 1984: 38)

The movement here from dreams, feelings and desires towards survival and change, from ideas into action through the naming of her strong demand for 'freedom' – including the implementation of that demand – shows the black mother/poet's urgent call for vast social change. As poet she will find words – her sister's or her mother's, her foresister's or her foremother's – to set against the white patriarchal words that colonise her.

Lorde's own mother Linda was a fierce disciplinarian who knew how to 'frighten children into behaving in public', a 'very powerful woman' who fired her daughter's imagination with stories of her home in Carriacou, a small island off the coast of Grenada (Lorde 1982b: 111). Lorde tells us in *Zami*: 'When I visited Grenada I saw the root of my mother's powers walking through the streets. I thought, this is the country of my foremothers, my forebearing mothers, those Black island women who defined themselves by what they did' (*ibid.*: 9). The dream of the homeland of Carriacou becomes closely bound up with desire for the mother – the desire for roots, for a homeland of fruits, trees and flowers, for a land peopled by her black mother's foremothers and other women.

The word *foremother*, according to Joanne Braxton, means a

female ancestor, 'one who has preceded and who has gone on, but by definition, foremother can also mean one who has gone in front, someone who has been a leader, someone who has stood at the foreground of cultural experience' (Braxton and McLaughlin 1990: xxv). The term includes all those women who have taken a leading role in contemporary politics or cultural life, those who have worked for the maintenance of Black relationships, and Black connection. Chinosole speaks of the related concept of the matrilineal diaspora as referring to the capacity of Black foremothers 'to survive and aspire, to be contrary and self-affirming across continents and generations. It names the strength and beauty we pass on as friends and lovers from foremothers to mothers and daughters allowing us to survive radical cultural changes and be empowered through differences' (in Braxton and McLaughlin 1990: 379).

Lorde's project of re-signifying difference and contesting 'mythical norms' defined as 'white, thin, male, young, heterosexual, Christian and financially secure' is crucially empowered through the figures of 'Foremothers (Lorde, in McEwen and Sullivan 1988: 270). The poem 'Call', which concludes her most recent book of poetry, *Our Dead Behind Us* (1986), particularly constitutes a sophisticated and strongly developed challenge to the power over minds of the figure of the white western male God. 'Call' is a prayer/poem addressed to Black African divinities 'whose names and faces have been lost in time' (Lorde 1986: 75). The poet calls upon the Black matriarchal warrior figure Aido Hwedo, holy ghost mother, symbolised in the poem as the Rainbow Serpent. The Black woman's faith in the 'most ancient Goddesses' of Black Africa is affirmed very strongly:

> I have not forgotten your worship
> nor my sisters
> nor the sons of my daughters
>
> my children watch for your print
> in their labours
> and they say Aido Hwedo is coming.
>
> I am a Black woman   turning
> mouthing your name as a password
> through seductions   self-slaughter
>
> and I believe in the holy ghost
> mother
> in your flames beyond our vision

Oya, Seboulisa, Mawu, Afrekete – goddesses from the ancient African capital of Dahomey – are set alongside historical and human heroines. 'Thandi Modise winged girl of Soweto' Rosa Parks and Fannie Lou Hamer, Assata Shakur and Yaa Asantewa, her own mother and Winnie Mandela are all invoked as images that affirm the Black woman as a warrior figure – shouting, ready and prepared to do battle against the white oppressor. The women sing and speak the Word (or the teaching) of the Black African ancestral inheritance. White male western deities have no place in this ancestral value and belief system. In deconstructing the power of the colonising white patriarchal God, Audre Lorde reconstructs a strong alternative system of faith that is centred in the black woman, and which she asserts in very powerful and polemical forms.

None the less, the pain of exploring the relation between her self and her mother has been, for Lorde, intense. The poem 'Story Books On a Kitchen Table' speaks of a Black mother who cannot accept her daughter's identification as lesbian. The poem records the mother's anguish at her daughter not 'becoming' a heterosexual adult. That said, anger does not prevent either of them from grieving deeply about their differences and the consequent separation from each other. In the poem, the lesbian daughter in her sexual difference has become her mother's 'nightmare':

> Out of her womb of pain my mother spat me
> into her ill-fitting harness of despair
> into her deceits
> where anger re-conceived me
> piercing my eyes like arrows
> pointed by her nightmare
> of who I was not
> becoming.
> (Lorde 1982: 35)

One of her own mother's 'deceits' is recounted in *Zami*, when her little daughter was spat on, an apparently commonplace event in New York in the thirties. Her mother is described ambivalently by the poet as fussing about 'low-class people who had no better sense nor manners than to spit into the wind no matter where they went, impressing upon me that this humiliation was totally random' (Lorde 1982a: 224). Lorde seems to be both grateful for and made uncomfortable by her mother's way of coping. As she explains, her mother's 'deceits' are grounded in her positive desire to protect her daughter from the humiliations of racism. When Lorde speaks of her mother's 'pain' and 'despair', however, we become aware that the two women are very different politically. Her mother still bears the scars from the traumas inflicted by the pernicious racism of white supremacist culture and dares not confront her oppressor. That the heterosexual mother cannot accept her lesbian daughter's sexuality also creates a difficult situation for both of them, but especially for the daughter who cannot and will not fulfil her mother's expectations of her. But it is because her black mother 'left in her place / iron maidens to protect me' that Lorde, the lesbian daughter, will survive. Coming to the painfully clear-sighted recognition that no 'white witches' will offer 'any kind enchantment / for the vanished mother / of a Black girl', the Black girl-child is under no illusions about what is possible in reality.

Despite her mother's 'going away' from her and her subsequent sense of loss, Lorde reclaims her powerful mother, seeing her as a 'Black dyke': 'to this day I believe that there have always been Black dykes around – in the sense of powerful and woman-oriented women – who would rather have died than use that name for themselves. And that includes my momma' (ibid.: 15). A large part of Zami is devoted to an account of her relationships with women, as mothers, friends and lovers: with her schoolgirl friend Genny (who commits suicide); with Ginger (her voluptuous first lover): with the unresponsive Bea; and then, in Mexico, a deeply fulfilling relationship with the mature and sophisticated alcoholic Eudora. And there are further loves – Muriel and Afrekete. Zami explores the gay scene of the McCarthyite fifties – as a role-playing world in which butch-femme conventions operated. Lorde felt unable to enter fully into adopting the 'mean' and 'tough' masculine image of the virile butch mode, nor could she identify with the 'cute' and 'passive' exaggeratedly feminine femme: 'I was given a wide berth. Non-conventional people can be dangerous, even in the gay community' (ibid.: 9). Lorde here speaks of her own marginality as a Black woman within that already marginal gay-girl world:

> Most Black lesbians were closeted, correctly recognizing the Black community's lack of interest in our position, as well as the many more immediate threats to our survival as Black people in a racist society. It was hard enough to be Black, to be Black and female, to be Black, female

and gay. To be Black, female, gay, and out of the closet in a white
environment, even to the extent of dancing in the Bagatelle, was
considered by many Black lesbians to be simply suicidal.

In such a world, survival was not always possible: 'Many of us
wound up dead or demented, and many of us were distorted by
the many fronts we had to fight upon. But when we survived, we
grew up strong' (Lorde 1982b: 225). Living as a Black lesbian in a
racist society involves living with constant fear. In her poem 'A
Litany for Survival', Lorde reveals how black women learn to be
afraid 'with our mother's milk':

> And when the sun rises we are afraid
> it might not remain
> when the sun sets we are afraid
> it might not rise in the morning
> when our stomachs are full we are afraid
> of indigestion
> when our stomachs are empty we are afraid
> we may never eat again
> when we are loved we are afraid
> love will vanish
> when we are alone we are afraid
> love will never return
> and when we speak we are afraid
> our words will not be heard
> nor welcomed
> but when we are silent
> we are still afraid
>
> So it is better to speak
> remembering
> we were never meant to survive.

(Lorde 1978: 31)

Black lesbians, compelled to stand outside of the definitions of
what will pass and what is acceptable, seem to have a choice: self-
destruction, that is, becoming something that will make it possible
to be taken inside the system, being assimilated, becoming an
insider, or finding alternative structures outside the system that
will allow, justify and acknowledge their existence. Survival in
Lorde's terms, when so many do not survive, is learning how to
move beyond fear, beyond despair, through love. In the words of

the quotation on the frontispiece of *Zami*: 'In the recognition of loving lies the answer to despair'. Black women dare not refuse to be conscious of what they are living through or feeling at any time. As Lorde affirms, the close scrutiny of that 'dark place' within is the route to survival: 'as we learn to use the products of that scrutiny for power within our living, those fears which rule our lives and form our silences begin to lose their control over us' (Lorde, in McEwen and O'Sullivan 1988: 269).

As we have seen, Lorde positions herself as a Black lesbian warrior, an identity constructed in strong resistance to the conventional structures of a white hetero-patriarchy. In claiming and affirming Black lesbian sexual difference, she has argued that Black lesbian survival depends on recognising and exploring difference – 'as a springboard for creative change within our lives' (*ibid.*: 270). Her template for survival is learning to talk across differences between woman and woman, Black and Black, Black and white, lesbian, gay and heterosexual: 'we have no patterns for relating across our human differences as equals. As a result those differences have been misnamed and misused in the service of separation and confusion' (*ibid.*: 269). Unacknowledged fear of the 'strangeness' of lesbian otherness, which lies at the root of that confusion, may remain guiltily ignored and unspoken, giving rise to the distortions and hostility of homophobia.

Internalised homophobia comes under close examination in Lorde's poem 'Letter for Jan'. In this 'letter' the poet reaches out to a silent and afraid woman, desiring her to move beyond her fear and loathing of what she imagines as a rapacious lesbian sexuality, to a point where she can experience lesbian sexual difference as non-threatening, even as 'full of loving':

> No I don't think you were chicken not to speak
> I think you
> afraid I was mama as laser
> seeking to eat out or change your substance

> (Lorde 1978: 88)

Fears of homophobic intensity link themselves, perhaps predictably, to the terrifying intrapsychic image of 'mama as laser', the devouring, avenging, guilt-producing, punitive mother. Does homophobia derive from this disavowed figure, angry, hated, condemned and ultimately projected onto the strong, independent, sexually free lesbian? In the poem, we encounter a 'Mawulisa bent on destruction by threat / who might cover you'. The fear to be acknowledged is that of being overwhelmed, seduced, and then drowning in the kind of exotic hothouse eroticism that could wipe out her voice, her identity, her own 'praise song'. In her essay 'The Uses of the erotic: the erotic as power', Lorde argues that the erotic as a source of power has been corrupted and distorted: 'we have been taught to suspect this resource, villified, abused, and devalued within western society' (Lorde 1984: 53). Suspicion, contempt and distrust of female erotic power fuel homophobic fears: lesbian sexuality in the first section of 'Letter for Jan' becomes seen as rampant and overbearing in its forms, comparable to the sexualised aggressions of macho-heterosexuality

> that would seduce you open
> turning erotic and delightful as you
> went under for the third time
> your own poetry and sweetness
> masked and drying out
> upon your lips

(Lorde 1984, 'Letter for Jan')

The fear is neither about the lesbian as she is nor lesbianism as it is commonly lived, but instead concerns 'me as I might have been – a too casual 'quick chic', a too powerful 'god mother', or someone who is ready 'to reject you back into your doubt / smothering you into acceptance / with my own black song'. This is an intrapsychic 'nightmare' figure bearing anger, ready to reject, able to 'swallow you into confusion', 'buy you up', 'burn you up'. Entering into that terror and that loathing is to enter into the fear of difference and otherness. Lorde identifies the therapeutic task as working with the distortion and 'darkness', the 'misnaming' that produced that particular silence, as well as exploring the moment of closure that so devastatingly prevented 'Jan' from speaking. The intrapsychic and sociopolitical work to be done is 'to extract these distortions from our living at the same time as we recognise, reclaim, and define those differences upon which they are imposed' (Lorde, in McEwen and O'Sullivan 1988: 270). The dangerous fantasy of the rapacious lesbian must be recognised for what it is: a disparaging homophobic stereotype which covers over, drowns, and so wipes out the specificities of lesbian identity:

When all the time
I would have loved you
speaking
being a woman full of loving
turned on
and little bit raunchy
and heavy
with my own black song

(Lorde, in McEwen and O'Sullivan 1988)

Lorde's insistence on exploring difference, and re-presenting lesbian sexual desire and lesbian eroticism in her own terms is a crucial political strategy:

The future of our earth may depend upon the ability of all women to identify and develop new definitions of power and new patterns of relating across difference. The old definitions have not served us, nor the earth that supports us. The old patterns, no matter how cleverly rearranged to imitate progress, still condemn us to cosmetically altered repetitions of the same old exchanges, the same old guilt, hatred, recrimination, lamentation, and suspicion.

(Lorde, in McEwen and O'Sullivan 1988: 275)

Blatantly exceeding the limits of what is discursively permitted within patriarchal discourses, Lorde's disturbing poem brings to awareness the suppressed negative in the homophobic response to lesbian difference.

All the poets I have looked at here, Broumas Rukeyser, H.D., Rich and, of course, Lorde – in their different way – subvert, contest or displace conventional heterosexist poetic discourses. Through these poets, different strategies – lesbian libidinal differences, sexualities and cultural identities, in at least something of their diversity and specificity – have disruptively entered language and history. Each poet develops a lesbian strategy of survival appropriate to the particular dangers they faced within their own location and historical situation. In all instances, their pain, celebration and courage are a testimony to their determination to survive despite marginalisation and homophobic ostracism. Indeed, constructing a poetic of survival demands just such a courageous strategy in which same-sex desire is represented in all its specificity and diversity, through a matrix that is textually, ontologically and culturally intelligible.

NOTES

1. This essay has appeared as a chapter in Joseph Bristow (ed.) (1992), *Sexual Sameness: Textual Differences in Lesbian and Gay Writing*, Routledge, London.
2. For further exploration of these issues see 'Mother daughter sister lover: Adrienne Rich's dream of a whole new poetry'. Chapter 9 in Yorke (1991).
3. I am grateful to Joseph Bristow for drawing attention to this figure.
4. Mythopoetic = mythmaking. Mythopoet = a myth maker. I use the term 'myth' to denote those messages emerging from patriarchal discourses, whether religious, historical, classical or cultural, which have functioned to organise our perceptions of reality. An exploration of these re-visionary processes of transforming such 'myth' within poetic discourses is offered in my *Impertinent Voices* (Yorke 1991). See also Rachel Blau DuPlessis, 'Perceiving the other-side of everything': tactics of revisionary mythopoesis', in R.B. DuPlessis (1985).
5. Judith Butler suggests that since '"identity" is assured through the stabilising concepts of sex, gender and sexuality; the very notion of "the person" is called into question by the cultural emergence of those "incoherent" or "discontinuous" gendered beings who appear to be persons but who fail to conform to the gendered norms of cultural intelligibility by which persons are defined. "Intelligible" genders are those which in some sense institute and maintain relations of coherence and continuity among sex, gender, sexual practice and desire' (Butler 1990: 17). Here the attempt is to claim for lesbian identity a conceived 'intelligibility' within discourse that affirms and celebrates the kaleidoscopic complexity of this matrix of desire.
6. Jane Gallop draws on Lacan's use of the term 'contiguity' to explore the patterns of feminine sexuality. She quotes: 'feminine sexuality appears as the effort of a *jouissance* enveloped in its own contiguité [Ecrits]'. Such *jouissance*, she adds, 'would be sparks of pleasure ignited by *contact* at any point, at any moment along the line, not waiting for closure, but enjoying the touching' (Gallop 1982: 30). Following the logic of Kristeva, I link this *jouissance* to the eroticism which 'is indissociable from the experience' of the m/other's body. See 'Julia Kristeva talks to Susan Sellers, A question of subjectivity', *Women's Review* 12 October 1986, p. 20.
7. See Chapter 9 in *Impertinent Voices*. How close Rich is to Irigaray may be seen in this passage which immediately precedes my quotation: 'Yet how do we stay alive when far from each other? That's the danger. How can I await your return if we don't remain close when you are far away? If something palpable, here and now, doesn't evoke the touch of our bodies? How can we continue to live as ourselves if we are open to

the infinity of our separation, closed upon the intangible sensation of absence?, Luce Irigaray, 'When our lips speak together', trans. Carolyn Burke, *Signs*, 6 (1), 1980, p. 77.

8. I should point to the contradiction that as well as being imposed by colonising missionaries, the Christian faith was also more or less willingly adopted by Black people in America. Many Black leaders have been willing to recognise the subversive potential inherent in the figure of Christ in his identification with suffering and oppression.

9. *Ibid.* p. 224. For a discussion of butch and femme roles, see Susan Ardrill and Sue O'Sullivan, 'Butch femme obsessions' and Inge Blackman and Kathryn Perry, who also discuss butch/femme style in dress in 'Skirting the issue: lesbian fashion for the 90s' both in *Feminist Review*, 34, 1990.

FOUR

Sappho and the other woman[1]

Margaret Williamson

Reading Sappho is a seductive project for a feminist. Although not the only woman poet known from antiquity, she is certainly the most significant.[2] Her poetic achievement was so legendary that a poem attributed to Plato calls her the tenth Muse[3] – an indication also of how transgressive was the role of woman poet. Another aspect of her fascination is her placing in history: around the turn of the seventh and sixth centuries BC, in a world still dominated by aristocratic power, contested though that power already was. She thus escapes the radical exclusion of women from public life that was a by-product of fully developed democracy in city-states such as Athens. She also precedes by two centuries the discourse of fourth-century philosophy, to which many recent theorists have allotted a privileged role in the genealogy of Western ideas of sexual difference.[4]

This chapter attempts to address what must be the fundamental question about Sappho: in what ways, if any, can she be said to be writing as a woman, even though she shares many aspects of poetic tradition with male writers? I shall approach it through a comparison of some of her poems with those of a male author of love poetry, Anacreon, who wrote a few generations later than Sappho. It must be said at the outset, though, that the difficulties entailed in reading her are formidable. The tantalising fragments of her poems reach us through over two and a half thousand years of neglect, random selection and censorship, and through the reconstructions of scribes, textual critics and papyrologists. And some of the accidents that have befallen her text seem simply too bad to be true. What accident was it, for example, that garbled the one word in the Ode to Aphrodite, Sappho's only complete surviving poem, that tells us whether the singer is in love with a man or a woman – and that in a poem where Sappho herself is, unusually, named as the singer?[5] At this point, as at many others, the would-be critic of Sappho cannot avoid the sense of peering through a series of fragmented and distorting prisms at a fragile and ever-receding text.

Two further factors adding to this sensation are, at one end of the process, our ignorance of the social circumstances in which Sappho wrote and sang and, at the other, the iconic status she has acquired for many twentieth-century readers. If the weight of previous centuries bears heavily on her texts, so, in the twentieth century, do the desires of many of their women readers today: to discover the originary voice of female poetic consciousness and, perhaps, of lesbian sexuality.

Even if many of them must now be put on one side,[6] these questions are worth mentioning for positive as well as negative reasons. One of the effects of the last twenty years or so of critical theory is liberation from some versions of empiricism: an acceptance of the desires motivating all reading. I make no apology, therefore, for subjecting the iconic figure of Sappho to an explicitly motivated reading which takes up one of the central questions of feminist theory: the relationship between language and gender.

Within classical studies, Sappho has increasingly been identified as a crucial (though not the only) figure in debates about gender in the ancient world. I single out three treatments in particular. For Jack Winkler, Sappho's exclusion from mainstream, masculine culture gives her a privileged, and paradoxically more inclusive, perspective on its dominant paradigms (Winkler 1990). Thus, in the Ode to Aphrodite, Sappho can write in counterpoint to Homer's epic epiphanies, embracing them from an ironic vantage point. Eva [Stehle] Stigers (1981), on the other hand, following Simone de Beauvoir, seems to indicate female biology as the basis in Sappho of an erotic reciprocity which evades the structures of phallic domination that elsewhere pervade archaic poetry. In a more recent piece (Stehle 1990), she draws on film theory to analyse the gaze in Sappho as a means of dissolving hierarchy.

My reading of Sappho, though in some measure influenced by both these writers, attempts to consider the question from a slightly different, and explicitly linguistic, angle. It involves looking at a feature of her writing which, though touched on by both Winkler and Stehle,[7] merits further exploration: the subject positions mapped out in her poetry. I shall be considering the different voices in her poetry, and the way in which they seem to construct the

positions of subject and object, self and other, the 'I', 'you', sometimes 'she' and occasionally 'he' positions. My concentration will be
mainly on love poetry and the configurations of individual desire:
this is, therefore, a partial sampling of her corpus.

The background to my discussion is provided by a challenge
issued by Plutarch. In the introduction to his essay on the virtues of
women, Plutarch both opens and forecloses the question under
consideration when he puts forward the proposition that 'the art of
poetry or of prophecy is not one art when practised by men and
another when practised by women, but one and the same' (*On the
Virtues of Women*, 243b). The truth of this statement can, he suggests, be tested by setting alongside each other the poems of
Sappho and of Anacreon. Although Anacreon was not an exact
contemporary of Sappho, the accidents of survival mean that we
have more of his love poetry than of any other archaic lyric writer,
making him an especially rewarding subject for comparison with
Sappho. Following Plutarch's suggestion, I begin, therefore, with an
analysis of self–other relationships in Anacreon, even though many
of the erotic structures identifiable in his work are paralleled in
other male love poets.[8]

SELF AND OTHER IN ANACREON

The relationship between self and other where desire is concerned
in Anacreon follows two distinct patterns. In the first, Love is personified as an adversary who either subdues the speaker or seeks to
do so. One boxes with Love, as in 396, flees him (400) or gives
thanks for having escaped his bonds (346). The mildest version of
his effect seems to be his summons to the speaker in 358 to dally
with a girl from Lesbos ('golden-haired Love strikes me with his
purple ball and summons me to play with the girl in the fancy san-
dals'). Other accounts of his impact represent it as violent, as in the
image of Eros as a smith (fragment 413) who strikes the speaker
with a bronze hammer and dips him in freezing water.
Occasionally, as in the poem about the girl from Lesbos, the object
of the speaker's passion is alluded to (see also 378), but the primary
relationship is one between Eros and the lover, who experiences
himself as either the victim or the adversary of a powerful external
force.

In another equally common pattern, the speaker addresses the object of his passion: the relationship is between the speaker and an addressee, an 'I' and a 'you'. What is noticeable here too is the tendency for the imagery to reflect an adversarial relationship: but this time it is the speaker who takes the dominant role. A good example is a well-known poem addressed to a sexually inexperienced girl, in which, by a common erotic metaphor, she is compared to an untamed foal whom the speaker imagines himself bridling and riding (417). This scenario of erotic domination is clearly also present in 346, which is also addressed to a youthful love object, a beautiful but fearful boy (or possibly girl); the poem goes on to allude to the hyacinth meadows in which Aphrodite tied her horses. It reappears, in wittily inverted form, in 360, in which the boy with girlish looks holds, says Anacreon, the reins of his soul. Here, therefore, Love's domination of the speaker has been replaced by the speaker's wished-for mastery of the addressee. Even when, as in 360, the relationship is humorously inverted, the basic pattern is one in which one side or the other must end up in control, and the integrity of the 'I' position is either completely secure or completely at risk.

We have, therefore, two main patterns, one involving Eros and the speaker, the other the speaker and a beloved. Both, however, are structured in essentially the same way: the self–other relationship is essentially one of domination. The repetition of this pattern suggests an overriding concern with establishing the boundaries between subject and object, and then with establishing the subject's control, in a kind of zero-sum competition of the erotic.

A few brief observations about this structure are called for. Firstly, this concern with maintaining the boundaries and the supremacy of the 'I' makes particular sense when related to the likely context of performance of these poems. The symposia, drinking-parties attended by aristocratic males, for which this poetry was almost certainly destined had a markedly political function: that of consolidating bonds between members of the group and of asserting their political dominance over those outside it. Recent work, inspired by Foucault, on male homosexual roles in classical Athens has demonstrated that the articulation of sexual roles in a public context has a political dimension: a male citizen's assumption of an active, dominant role in his sexual life is an index of his capacity as a citizen.[9]

The situation of aristocratic symposiasts in the archaic period resembles in some ways that of citizens in classical Athens. They too were members of an élite whose privileges distinguished them sharply from other members of the community and were jealously guarded. Studies of symposiastic groupings have emphasised their importance as a defensive formation against the threat to aristocratic power and privilege posed by hoplite warfare and the wider distribution of wealth.[10]

It has long been accepted by critics of archaic lyric that at least some symposiastic poetry is directly related to the political aspirations of its audiences: that exhortations to military virtue and patriotism, for example, express a collective ideal. Love poetry, though, has traditionally been interpreted as belonging to a more individual, confessional mode.[11] The patterns sketched above, however, suggest that its rhetoric of exclusivity and supremacy is employed in the interests of a collective, rather than an individual, identity. It is the aristocratic group as a whole whose identity in relation to an other is figured in the structures of love poetry. The performer of a song ostensibly addressed to his beloved may be singing *about* his erotic mastery of a beloved other. He is singing it, however, not to that beloved boy or girl but to those occupying the same subject position as himself; and in so doing he repeats a gesture of mastery in which all of his audience are implicated.

This analysis of the ways in which social context informs love poetry also helps to make sense of the other pattern of subject–object relations in Anacreon: that between the speaker and Eros. The shattering effect of Eros on the 'I' is tolerable only if the agent, rather than being an individual other, is a personification or deity. To regard this threat as the effect of another human individual would be unacceptable for the community of aristocratic subjects to which singer and audience both belong. We shall return to this question of singer and audience in relation to Sappho.

The last point to note before embarking on a comparison with Sappho is that, in the pattern involving two human individuals, subject and object positions are gendered, but their relation to biological sex is a mediated one. Thus, though the 'I' is always an adult male, the other is always younger but can be either male or female. The subject–object polarity is articulated both with gender and with relations of power, so that to occupy the position of love object is also to occupy the weaker, feminine position, regardless of one's sex.

SAPPHIC VOICES AND THE OTHER

To turn to Sappho at this point is to enter a completely different world, in which the range of voices, positions and self–other relationship in the expression of desire is far wider and far more subtly modulated. To illustrate this I shall look first at a very fragmentary poem, number 22. The parts of this text that are legible, including editorial supplements, are, in translation, as follows:[12]

> . . . task . . . lovely face . . . unpleasant . . . otherwise winter . . . pain(less?)
> . . . I bid you, Abanthis, take (your lyre?) and sing of Gongyla, while
> desire once again flies around you, the lovely one – for her dress excited
> you when you saw it; and I rejoice: for the holy Cyprian herself once
> blamed me for praying . . . this (word?) . . . I wish . . .

At the point at which these fragments begin to be intelligible, the speaker commands a second woman, Abanthis, to celebrate in song her desire for a third. This is evidently not the first time Abanthis has felt such desire, as the adverb 'once again', traditionally used of the renewed onset of love, suggests. This is confirmed in the next strophe by the description of Gongyla as 'the lovely one', and an account of the way in which her appearance excited Abanthis' longing. The speaker then, with the explicit statement 'and I rejoice', takes up for the first time her own stance in relation to this scenario.

But is it really the first time? A closer look at the poem suggests that 'once again' haunts this entire scene in a way that has from the beginning drawn in the speaker too, and that begins to open up some of the differences between this and the erotics of Anacreon. In this poem there is a subtle process of association between different subject positions in operation throughout, which has the effect of eliding them, blurring without removing their boundaries. The person I have so far called a speaker is in fact, of course, a singer (this is, after all, *literally* lyric poetry): it is in song that she bids Abanthis sing. The process of elision between the 'I' and 'you' positions is compounded further when the speaker proceeds herself to name Abanthis' desire: she is doing, in that second strophe, what she has commanded Abanthis to do in the preceding one. It is significant too that, just as desire is distributed among different speakers, so too it is distributed through different moments in time: the desire which was excited (repeatedly, apparently) in the past is to be spoken in the future as well as the present. The positions from which desire is articulated and the moments of its articulation, therefore, constantly shift and merge into one another. What is constant is the movement of desire itself through the poem.

In fragment 96, of which we have much more, a similar process can be traced. The leastdamaged part of the text translates as follows:

> ... Sardis ... often turning her thoughts in this direction ... (she honoured) you as being like a goddess for all to see and took most delight in your song. Now she stands out among Lydian women like the rosy-fingered moon after sunset, surpassing all the stars, and its light spreads alike over the salt sea and the flowery fields; the dew is shed in beauty, and roses bloom and tender chervil and flowery melilot. Often as she goes to and fro she remembers gentle Atthis and doubtless her tender heart is consumed because of your fate ...

Once again the singer, the 'I' of the poem, speaks to 'you' and 'she', both female, of their desire. A distant 'she', a woman now (probably) in Sardis, the capital of Lydia, is described as turning her thoughts in this direction. Then the poem modulates into the past in order to describe her desire for the speaker's interlocutor, the 'you' of the second strophe. The focus now shifts back through both time and space to the woman in Lydia, who in her present surroundings is likened, in an extended simile, to the rosy-fingered moon; and finally her desire for Atthis (who I am assumed to be the 'you' of strophe 2) is recapitulated through her memory.

Here we can see an even more subtle and elusive play of desire at work, which once again works partly through an elision of the speaking positions. The singer is again associated through her song with the 'you' of the second strophe: the woman now in Lydia, she says (or rather sings), 'took most delight in your song'. This time, though, the effect of the speaker's implication in the other woman's desire is even more complex than in fragment 22. The singer sings of a song which aroused desire, thereby performing through her poem an act designated within it as erotic, and thus constructing herself as a potential object of desire. She also, though, enacts desire from the subject, speaking point of view when she turns to the lengthy simile which names in song the woman's beauty. As in fragment 22, this effect simultaneously represents and bridges the gaps between subjects, but without erasing them. It is this effect which I am trying to capture by the term 'elision', with the distances between the three speaking positions of the poem figured, on this occasion, through space as well as time. When finally she returns to the Lydian woman's desire for Atthis, in the sixth strophe, it is in a way marked by distances of both space and time: her longing for Atthis is possible only through the memory which bridges those distances.

It is evident from these two poems, and others besides, that there is a constant process of subtle and multifarious shifts going on between the speaking voices, and the subject positions, in Sappho's poetry. 'I', 'you' and 'she' (and in fragment 96 we should also add 'we') are never clearly differentiated, securely demarcated positions, but are constantly linked in a polyphonic, shifting erotic discourse, a kind of circulation of desire in which the gaps between subjects, figured through time and space, are at the same time constantly bridged by the operations of love and memory.[13] How different from the monologic erotic discourse of Anacreon, in which the main form self–other relationships seem to take is that of struggle which will end in the mastery of one over the other.

There are several major points of contrast here with Anacreon. The fact that this is a female voice speaking, astonishing though that is when one thinks of the silences that surround it, is only the beginning. Much more important is the way in which this female voice has been able to avoid speaking from the feminine position occupied by the addressees of Anacreon and of other male love poets. Instead we have a polyphony of voices whose neither-one-nor-two,[14] neither-subject-nor-object, relationship successfully both evades and contests the polarities found in Anacreon, and inscribed in the tradition in which he writes.

It is important to note, however, that though the boundaries between subjects are elided, they are not dissolved: there is a constant spacing effect between speaking positions. The most obvious way of achieving this is through the gaps of space and time found throughout Sappho's poetry. A second way, which we may note in passing, in which this spacing effect is achieved in Sappho is through the use of reported speech. This too is highly characteristic of her, and the Ode to Aphrodite (poem 1), combining reported speech with a set of complex temporal shifts, is an obvious example. Both resources are lacking in Anacreon, whose much sharper subject–object division does not require them: his poetry takes place for the most part in an undifferentiated present, and makes little use of reported speech.

One of the most important contrasts with Anacreon, however, takes us back to the relationship between singer and audience. I suggested for Anacreon an isomorphism between the self–other relationship within the poetry and that of its symposiastic audience with the world outside the symposium. For Sappho we are, of course, lacking historical information about who listened to her songs. The analysis offered so far of her poetry offers, however, a way of reading relationships with and between the members of her audiences within the poems themselves.

In the two fragments of Sappho considered so far, numbers 22 and 96, the singing voice itself is an important way of achieving the effect of elision between speaking positions. In this circulation of desire, the singing voice plays a crucial role in that it both arouses and expresses desire, linking all the female figures who speak and are spoken of in the poem and making them both subjects and objects of desire. Not only this: the self-referential allusions to song also, I have suggested, return upon the subject of enunciation, the poet, and draw her in too. There is, thus, a second kind of elision: between the enunciated 'I', named within the poem, and the singer who is doing the enunciating – between enunciating and enunciated subjects.[15] Conversely, the addressee, the desired and desiring other, is not limited to the ostensible addressee of each poem, but ultimately draws in the entire circle of women. If song itself both arouses and expresses desire, then to sing at all is to enter into an open-ended, unbounded erotic dialogue with the entire group: the erotics of Sappho's poetry implies, therefore, a community of singing, desiring, women. The contrast with poems of Anacreon in which a beloved other is addressed lies in the fact that in them the speaking positions within and outside the poem are insulated from each other by the gap between ostensible and actual addressee.

My analysis has so far depended, however, on poems which evoke an all-female world. But there are others. If, in the poems so far considered, Sappho successfully evades the gendered polarities found in Anacreon and other male love poets, what of those poems in which the masculine intrudes upon this secluded world? Can her implication with a community of singing, desiring female subjects always provide a position from which to contest the position of feminine, object, other?

I shall address this question by looking at two more poems, each of which involves explicit opposition to the masculine. Perhaps Sappho's best-known poem is fragment 31, which famously charts the speaker's distress as she looks at a beloved woman in the company of a man:

> He seems as fortunate as the gods to me, the man who sits opposite you and listens nearby to your sweet voice and lovely laughter. Truly that sets my heart trembling in my breast. For when I look at you for a moment, then it is no longer possible for me to speak; my tongue has snapped, at once a subtle fire has stolen beneath my flesh, I see nothing with my eyes, my ears hum, sweat pours from me, a trembling seizes me all over, I am greener than grass, and it seems to me that I am little short of dying. But all can be endured, since . . . even a poor man . . .

What the poem says on a surface level is obvious enough, even if it has given rise to a good deal of discussion as to the man's identity. What is important for present purposes is only that he is male.[16] As the speaker looks at him, he in turn, like the female lovers in the poems discussed before, is listening to a beloved woman's desire-arousing voice. The spectacle of her rival's relation to this woman then, on the level of surface meaning, causes the speaker such pain that she has the sensation of bodily disintegration. The final, damaged fragments suggest some kind of recovery, but cannot be interpreted with confidence.

What is of interest here is the way in which the poet's disintegration is represented in terms of speaking positions. As in previous poems, the addressee of this poem is herself speaking – but to her male companion, not to the singer of the poem. One of the consequences, within the poem, is the cessation of the singer's own voice. But the breaking of the erotic dialogue between female speakers is not the only cause of the disintegration. The other, I suggest, within the rhetoric of the poem, is the introduction of an objectifying gaze, whose direction is represented grammatically. The main body of the poem is framed by a very significant verb: 'to seem'. At the opening, the single Greek word translated as 'he seems' constructs the male lover as the object of the speaker's gaze. But the direction of that gaze is reversed within the poem, when the speaker herself becomes the object of a gaze: the last phrase reads literally 'I seem to myself'.

There are two ways of interpreting this reversal, both of which can be taken to be in play simultaneously. The repetition of the verb has, to begin with, the effect of suggesting a simple reversal of the gaze with which the poem opened: as she looked then at her male rival, he now looks at her. The physical disintegration of the speaker can be understood therefore as the consequence of her becoming the object of male gaze. But more important than the sex of the gazer is the way in which the gaze itself reintroduces what was absent from the previous two poems, namely a polarised division between subject and object positions.[17]

Linked with the introduction of this division is the fact that the fragmenting of the female speaker's self, and body, occurs not only on the literal level of description, but also linguistically, as can be seen first from the description of herself as 'greener than grass', and then from her use of the word 'I seem'. With this verb the subject's position itself becomes a divided one, since it involves the speaker in representing herself to herself from another's perspective, and therefore in splitting.[18] One can, then, read this disintegration of the female subject as the consequence of her move from being the subject of the gaze to being its object: a move which itself depends on the fact that the gaze demarcates these positions far more sharply than Sappho's more customary mode of engagement with others, the voice. Subject and object positions, in the phrase 'I seem to myself', then collide or conflict rather than, as in the previous poems, being elided.[19] It is worth noting too that the spacing effects which made that elision possible in the earlier poems are missing here: the tense of this poem, unlike many others of Sappho's, is a continuous present. It seems, therefore, that engagement with a masculine world is reflected in the range of techniques used as well as in terms of content.

It is of course possible to align the movement of this poem with the scenario of domination envisaged in Anacreon and to see this as, so to speak, the beloved's eye view of things: a brief attempt by the object to speak. No doubt there is no accident in the fact that we have a female speaker describing the disintegration brought about by a male gaze. But it is important to separate the idea of gendered subject positions from that of gender in a simple sense, even if, as here, they happen to coincide. What has changed between this and the earlier poems is not just the introduction of a male figure: it is, more importantly, the introduction of a gendered subject–object polarity, in which the speaker appears momentarily to be in the subject position (subject of the gaze) but is then forced also into that of its object. It is the resulting contradiction that causes her disintegration into a mute fragmented body. The example of this poem suggests, then, that it is not the mere assumption of a speaking position by a woman that counts, but the negotiation of the subject–object polarity: in other words the successful negotiation of the feminine, rather than the female, position.

In my final example, the speaker once again engages with the masculine. Fragment 16, the Anactoria poem, with its apparently self-conscious allusion to both dominant cultural values and poetic tradition, presents us quite explicitly with a woman challenging her marginal position in the culture. This time the speaker emerges from her encounter on a very different note; and once again the key to understanding why is the way in which the speaker is positioned within the poem.

> Some say a host of cavalry, others of infantry, and others of ships, is the most beautiful thing on the black earth, but I say it is whatsoever a person loves. It is perfectly easy to make this understood by everyone: for she who far surpassed mankind in beauty, Helen, left her most noble husband and went sailing off to Troy with no thought at all for her child or dear parents, but (love) led her astray . . . lightly . . . (and she?) has reminded me now of Anactoria who is not here; I would rather see her lovely walk and the bright sparkle of her face than the Lydians' chariots and armed infantry.

The categories with which the poem plays are easily identified. The culturally prestigious, and masculine, values of militarism and heroism are evident at the beginning and (what I take to be[20]) the end of the poem, as well as in the allusion to Troy and the account of Helen's abandoned husband as 'her most noble husband' – a description with strong connotations of military prowess. However, there are also reminders of the ways in which women are valued within the culture – in terms of their beauty, and of their role within marriage and the family.

It is not difficult to see how, even on first reading, the poem challenges these values. In the first strophe the emphatic 'but I say' announces a strong and explicit challenge to a society which, collectively, values militarism above anything else, and claims the right to substitute an individual's desire – 'whatsoever a person loves' – for that collectively sanctioned one. The markedly general phrasing of the opening then gives way to an example which defines the substituted desire as sexual, and a woman's: that of Helen, who left 'her most noble husband' and went to Troy. A comparison with the treatment of Helen by Alcaeus, a male contemporary of Sappho's, also from Lesbos, exposes the rehabilitation that is going ,on here: far from suppressing the consequences of her action, one of

Alcaeus' two treatments of Helen (42) singles her out as the cause of Troy's destruction, and contrasts her with the virtuous and fertile Thetis; the other (283) stresses her limited responsibility for her actions. She was, according to Alcaeus, 'crazed' by Paris when she followed him over the sea, and it is his transgression, not hers, against the laws of hospitality and exchange that is stressed. In Sappho's version, as Page duBois (1984) has pointed out, Helen is not the object of exchange (or theft) between men, but celebrated as 'an actant in her own life, the subject of a choice, exemplary in her desiring' (p. 102). The poem suggests, therefore, a double reversal of established values: love is to be valued above war, and women are to take on an active, desiring subjectivity.

But this concentration on the strategy of substitution expressed in the opening strophe is vulnerable. Deconstructive criticism has taught us to read utterances as threatened by the repression on which they are founded, and the poem's attempt at mastering the values and paradigms of Greek culture seems to lay itself open to being read in this way. From such a perspective, the insistent repetitions ('perfectly', 'everyone', expressed in Greek by variants of the same word: *panchu, panti*), like the emphatic 'but I say', suggest the fragility of the opening proposition rather than its strength. The claim to revalue militarism by means of language, to set in motion and then to control a process of linguistic substitution, sets up a structure which is open to reversal – and which is, within the poem, reversed. The presentation of Helen's desire makes the substitution she performs an ambiguous and unstable one: its object, Paris, is indicated only metonymically by a phrase – 'to Troy' – which also connotes war and the destruction catalogued by Alcaeus. The values repressed by the speaker in the first strophe seem to return here, then, as well as in the final strophe where the Lydian army is the measure of Anactoria's value to the speaker. According to this account, Sappho's revaluation is only the obverse of Alcaeus' in his poem 42, which was also announced as structured within language by the opening phrase 'as the story goes'; and the movement of the poem as a whole is that of a desire for linguistic mastery which is threatened and dispersed by the otherness it seeks to control.

I began my argument with an attempt to examine Plutarch's assertion that the art of poetry was undifferentiated by gender. If my earlier analyses of Sappho have tended to prove him wrong, fragment 16 seems thus far to bring us up against an uncomfortable relativism *vis-à-vis* Sappho and Alcaeus. Once again, however, it is the relationship between the subject positions in fragment 16 which is the key to Sappho's distinctiveness. In this poem they are linked with another crucial element: the quintessentially female figure of Helen.

The dualities which Helen embodies have been persuasively out lined by Ann Bergen (1983). In Herodotus's account of the origins of the long-standing hostility between Greeks and Persians – which includes the Trojan War – the women who move from one side to another, as marriage or love partners, have an ambiguous status: they are both subjects and objects of the exchange (or theft). Helen, who is also part of this self-renewing sequence of exchange, theft and reparation, partakes of this ambiguity in a way we can glean from the poems of Sappho and Alcaeus just considered. That is, she both chooses Paris and is chosen by him, both abandons and is stolen from her husband, exchanges and is exchanged. This pattern conforms, of course, to Levi-Strauss' analysis of the position of women in both kinship and linguistic structures as that of both signs and generators of signs (1968: 60–2). The duality can be found on a linguistic level too in the *Iliad*, where Helen is first encountered weaving in a tapestry the narrative of the war (3.125–8). She is, thus, both subject and author of the narrative, its weaver and her-self woven into it by the rhapsode, the 'stitcher-together' of tales. Like the Sapphic singing voice, therefore, she elides the positions of enunciating and enunciated subject.

This duality is, no doubt, part of what motivates Sappho's inter-ception of Helen in her long wandering through Greek literature. But the way in which she is drawn into the chain connecting the three female figures of the poem – the speaker, Helen and Anactoria – is also important, and it draws on the fluidity of subject positions which we have traced elsewhere. The link between the three female figures of this poem, once again formed partly by ver-bal repetition, is one that has eluded some of the poem's critics. The author of a standard commentary on Sappho, for example, says apropos of Helen's first appearance: 'It seems . . . inelegant to begin this parable, the point of which is that Helen found [the most beau-tiful thing] in her lover, by stating that she herself surpassed all mortals in this quality' (Page 1955: 53). But what he is objecting to is the poem's most crucial move, and it is signalled precisely by the way in which the description of Helen, 'who far surpassed mankind in beauty', echoes the opening reference to 'the most beautiful thing', once again using variants of the same Greek word (*kalliston*, *kallos*). The effect of this repetition is to hint that Helen is the object of the speaker's desire, announced in the first strophe. Helen then, in the next strophe, becomes herself a desiring subject, who goes away to Troy. But her oscillation does not end there. Another verbal echo links her with the absent Anactoria: the word translated as 'walk', *bama*, is formed from the same verb as that for 'went' in the account of Helen's journey to Troy, *eba*. The speaker, thus, is a desiring subject: Anactoria, at the end, is a desired object; but Helen, in between, by means of the now familiar elision, is both.

It is this elision which slides out from under the tyranny of the opening propositions, and implicates both the speaker and Helen in an endless chain of substitution in which each is both subject and object, speaker and spoken. This, more than the opening challenge, is the move by which the poem really subverts the discourse in which it is framed, and we can see this in the resulting disruption and instability of gender categories. In sailing to Troy, leaving behind her family, for example, she imitates the action of the Homeric heroes; but this assumption of a male role at the same time enacts the female speaker's erotic impulse. In leaving 'her most noble husband', to go to Troy, she rejects but also embraces each of the competing values in the first strophe – the object of individual desire and the values of heroism and militarism. We could multiply these antitheses indefinitely, and yet they could hardly mimic the text's resistance to them. The elision of subject and object results, then, in the confounding of mythical categories of gender: and it is here that the elision in Sappho of what is elsewhere a gendered polarity has its most radical effect.

CONCLUSIONS

The rejoinder to Plutarch which emerges from this reading of Sappho is, therefore, a fundamentally and fruitfully ambiguous one. Sappho writes, we can say, as a woman precisely to the extent that she writes as not-a-woman: from a position, that is to say, which undercuts and contests the hommosexual structures defining feminity. We may wish to ask further what defines this position: is it to be located in linguistic or psychic structures or, indeed, the female body?

This study hints at a further possibility. We can hardly talk of Sappho's social situation as the background to her poetry: the sparsity of our information renders the distinction between foreground and background untenable. What I have done is, *faute de mieux*, to read a social context within, rather than behind, the poetry. The exercise suggests that the gendering of Sappho's poetic discourse takes place through that of her audience; and, furthermore, that gender is a matter of relations of power at least as much as of biological sex. It is the fact that she addresses an audience of equals, of singing, desiring women whose song and desire endlessly refract her own, that makes possible her characteristic mode of address: to the other woman of my title.[21]

Since this is explicitly a motivated reading, I may perhaps be allowed to end by introducing another woman into my account of the Anactoria poem. You may think she is already there: the reader. The disruption of gendered positions which I have traced in relation to the figures of the poem has as its correlate that of the reader's position. The opening 'some say' of the poem bears ambivalently on the gender of the reader. Gendered in Greek to the extent that 'mankind', for example, is in English, it apparently contains the male reader only to assimilate his desire to that of the female speaker and of Helen: but a female reader is from the beginning both uneasily contained and excluded by it. It is from this fragmented position that reader and poem conduct their negotiation with gender, a negotiation which when it pauses in the last strophe has at least won a place for Anactoria alongside those massed and glorious armies. The place and the moment which Anactoria inhabits may be distant, conditional and fleeting, but I think we can claim this as a kind of victory.

NOTE ON TEXTS AND TRANSLATIONS

Quotations from Sappho and Alcaeus are from the plain prose translation in the Loeb edition (Campbell 1982), which like all other current texts of Sappho depends to some extent on editorial reconstruction. See Campbell's notes on the most disputed passages. For more detail, see Page (1955). The fullest recent scholarly edition is

Voigt (1971). For a verse translation, see Balmer (1992). Translations of Anacreon can be found in Campbell (1988), and all the ancient poets referred to in this chapter are translated in West (1993).

NOTES

1. Earlier versions of this paper were given at the universities of Southampton (1988) and Oxford (1991): my thanks to those audiences for their comments.
2. Other ancient women poets are now receiving increasing attention: for an overview, see Snyder (1989), with references.
3. *Palatine Anthology*, 9.506. Despite its traditional attribution, this is probably among the many epigrams written in the Hellenistic period and passed off under the names of classical authors: see Page (1981) 125–7. The 'tenth Muse' label rapidly became a cliché in allusions to Sappho.
4. Two particularly relevant to this essay are Foucault (1987), whose genealogy of modern sexuality barely reaches back beyond the fourth century BC, and Irigaray (especially 1985a) on whom see below, nn. 14 and 21.
5. Only one word in poem 1, the Ode to Aphrodite, indicates the gender of the beloved. The manuscripts on which modern texts are based give three variant readings of the text at this point, none of which can be correct because none both makes sense and fits the metre and dialect. The currently accepted reading, which makes the beloved female, depends on an emendation which was proposed only in the nineteenth century. It is defended in his edition by the German philologist Bergk (1843[2]) with the simple statement that 'we are dealing with the love of a *girl*' (de *puellae* amore agitur). He reaches this conclusion mainly on the basis of Sappho's other poems.
6. On the textual transmission of Sappho's poems, and on the question of whether she can be described as lesbian in the modern sense, see Chapters 2 and 4 of my forthcoming book on Sappho (Harvard University Press).
7. See, e.g., Winkler (1990: 167) 'Sappho's poem 1 ... contains several personal perspectives, whose multiple relations to each other set up a field of *voices* [my emphasis] and evaluations'.
8. See [Stehle] Stigers (1981), who gives examples also from Archilochus and Ibycus, and comments: 'The man is helpless, stricken by the power of Eros or Aphrodite, but toward the particular boy or girl who attracts him the man is confident and prepared to seduce' (1981: 46). She attributes these patterns to 'male sexual psychology' (50).

9. See in particular Halperin (1990) and Winkler (1990). Both draw on Foucault's work on sexuality, especially Foucault (1987). See also Dover (1978).

10. On symposia, see Murray (1983a), (1983b), (1990) and (1993); Rossi (1983); Vetta (1983).

11. For an overview of current critical positions, see Slings (1990), with references.

12. This poem survives only in a badly damaged version on papyrus, and some of the readings translated here depend on editorial supplements which are controversial: Balmer (1992) translates a different text. The main trend of my argument can, however, be defended even without the conjectural supplements on which both translations depend.

13. I prefer to speak of the elision of subject positions, and of a circulation of desire, rather than, as Stigers (1981), followed now by Skinner (1993), does, of reciprocity and mutuality. The latter description seems to me to take insufficient account of the transaction's embeddedness in social and linguistic practice. Another way of putting this, on a linguistic level, would be to say that it overlooks the effects of *différance* (Derrida 1973).

14. As the terminology shows, this analysis is influenced by the work of Luce Irigaray: see particularly (1985b). On the use of Irigaray by classicists, see now Skinner (1993), and below, n. 20.

15. Calame (1986) applies this distinction to the analysis of Greek poetry, though he has very little to say about Sappho.

16. Several scenarios have been proposed: see Page (1995). The tendency in more recent criticism is to read the opening as a rhetorical trope ('whoever sits opposite you . . .') rather than a reference to a real figure: see Winkler (1990: 179).

17. See Stehle (1990), whose fuller (and very powerful) treatment of the gaze attributes to it some of the blurring and de-hierarchising effects linked in this essay with the voice.

18. It is significant that the use of the verb 'appeared' is identified by Barthes as a sure indication of the move from personal to impersonal narration: a move which also, according to his categories, occurs in this poem. See Barthes (1977: 112). See also, on non-dialectical self–other relations, Jefferson (1989).

19. The context of this poem in Longinus' account provides a fascinating sideline on this discussion. Longinus, to whom we owe the survival of most of this poem, famously celebrates it as an example of poetic unity: he marvels at Sappho's 'selection of the most important details and her combination of them into a single whole' (*On the Sublime*, 10.3). This in itself seems surprising, given the poem's stress on *dis*-unity. And yet one detail of the text he quotes raises at least the possibility that he was more alive to the text's disintegration than his

argument allows. The phrase 'to myself', occurring immediately after 'I seem', can be construed as an attempt to heal the division between subject and object, even though in so doing it also serves to highlight it. Longinus, however, in the text transmitted to us, omits it altogether, though he continues his quotation with a few words which apparently come after it. The missing words have been restored only through the insertion of a further papyrus scrap (fragment 213): Longinus' version of the line reads simply 'I seem', omitting the telltale recuperative phrase. On the context of this omission in Longinus, see Hertz (1985).

20. The papyrus on which this poem was found continues with damaged sections of three more lines. Most editors think they are the beginning of another poem; some think they continue this one. I should make clear my assumption that the speaker is, as in almost all Sappho's poems, female.

21. As implied in Irigaray's pun *parler-femme / par les femmes*. This is an important qualifier of her other famous punning term, *hommosexualité*. Taken together, they suggest that women can escape the constraints of patriarchal discourse, but on the basis of social practice. Analyses of ancient culture in terms only of *hommosexualité* lead to the distortions which are contested, rightly, by Skinner (1993). On the complexities of *parler-femme*, see especially Whitford (1991: Ch. 2). Irigaray's later work (1986) suggests that divine paradigms may also be a basis for this concern for other women: the importance in Sappho of Aphrodite offers some confirmation of this. See also Cantarella (1992) on the different relationship to power-structures for women, which (she argues) meant that homosexual love did not symbolise the transmission of power as it did for men.

FIVE

'Her wench of bliss': gender and the language of Djuna Barnes' Ladies Almanack[1]

Deborah Tyler-Bennett

This essay does not represent a close linguistic reading of Djuna Barnes' text, *Ladies Almanack* (Barnes 1928a) but considers the way in which the text engages gender archetypes, and thus subverts and explores older verbal and visual forms, such as ballads, almanacs and chapbooks. Barnes was born in Cornwall-on-Hudson, New York State, in 1892, and died at Patchin Place, Greenwich Village, in 1982. She is chiefly remembered for her novel *Nightwood* (Barnes 1936) and for the increasingly reclusive lifestyle which has been represented as typifying her old age. Barnes occurs as an 'exotic' figure in many memoirs of the 'modernist' period, and *Ladies Almanack* has come to be regarded as a who's who of the lesbian salon of Natalie Clifford Barney. Barnes' use of language, it will be argued here, deliberately inverts known devices from the sixteenth and seventeenth centuries, thus allowing borders (chronological, historical and between genres) to be crossed. Barnes' usage of historical phrases (both 'legitimate' and 'underground'), her use of verbal listings and elliptical and rhythmical line structures, create an almanac which is difficult to fit in to current definitions of 'modernism', a term which remains, itself, problematic, as Bonnie Kime Scott notes (Scott 1990: 10–11). This essay demonstrates how Barnes' use of language enables her to re-evaluate the almanac form in terms of gender.

Indeed, in engaging with the almanac form, a form, with exceptions, most often used by men, Barnes both reconsidered and transmuted that form. By so doing, she was writing into the past whilst creating a picture of lesbian history which did not depend on *fin-de-siècle* stereotypes. In 1927, one year before the publication of *Ladies Almanack*, Barnes wrote a preface to the posthumous 'selected letters' of her friend, the poet Elsa, Baroness Von Freytag

Loringhoven, published in *transition* magazine (Barnes 1928a: 19). In her preface, Barnes stated: 'such of her things as are in my possession, letters written in her time of agony . . . I now give parts, as they make a monument to this her inappropriate end, in the only fitting language which could reveal it, her own' (Barnes 1928a: 19). Freytag Loringhoven, a German exile, had constantly written of her struggle with the English language and this difficulty with grammar and syntax has also been applied by certain critics to Barnes herself (Field 1985). Barnes had little formal schooling and thus her emphasis on the Baroness's 'own' language is important, firmly linking language to the concept of self outside academic constraints. In moving and desperate letters, written shortly before her suicide, the Baroness outlined the difficulties of being a woman writer. It might be argued that, like her, Barnes suffered from a horror of being categorised and thus created works which fitted into many literary and artistic categories. Therefore, when Marianne Moore commented that 'reading Djuna Barnes is like reading a foreign language, which you understand' (Broe 1991: 155), she outlined a vital part of Barnes' aesthetic.

Moore's comment might be applied to a reading of *Ladies Almanack*, a text which has, until recently, been dismissed as a comic 'diversion' amongst Barnes' serious works (Field 1985: 124–5). Despite new readings of the text by Susan Snaider Lanser (Lanser 1992: xv-xlv), Karla Jay (Jay 1991: 184–91), and Fran Michel (Michel 1991: 170–83), *Ladies Almanack* remains the least discussed of all Barnes' works. Yet it is a vital work, as Lanser suggests, not merely in terms of Barnes' career as a whole, but in histories of the lesbian novel (Lanser 1992: xv-xlv).

Ladies Almanack was privately printed in Paris in 1928, by Maurice Darrantière on behalf of Djuna Barnes (Field 1985: 124–5). It was published under a pseudonym which had an eighteenth-century ring to it, 'a Lady of Fashion'. This may have also referred to a private joke as Natalie Barney's lover, Romaine Brooks (Cynic Sal in the text), had been photographed as 'a Lady of Fashion' in 1908 (Secrest 1974: 163). The original print-run consisted of 1,050 copies, the first fifty of which possessed illustrations hand-tinted by Barnes herself. It was to have been distributed by Edward Titus, who lost confidence in the volume when he saw its lesbian content, and was thus privately distributed among friends (Field 1985: 124–4). Thus the text became notorious, both for what it contained and for the way in which it was sold. As a satire on Barney's circle, the text was also both a public and a private work.

As the study by Karla Jay reveals, the text is usually discussed more in terms of who it satirised than in terms of its form (Jay 1991: 184–94). However, it could be argued that a discussion of form is crucial to an understanding of the piece as a whole. A cast-list, including Barney, has been applied to the text from Barney's annotated copy (Field 1985: 124–5). Yet, by applying this type of literary 'who's who' to the piece, ideas concerning the text's exploration of gender are omitted. Essentially, the text is a pastiche which employs terminology from sixteenth- and seventeenth-century popular literature – ballads, chapbooks, almanacs, hagiographies, conduct-books and bestiaries – as well as containing private jokes which refer to Barney's own circle. In *Border Traffic*, Maggie Humm quotes Frederic Jameson's description of pastiche as a product of postmodernism, 'each group comes to speak an "idiolect", a curious private language of its own which is spoken at the moment when pastiche appears and parody has become impossible. Pastiche is blank parody that has lost its sense of humour . . . this is a condition of marginality' (Humm 1991: 15). Humm rightly discusses the problems of relating statements such as this to writings by women. The pastiche of the *Ladies Almanack* is one which very definitely retains its bawdy and irreverent sense of humour. Using pastiche, the text quite clearly effects the type of border crossing which Humm describes as issuing 'a profound challenge to the literary canon, and to the very process of criticism as an exercise in gender proprieties' (*ibid*.: 9). By means of an eclectic blend of secular and religious imagery, Barnes' text crosses several borders, including those of gender, class and history.

When asking about the sources of the work, Barnes' biographer, Andrew Field, was given an evasive reference to 'some old French albums which' she had 'picked up in the bookstalls of Paris' (Field 1985: 125). The text, which begins in the style of a conduct-book, is referred to as 'the book which all ladies should carry' and is a lesbian re-working of several antique forms (Barnes 1928b: 5). By deliberately imitating both chapbook conventions and the almanac tradition, Barnes is not only re-working male-dominated conventions but also acknowledging the way in which many of these forms covertly refer to women's history. In the past, as work by Elaine Hobby reveals, texts which suggested that 'all ladies' should carry them were often instructive manuals, a good example of this being the conduct-books of the seventeenth and eighteenth centuries (Hobby 1988: 8). In rewriting the instruction book, a work intended for a young female audience, Barnes re-evaluates a past form in terms of lesbianism. The title page, which is famous more for its parodic element than for the gender implications with which it presents the reader, is concerned with outlining all aspects of the female condition. If this is compared with the headings of tracts from the seventeenth-century, such as *Mundus Muliebris* by John and Mary Evelyn (Evelyn and Evelyn 1690), both the quality and clarity of the parody become obvious.[2] The introduction to *Ladies Almanack* describes a cycle of moons and tides associated with femininity, which re-writes the traditionally male calendar of the almanac. Thus Barnes creates an idea of woman's time connected to birth, menstruation, pregnancy and menopause. This can be contextualised historically for, as with the seventeenth-century almanac-maker Sarah Jinner, Barnes can be regarded as placing a new context upon a yearly calendar of times, thus privileging the 'moons and tides' of women above conventional time-scales (Hobby 1988: 181–2). Barnes' text reminds the reader that women, such as Sarah Jinner and Mary Holden, both of whom created women's almanacs, are able to alter time-scales and, by so doing, creates a female calendar in which her heroine (Evangeline Musset) and her heroine's circle can exist.

Musset, 'as fine a wench as ever wet bed', celebrates her lesbianism over the seasons of her life (Barnes 1928b: 6). She and her countless lovers are watched by the almanac's one heterosexual character, Patience Scalpel. Scalpel, whose very name is emblematic of her critical nature, wonders at these women who are transmuted by Barnes into figures from baroque art: 'she saw them gamboling on the Greensward, heard them pitch and moan within the Gloom of many a stately mansion; she beheld them floating across the Ceilings, (for such was art in the Old Days) diapered in *Toile de Jouy* and welded without Flame, in one incalculable embrace' (*ibid.*: 11). In making a linguistic reference to the 'cherubs' which filled Renaissance and Baroque art works, Barnes combines both the religious and the secular, as the cherubs (divine children) are replaced by Musset's friends (secular figures). Thus an angelic hierarchy is secularized (as it becomes one with Musset's lesbian circle), as secular women form a kind of celestial tableau, or lesbian heavenly chorus. Quite often, at the conclusion of certain passages, the women are frozen in tableaux. The 'incalculable embrace' is typical of this use of language: the tableau, taken as it is from visual art and transmuted into verbal art, implies that Musset's type of sexuality will remain for eternity. Patience Scalpel does not deny this sexuality but neither does she understand it.

As Dame Musset remains surrounded by seraphic women for much of the text, it is perhaps inevitable that she will be beatified at the work's conclusion. Even her birth re-writes the biblical concept of creation:

> There was heard from under the dome of heaven a great crowing, and, from the midst, an egg fell to earth and striking, split and hatched and from out of it stepped one saying 'Pardon me, I must be going!' And this was the first Woman born with a difference. After this the angels parted, and on the face of each was the Mother look. Why was that?
>
> (Barnes 1928b: 26)

This biblical pastiche combines the ornate phraseology of biblical texts with commonplace speech; for example, after the 'great crowing' and the egg falling majestically to earth, one expects a miraculous and mysterious birth, but the commonplace statement 'Pardon me, I must be going!', totally undercuts this. The angels, who, it is implied, have created the egg, re-write a portion of the Bible for themselves, becoming active creators rather than passive spectators. This is birth without male participation and Barnes' angels appear to be androgynous. Yet it is not only the Bible which is parodied skilfully by Barnes. In her ballad 'Lists and Likelihoods', she re-writes the misogyny of sixteenth- and seventeenth-century ballads by creating a list of lesbian archetypes which poke fun at early ballad depictions of women as either shrill viragos or the victims of male cruelty. Barnes replaces misogynistic archetypes:

> The Vixen in the coat of red,
> The Hussy with the honey head,
> Her frontal Bone soft lapped up,
> With hempen ringlets like the Tup,
> The Doxy in the Vest of kid,
> Rustling like the Katie-did,
> With Panther's eyen dark and wan,
> And dove's feet to walk upon.
>
> (Barnes 1928b: 60)

At first glance, this listing appears to invoke a selection of female archetypes, but it also hints at the lesbian possibilities behind such stereotypical images. Words such as 'Vixen', 'Hussy', and 'Doxy' were, as Salgado and others have noted, traditionally linked to prostitution (Salgado 1972). Yet here, Barnes uses them in a more positive light, as the women possess a type of fierce aloofness which enables them to transcend the stereotypical language allotted to them. The animals and birds listed link them to the medieval bestiary, where animals and humans merge to form fantastic beasts, such as the Siren (Benton 1992: 36). As Barnes herself created a bestiary, *Creatures in an Alphabet* (Barnes 1981), the use of linguistic devices from the form in other texts is not surprising.

In the verse which follows, Barnes lists archetypes of lesbianism: the feminine lesbian: the mythic 'mannish' lesbian (defined by Esther Newton (Newton 1984: 557–75) and the Lesbian History Group amongst others (Lesbian History Group 1989: 217–18), described here as the 'starry Jade with Mannish stride' (Barnes 1928b: 60); and the 'masculine' sportswoman. Here, Barnes employs myriad terms which were deployed in caricatures of lesbian life but undercuts them, revealing the humour which many previous writers failed to recognise. In late nineteenth-century writings, such as those by Louys and Gautier, lesbianism, as Lillian Faderman has pointed out, was presented as a diseased state, evil and exotic (Faderman 1985: 369). Such nineteenth-century symbolist writers defined the lesbian body by deploying a discourse of disease. Faderman perceives these *fin-de-siècle* notions as also occurring in Barnes' work but this can be strongly contested (Faderman 1985: 369). In parodying these verbal representations of the female body, Barnes reveals that works on lesbian sexuality could be both humorous and celebratory. As Lanser notes, Dame Musset's name could be seen as parodic, as Alfred de Musset was one such symbolist writer (Lanser 1992: xxix). Likewise, Barnes' ballads run counter to symbolist prose, as they provide positive female images. For example, women described in the ballad vary from a trapeze artist to a queen who seeks out her own 'wench of bliss' (Barnes 1928b: 60). This makes the point that there is no such thing as a 'typical' lesbian, as lesbians can come from all walks of life and all class groups. Stereotypical doxies, hussies and viragos, who previously inhabited misogynistic ballads, chapbooks and, later, novels, are transmuted into amazonian and liberated figures. Thus the discourse of desire, as the women are depicted as both strong and active and thus oppose the 'decadent' image of the passive, invalided woman.

As is obvious, naming is very important to the text as a whole. Many of the names used are doubly emblematic, redolent both of actual members of Barney's circle and of female archetypes. Lady Buck-and-Balk and Tilly Tweed-in-blood are archetypes meant to refer to Radclyffe Hall and her lover, Lady Una Troubridge (Field 1985: 124). Buck-and-Balk and Tweed-in-Blood employ language similar to that used in Hall's *The Well of Loneliness* (Hall 1928) to describe their ideas on marriage between women. As with women listed in the ballad, they are defined by their basic characteristics: 'Lady Buck-and-Balk sported a monocle and believed in spirits. Tilly Tweed-in-Blood sported a stetson and believed in marriage' (Barnes 1928b: 18). Unlike Dame Musset, the two are pacifists who plead for tolerance. Musset dismisses their gentle discourse, scorning their delicacy and innate seriousness and responding with a violent discourse of her own. The two plead for lesbianism to be sanctioned by marriage, and for monogamy, which, if bound by law, should only be nullified by the courts. Their language includes words such as 'love', 'hearts', 'pity', 'dear', 'need' and 'poignancy' (Barnes, 1928b: 19), whereas Musset's discourse (which suggests that differences are best settled by duels) is full of terms such as 'struck', 'fowling-piece' and 'terror' (*ibid*.). Musset's discourse is one of strength, whereas Buck-and-Balk speaks of 'morals' (*ibid*.).

Such differentiations between discourses (whether between Musset and the two Englishwomen or between Musset and Scalpel) fill the text. Also typical is the way in which Barnes carefully adhered to the almanac form, making the cycle of Dame Musset's life appear to be inevitable. Each month comes to represent a period of Dame Musset's life and each ends on a different note. For example, June ends with a positive couplet:

Of such is high and gaming pride,
of Woman by a Woman's girlish side.

(Barnes 1928b: 40)

This note is then carried through July, where women are shown to be ideal partners for each other (Barnes 1928b: 43). However, as the cycle continues, it becomes clear that this affirmation cannot last as Dame Musset is growing older (*ibid*.: 68). August brings 'distempers' and concludes in confusion with the rattle of 'memory bones' (*ibid*.: 54). Such confusion creates a class border crossing, as it affects both high and low alike and is composed in true almanac form:

'some dropping Tea-pots and Linens, Some Caddies and Cambric, some Sea-weed and saffron, some with Trophy Skulls and Memory Bones, gleanings from Love's Labour lost' (ibid.). As has been indicated earlier, these portions of the text, with their complex couplings of words, reflect Musset's life cycle, as they describe the motions of the tides and seasons traditionally connected with femininity. Thus, the discord of August is followed by the displacement of September. In the text, Barnes makes a statement which might be used as a coda for the work as a whole: 'the very condition of Woman is so subject to Hazard, so complex, and so grievous, that to place her at one moment is but to displace her at the next' (ibid.: 55). This could also be applied to Barnes' aesthetic as a whole.

The shifting boundaries of femininity are also charted in the various 'border crossings' effected by the language of the text. By the time that the last seasons of the year are reached, Dame Musset is old and dying. Dame Musset will die in December when it is 'right' for her to die, thus completing the text's cycle. She is buried by a troop of mourning women, and her tongue, a parody of Shelley's heart perhaps, refuses to burn in the funeral pyre (ibid.: 84). This might also recall an inversion of the traditional image of the scold's tongue, creating a symbol of the undeniable power of women's language.

What I wish to suggest in this essay is that by using a language appropriated from old texts, frequently texts of a misogynistic nature, Barnes places the lesbian woman at the centre of the picture rather than at its margins. Thus, she foregrounds the sense of a lesbian past. Just as Janet Todd suggests that in works by Aphra Behn 'the wit is in the appropriation' of themes and linguistic tropes from earlier works (Todd 1989: 12–36), this might also be said to be true of Barnes, whose plural text uses many forms, but remains peculiarly difficult to categorise. In other words, Ladies Almanack is a text where use of pastiche enabled Barnes to place the lesbian self at the centre of history. This placing is achieved by a use of language which invokes opposition, combining the religious with the secular, the human with the animal, the violent with the passive, and the woman with the saint. Dame Musset's tongue, which 'would not suffer ash' (Barnes 1928b: 84), might therefore stand as a metaphor for the power of her speech and the strength of her image. If Barnes' Musset is, at the text's conclusion, beatified, then she also provides a secular symbol as she reverses the misogynistic archetype of the scold and remains 'unbridled' to the last.

NOTES

1. I would like to thank Dr Martyn Bennett, Katherine Cockin and the Feminist Research Group, Loughborough University, for their help and support.
2. The title pages of *Ladies Almanack* reads: 'Ladies Almanack; showing their Signs and their Tides, their Moons and their Changes; the Seasons as it is with them; their Eclipses and Equinoxes; as well as a full Record of diurnal and nocturnal Distempers'. *Mundus Muleibris* reads: 'Mundus Muleibris; or the Ladies Dressing-Room Unlocked and her Toilette Spread in Burlesque, Together with the Fop's Dictionary'.

GENDER/GENRE

SIX

Cyborgs and cyberpunk: rewriting the feminine in popular fiction [1]

Jenny Wolmark

The relationship between feminism and popular fiction has received a great deal of critical attention in the last few years, most of which has been directed towards romance fiction as the genre in which female desire is most clearly foregrounded. Science fiction, on the other hand, has received relatively little critical attention, although there is now a considerable body of work written by women that articulates feminist concerns.[2] This inattention is hardly surprising since science fiction is a genre that is dominated by the masculine, not least in its emphasis on the language of 'hard' science, and the privileging of the masculine in scientific discourse has long operated as an exclusionary device as far as women are concerned. Since the 1970s, however, the masculinist hegemony within the genre has been persistently challenged by women writers of science fiction,[3] and many of the narratives that have been produced have been strongly influenced by feminism, as is evidenced by the way in which gender and identity have been placed at the centre of such narratives. In this chapter I shall be discussing some key writing strategies used by feminist writers of science fiction to subvert the generic stability of science fiction, thereby creating an environment of uncertainty within which conventional constructions of sexual difference can be questioned. I am primarily concerned with the use of narrative structures and codes drawn from other genres in which the feminine is not marginalised, such as romance fiction, and with the rewriting of the dominant metaphors of science fiction to create a conceptual and linguistic space within which the feminine can be coded as hegemonic. The metaphor of the cyborg, and its positioning in relating to cyberpunk, provides the focus for my argument that these strategies have been profoundly disruptive for the genre as a whole because, in challenging the dominance of the masculine in discourses about technology, they challenge the constraints of both genre and gender.

Although the term 'cyberpunk' is one that is now used to describe cultural productions across a range of media, particularly film, video and performance, it first emerged in the 1980s as a sub-genre of science fiction. Cyberpunk constitutes a major intervention into the genre, and the writer whose name remains most clearly identified with it is William Gibson, although other writers such as Bruce Sterling, Lewis Shiner, Rudy Rucker and John Shirley were equally involved in promoting the idea that cyberpunk was a 'movement'. Cyberpunk writing combines the language of informa-tion technology with the spatial and temporal dislocation that is characteristic of science fiction. The innovative syntax of cyberpunk draws on the rhetoric of postindustrial technology to present fic-tional landscapes that are ironic and playful, both in their simulation of surface reality and in their apparent effacement of the boundaries between inner and outer worlds. A notable feature of cyberpunk writing is its speed and dazzle, and in his introduction to the cyberpunk anthology *Mirrorshades*, Bruce Sterling describes the impact of its prose as resembling the kind of 'sensory overload' that is 'the literary equivalent of the hard-rock "wall of sound"' (Sterling 1988: xiii). Cyberpunk writing has also been compared to the editing process involved in video and computer graphics, pri-marily because it simulates the instantaneity and depthlessness of the visual image. Such a simulation derives from cyberpunk's post-modern emphasis on signifiers rather than on the signified, and cyberpunk narratives are celebrated for their distance from the familiar linear structure of most science fiction narratives.

The multiplicity of signs in cyberpunk emphasises surface style as an emblem of a depthless present, and as such it is taken as an indication of the instability of language itself. Such linguistic insta-bility has been discussed by Fredric Jameson who, appropriating Lacan's account of schizophrenia, describes a situation in which the relationships between signifiers collapse, so that 'when the links of the signifying chain snap, then we have schizophrenia in the form of a rubble of distinct and unrelated signifiers' (Jameson 1992: 26). A different account of this unstable and postmodern linguistic environment draws on an analogy between cyberpunk writing and video processes, particularly the cut-and-mix collage techniques of music videos: George Slusser describes words as being 'like MTV images . . . disarticulating coherent discourse into semicoherent pulsations, turning each single, disoriented word into a "womb" that spawns its own, hyperverbal, harmonics and dissonances' (McCaffery 1991: 341). The discontinuity that is the dominant stylistic feature of music videos is incorporated into cyberpunk writing, so that it becomes a kind of 'optical prose' (*ibid*.). The preoccupation with style, with the sign itself rather than with what it refers to, together with its fragmented, discontinuous narratives, suggests that cyberpunk is part of the crisis of representation expressed in other postmodern cultural productions. Cyberpunk and feminist science fiction can, then, be thought of as occupying similar territory.

The emphasis on video and computer technology both in cyberpunk writing and in writing about cyberpunk appears to question the status of fiction as a mode of representation, and indeed the status of writing itself. Brooks Landon suggests that, within postmodern culture, cyberpunk writing 'almost demands a reexamination of the status of writing in that culture. In so far as cyberpunk writing directs our attention to MTV, *Max Headroom*, and computer-generated graphics which are rapidly becoming indistinguishable from "real" images of our referential world, it compels us to question the nature of representation in our world – and our traditional assumptions about the nature of fiction and narrative (McCaffery 1991: 242). Since these are the kinds of questions about cultural forms that are raised within the ironic and self-reflexive practices of postmodernism, cyberpunk has therefore to be situated within the overlapping frameworks of postmodernism and science fiction. Because of its ambiguous positioning, cyberpunk demonstrates the apparent erosion of the boundaries between 'high' and popular culture that Fredric Jameson in particular has identified as a consequence of the 'cultural logic' of postmodernism (Jameson 1985: 112). The increasingly uncertain generic outlines of both science fiction and mainstream postmodern fiction have provided an alternative 'space' within which feminist science fiction has been able to develop, but the erosion of boundaries is also a source of gendered anxiety. As Andreas Huyssen has pointed out in his essay 'Mass culture as woman: modernism's other', historically, mass culture 'is somehow associated with woman while real, authentic culture remains the prerogative of men' (Huyssen 1986: 47). The modernist fear of the encroachments of popular culture resulted in the exclusion of the popular from the realms of 'authentic' culture, enabling it to be feminised and posited as modernism's 'other'.

The distinction between the feminised, 'everyday' nature of popular culture and the realms of the aesthetically significant, and therefore masculinised, nature of high culture is reiterated in Brian McHale's otherwise interesting account of the convergence of cyberpunk and mainstream postmodern fiction in the 1980s. Although he acknowledges the 'Traffic between cultural strata', he is concerned that this 'traffic' should not be regarded as in any way altering the fixed and hierarchical relations between those strata. In McHale's view, the relations between science fiction and postmodern fiction are to be seen as 'independent but parallel developments' in which the cybernetic interfaces of cyberpunk 'typically serve the function of literalizing and updating traditional literary elements' (McCaffery 1991: 318–19). This restatement of the boundaries between science fiction and postmodern fiction constitutes an expression of precisely those gendered anxieties regarding the erosion of clearly marked distinctions between high and popular fiction that are described by Huyssen. Both cyberpunk and feminist science fiction not only endorse the existence of the unstable and collapsing boundaries within postmodern culture, but they also contribute to the threat of disintegration. For feminist science fiction in particular, the threat of disintegration cannot be considered in entirely negative terms, since it contains possibilities for the rethinking of difference, and of gendered cultural and social relations.

It is appropriate at this point to examine cyberpunk's own claims to difference. Many of the claims for, and descriptions of, cyberpunk that come from within the field itself express the same gendered attitudes and anxieties already discussed, not least in their own literary pretensions. Timothy Leary, for example, demonstrates this quite clearly in an article called 'The cyberpunk: the individual as reality pilot', in which this guru of 1960s drug culture re-presents history in the light of cyberpunk. He not only finds in the cyberpunk a hero for modern times, but he also finds that the past is conveniently stuffed full of cyberpunk heroes:

> Every stage of history has produced a name and a heroic legend for the strong, stubborn creative individual who explores some future frontier, collects and brings back new information, and offers to guide the gene pool to the next stage . . . Self-assured singularities of the Cyber Breed have been called mavericks, ronin, free-lancers, independents, self-starters, nonconformists, oddballs, troublemakers, kooks, visionaries, iconoclasts, insurgents, blue-sky thinkers, loners, smartalecks.
>
> (McCaffery 1991: 245–6)

This celebration of difference is singularly male-oriented, as is cyberpunk itself, and the idea that cyberpunk was a 'movement' was generated by a small group of successful self-publicists, all of whom were white and male. Bruce Sterling's introduction to the cyberpunk anthology *Mirrorshades* explains that the writers in the book 'have come to prominence within this decade. Their allegiance to Eighties culture has marked them as a group – as a new movement in science fiction'. He goes on to quote some of the labels given to the group, such as 'Radical Hard SF, the Outlaw Technologists, the Eighties Wave, the Neuromantics, the Mirrorshades Group' (Sterling 1988: vii). Cyberpunk is defined by its contemporaneity but also by its masculinity, as is indicated by the inclusion of only one woman writer, Pat Cadigan, in the anthology.

The combination of computer technology and the oppositional ethos of punk and rock music that gave rise to cyberpunk is, like science fiction itself, inscribed with the masculine. Cyberpunk heroes are the hackers, street-wise rock'n'roll heroes who wear mirrorshades and do 'biz' in the urban sprawl, dealing in designer drugs, information technology and stolen data. The cyberpunk hacker is a 'computer cowboy' who jacks into the matrix of cyberspace by means of implanted cranial sockets. He is the postmodern equivalent of the *flâneur* described by Baudelaire, strolling anonymously and heroically through the chaotic streets of the modern city. But, as Janet Wolff has pointed out in her essay on the 'invisible flâneuse' (Wolff 1990), women could not inhabit the streets in the same way, and to be there alone was rarely a matter of choice. Since there was no place for 'respectable' women in the public places and on the streets of the city, they had no option but to retreat to the private world of the suburbs. In analogous fashion, the postmodern streets and spaces of cyberpunk seem distinctly inhospitable to women. Despite the stylistic innovations of cyberpunk, then, its narratives continue to privilege the masculine both in their celebration of technology and because its themes stem from the familiar male-dominated territory of sex, drugs and rock'n'roll. Cyberpunk presents us with masculine pleasure mediated through technology.

William Gibson's 1986 novel *Neuromancer* was the first novel to be referred to as cyberpunk, and it contains numerous cross-references to other genres and to codes drawn from information technology, hard-boiled detective fiction and science fiction. The hero of the novel is Case, a burnt-out hacker down on his luck and hustling to survive in Night City, described as being 'like a deranged experiment in social Darwinism, designed by a bored researcher who kept one thumb permanently on the fast-forward button. Stop hustling and you sank without trace, but move a little too swiftly and you'd break the fragile surface tension of the black market; either way, you were gone, with nothing left of you but some vague memory . . .' (Gibson 1986: 14). The language of this extract is deliberately reminiscent of the hard-boiled detective genre, in which lone heroes engage in righteous battle in mean city streets. Gibson's eclecticism and generic boundary-crossing are characteristic of cyberpunk's postmodern feel. It is situated somewhere within the gap between parody and pastiche that is described by Fredric Jameson, where the stylistic mimicry of pastiche is an emptier version of the satirical and critical intentions encountered in parody, making it a 'neutral practice' (Jameson 1992: 17). The opening line of the novel could be said to conform to the notion of such a neutral practice, 'The sky above the port was the color of television, tuned to a dead channel' (Gibson 1986: 9), where the laconic intonations of the language act solely as reminders of another genre, rather than as a critique of it. However, when Gibson goes on to describe the mean streets of the urban sprawl in terms of an information map, which in turn is described in the heightened prose that is reminiscent of William Burrough's writing, then the language has a more obviously parodic feel to it:

> Program a map to display frequency of data exchange, every thousand megabytes a single pixel on a very large screen. Manhattan and Atlanta burn solid white. Then they start to pulse, the rate of traffic threatening to overload your simulation. Your map is about to go nova. Cool it down. Up your scale. Each pixel a million megabytes. At a hundred million megabytes per second, you begin to make out certain blocks in midtown Manhattan, outlines of hundred-year-old industrial parks ringing the old core of Atlanta . . .
>
> (Gibson 1986: 57)

By rendering the silent and often secret numerical exchanges of cybernetic systems as high drama, the language and the implicit power structures of information technology are parodied by being made highly visible. Cinematic metaphors of zoom and close-up are used in conjunction with metaphors from information technology as an ironic reminder of the essentially closed environment of cybernetic systems and of the privatised power that they represent. However, although the language of information technology is parodied by being reworked in terms of the metaphoric and the poetic, the extent of the parody is ultimately ambiguous because of the covert romanticisation of technology that is also present. This ambiguity suggests that cyberpunk cannot finally be categorised as either pastiche or parody, but lies somewhere between them, and the most troubling consequence of this is that the gendered power relations of cybernetic systems are, in the end, uncritically replicated.

The masculine inflection of cyberpunk can also be seen in other areas of cultural production, such as film and performance. Like cyberpunk, Ridley Scott's film *Blade Runner* borrows from film noir, and Dekker's world-weary voice-over evokes a similar moral alienation from futuristic city streets that are a chaotic jumble of conflicting messages and signs. Anxieties about identity are expressed in the film through the conflict between human and non-human. The non-humans are replicants, genetic constructs that are perfect simulations of humans, but with enhanced physical abilities. Four of the replicants have escaped from their environment of control, and have returned to Earth: Dekker's job is to destroy them. They desire confirmation of their humanity, but neither of the sources that programmed them into existence, the genetic scientist and the head of the Tyrell Corporation, will grant them that recognition, so the replicants kill both men. This radical refusal of the replicants to submit to the law of the father is corrected in the film by means of a fifth replicant, Rachael, with whom Dekker falls in love. Her survival is ensured precisely because she does submit to the law of the father, in this case Dekker, and they escape together from the city. Anxieties about identity are thereby resolved in favour of the masculine. A further example of the masculine inflection of cyberpunk is provided by the American performance group Survival Research Laboratories, the members of which are amongst a growing number of techno-artists whose intentions are to use technology in their art in order to question it. The SRL has used weapons technology and explosive material in its work, some of which blew off part of the hand of group member Mark Pauline. Pauline acknowledges the criticism that their work could be seen to reproduce the gendered power relations implicit in technology, and he also admits in the same interview that the SRL 'is mostly white guys' (*I-D* 1992: 23–4).

The narratives of cyberpunk, then, seem to reveal a deep anxiety about the disintegration of the unitary self. This is indicated in Bruce Sterling's introduction to *Mirrorshades*, in which he says, 'Certain central themes spring up repeatedly in cyberpunk. The theme of body invasion: prosthetic limbs, implanted circuitry, cosmetic surgery, genetic alteration. The even more powerful theme of mind invasion: brain–computer interfaces, artificial intelligence, neurochemistry – techniques radically redefining the nature of humanity, the nature of the self' (Sterling 1988: xi). Clearly, in the context of cyberpunk, the 'self' is defined as masculine. The recurring theme of the interface between human and machine is explored in the science fiction narratives of cyberpunk by means of the metaphors of the matrix and cyberspace. As a place of semiotic excess, cyberspace blurs the distinction between reality and simulation, self and other, thus calling identity into question. It has the potential to be a new and heterogeneous space of desire, but because it is dominated by the masculine, it becomes a place in which loss of identity is to be feared. Anxiety and uncertainty about redefinitions of the 'nature of the self' suggest that gender is a key 'semiotic ghost' of cyberpunk, and the monstrous interface between human and machine threatens the very masculinity that is at the heart of cyberpunk narratives.

There is, however, a significant contrast to be made between cyberpunk's version of the monstrous interface, and that contained in feminist science fiction. In feminist SF narratives, the monstrous interface is celebrated as an opportunity to replace binary divisions between self and other, nature and culture, by other partial relationships and identities. The argument for the enormous potential of hybrid, or cyborg, identities has been put forward by Donna Haraway, who suggests that the metaphor of the cyborg can be a powerful means of challenging the binarisms that structure the dominant social and sexual relations of our culture. Haraway defines a cyborg as a 'cybernetic organism, a hybrid of machine and organism, a creature of social reality as well as a creature of fiction' (Haraway 1985: 65). Cyborgs are transgressive monsters that problematise the whole question of identity and difference, and the metaphor is an enabling one for feminist science fiction because it addresses the relations between technology, power and gender, a debate in which cyberpunk has been largely unwilling to engage.

Despite the apparent intransigence of cyberpunk, feminist science fiction has nevertheless had a profound but unstated influence on it, and as Samuel Delany suggests, 'the feminist explosion – which obviously infiltrates the cyberpunk writers so much – is the one they seem to be the least comfortable with' (Tatsumi 1988: 9). The work of Joanna Russ has been particularly important in this respect, and her science fiction novel *The Female Man*, first published in 1975, has had a considerable impact on the genre in general, including cyberpunk. Russ uses the familiar SF convention of parallel universes and time zones to describe the alienation and fragmentation that women experience within patriarchal society and culture. There are four 'voices' in the novel, belonging to four women from different universes, and each narrative voice demonstrates a different possible existence for women. Joanna inhabits a time very similar to our own contemporary reality; Jeannine lives in a world where the Depression never ended and World War II never began; Janet comes from a utopian future in which men do not exist; in Jael's universe, women were the victors when the 'battle of the sexes' had become literal war. Jael, with her 'weaponry' of retractable steel claws and teeth, reappears in Gibson's *Neuromancer* as the character Molly Million, a hard-bitten freelance mercenary whose mirrorshades are grafted into her skin and who has retractable razors under her fingernails.

Russ's novel is notable for the way in which she playfully fragments narrative and sentence structure, and as the four women move between each other's universes, offering ironic commentary on each of them, the four voices in the narrative both overlap and conflict. The shifting and uncertain narrative focus and the fragmented narrative allow the text to masquerade as incoherent, and the masculine drive of conventional SF narratives is therefore disrupted. As the title of the novel indicates, when signifiers are cut free from signifieds defined solely by the masculine, different kinds of gender definition become possible. Through the central image of the female man, the narrative enters what Elaine Showalter has called the 'wild zone' of language (Showalter 1985: 262), where that which is repressed in language can be revealed. Russ explores the way in which feminity is both defined by and confined by conventional language uses, and she uses the image of the female man to suggest the possibilities of appropriation, whereby new meanings can emerge from old structures. The irony inherent in such appropriations is fully understood by Russ, as one of the narrative voices indicates: 'If we are all Mankind, it follows to my interested and righteous and rightnow very bright and beady little eyes, that I too am a Man and not at all a Woman ... I think I am a Man; I think you had better call me a Man; I think you will write about me as a Man from now on and speak of me as a Man and employ me as a Man and recognise child-rearing as a Man's business' (Russ 1985: 140). Although the image of the female man is located within the context of a science fiction narrative, the feminist content of its meanings escapes the semantic confines of such a context. The female man re-creates herself in and through language and is empowered by her acquisition of the masculine. She is a cyborg construction, a partial subjectivity that refuses closure around definitions of either masculinity or subjectivity, and thus defers the notion of a fixed identity.

Other feminist science fiction texts are less linguistically and structurally ambitious than *The Female Man*, but they also raise the issue of gender identity by means of the cyborg metaphor. Cyborgs can be found throughout Vonda McIntyre's work, but particularly in *Superluminal* (1984), in which McIntyre uses the metaphor of the cyborg to question the cultural construction of gender. The two central female characters in the narrative escape the confines of socially and culturally determined definitions of gender by means of biological alteration. One of them, Laenea, has her biological heart replaced by a microelectronic device in order that she can become a space pilot, and the other, Orca, has been genetically altered to enable her to live on land and also in the oceans, so that she and others like her can communicate with the ocean-dwelling cetaceans. McIntyre uses conventions from both romance and quest narratives in her work, and the way in which constructions of gender and identity are embedded in language and narrative is revealed by such generic boundary-crossing. For example, the opening line of *Superluminal*, 'She gave up her heart willingly', would be equally at home in a romance narrative, although here it refers to the technological processes of surgery and prosthesis. Laenea sacrifices her heart not in order to subordinate her own interests to those of a man, as is usual in romance fiction, but to serve her own interests, and thus the ironic combination of cliché from romance fiction with the science fiction convention of future technology is deliberately unsettling. The language of technology and 'hard science' with which the male-dominated narratives of SF are most commonly associated is here rendered in terms of the feminine, as romance, and this undermines the binary certainties of scientific discourse that are constantly recalled in science fiction.

The generic boundary-crossing that is a persistent feature of feminist SF in general, and of *Superluminal* in particular, subverts the linguistic and narrative expectations of genre. The dominance of masculine pleasure in the narrative structures of science fiction is undercut by the emphasis on female pleasure that is central to romance narratives, and this unexpected juxtaposition of romance and SF reveals the relations of domination and subordination that are embedded in popular genres.

In common with other feminist science fiction writers, McIntyre reworks generic conventions to include the feminine, and the incorporation of unexpected and potentially incompatible elements from other genres undercuts the masculine inflections of SF. The cyborg thus becomes a signifier for the radical instability that feminist science fiction has introduced into the genre. Through the metaphor of the cyborg, McIntyre is also able to present masculinity in a different way. The central male character in *Superluminal* is also a cyborg, in that he has undergone a biological transformation: by surviving a plague-inducing virus, his sense of time is changed in such a way that it irrevocably alters all human understanding of the space–time continuum. In conjunction with this major change, he is not characterised as the heroic male figure that would be expected to dominate in a science fiction narrative: instead, he spends most of the narrative out of his depth and remarkably dependent on the two female characters.

The partial and incomplete nature of cyborg identity provides a useful way of thinking about the construction of identity in terms of race and gender, and the work of the black feminist science fiction writer Octavia Butler is particularly concerned with this issue. Postmodern anxieties about the disintegration of the unitary self which figure strongly in cyberpunk are also a major concern of Butler's recent *Xenogenesis* trilogy. Such anxieties are explored throughout the novels, by means of a vocabulary that emphasises transformation, metamorphosis, merging and bonding. In the trilogy, the world has been devastated by nuclear war and the remnants of humanity are rescued from extinction by an alien race called the Oankali. The aliens are a race of gene traders, and in return for rescuing humanity they want a genetic exchange with humans. The central character in the first novel *Dawn* (1988) is Lilith, a black woman survivor who is given the task of telling the remaining humans that the price for their survival is a genetic exchange that will result in the eventual extinction of the human race in its present form. The implied power structure in the relationship between humans and the Oankali is, for Lilith and other humans, reminiscent of the power relations of slavery, an issue raised throughout Butler's work. The complexity of those relations is explored in the narrative as it is made clear that the Oankali face the same possibility of extinction as humanity if no gene trade takes place.

The aliens are described as being 'seduced' by the genetic possibilities of humans, and this is contrasted with the xenophobia expressed by some of the humans. Lilith eventually takes an Oankali mate, as do other humans, and the remaining novels in the trilogy, *Adulthood Rites* (1989) and *Imago* (1990), are narrated from the point of view of Lilith's children. The children are genetic constructs, the product of genetic exchange between humans and Oankali, and as constructs they are also cyborgs. 'Otherness' is constantly redefined in the trilogy, since it is represented not only by the alien Oankali, but also by Lilith as a black woman, and by her children as human–alien constructs. The shifting definition of human and alien in the narrative allows Butler to explore the social and cultural construction of identity and difference, and the science fiction convention of the alien is rewritten to become a metaphor for the erosion of boundaries between self and other, human and alien. It is the radical developmental possibilities of the dissolution of boundaries between self and other than are seized on in Butler's novels. This interest in merging and dissolution is in stark contrast to the anxiety at the 'invasion' or loss of self expressed in cyberpunk. In cyberpunk, only Artificial Intelligences merge; where there is a merging of human and machine, it is at the expense of the human, which is rendered down to become merely information on a microchip. In Butler's work, however, metamorphosis is used to oppose both universalist and masculinist definitions of self and other.

The ambiguous consequences of the human–machine interface are examined in Pat Cadigan's cyberpunk novel *Synners* (1991). The narrative depicts an environment in which the technology of the interface is taken for granted, hacking is an accepted part of youth culture, and virtual reality has been appropriated by the advertising and leisure industries. Technology has thus been domesticated, and the mystique of the interface that is so apparent in other cyberpunk texts is therefore undermined. Cadigan attempts to dissolve the alliance between masculinity and technology that is characteristic of cyberpunk by providing a narrative account of the social and cultural consequences of the technology, rather than an uncritical celebration of it. In a reminder of cyberpunk's debt to both MTV and rock'n'roll, the 'synners' of the title are video artists who produce music videos using the technology of the interface to synthesise images and rock music. The narrative concerns the development of cranial sockets that allow the synners' own input to be fed directly into the brain of the consumer, an unexpected consequence of which is that the entire information network becomes sentient. Its sentient form is, however, unequivocally masculine, and the possibilities inherent in the metaphor of a sentient information system for exploring other definitions of identity are not ultimately pursued in the narrative. Although Cadigan's cyberpunk narrative contains strong female characters and a more subtle response to the notion of the interface than is present in much cyberpunk writing, it is still subject to the limits of cyberpunk. Within the predominantly masculine narratives of cyberpunk, the erosion of boundaries such as those between self and other, reality and simulation, is not a preferred option, and the potential instability of gender and identity that is implied in the interface continues to be regarded as a threat.

Cyberpunk has situated itself centrally in postmodern cultural practice, particularly with its self-conscious crossing of generic boundaries, both within popular culture and across the binary division between high and popular culture. The rich and stylised vernacular of cyberpunk, by means of which it simulates the rapid flow of information, has provided a source of linguistic experimentation, as has the appropriation of the metaphor of the interface within cybernetic systems. However, despite the fluidity of its narratives, cyberpunk has persistently retreated from the implications of its own metaphors regarding the dissolution of fixed identities at the interface. In contrast, the generic boundary-crossing of feminist science fiction has produced narratives in which altered definitions of self and other are comprehensively explored, and it is the cyborgs of feminist SF that are finally able to disrupt the narratives of power that are embedded in the distinctions between human and machine, self and other, human and alien.

NOTES

1. This chapter is an earlier version of 'Cyberpunk, cyborgs and feminist science fiction', in Wolmark, (1993).
2. Critical works in which the focus is on feminist science fiction are: Lefanu, (1988) Armitt (1991), Barr (1981), Cranny-Francis (1990).
3. There are many other significant contributors to feminist science fiction apart from those writers mentioned in the text. For example: Suzette Haden Elgin, Sally Miller Gearhart, Suzy McKee Charnas, James Tiptree Jr, Joan Slonczewski, Emma Bull, Mary Gentle, Lisa Tuttle, Gwyneth Jones and Sue Thomas.

SEVEN

Claiming the speakwrite: linguistic subversion in the feminist dystopia

Elisabeth Mahoney

> With the deep, unconscious sigh which not even the nearness of the telescreen could prevent him from uttering when his day's work started, Winston pulled the speakwrite towards him, blew the dust from its mouthpiece, and put on his spectacles.
>
> (Orwell 1983: 37)

Winston Smith, in Orwell's *Nineteen Eighty-Four*, works at the Ministry of Truth, rewriting old articles and news stories in *The Times*, the Party paper in Oceania. He is fluent in both Oldspeak and Newspeak, moving easily between the two as he refashions texts. He is thus more than a passive consumer of Party propaganda: Winston is involved in the reproduction of discourse which maintains both Party power and his position within its ideology. It is thus absolutely appropriate that he should work with a 'speakwrite', raising as it does the question of speaking correctly or in such a way as to gain or maintain the 'right to speak'. It also suggests an unproblematic relationship between speaking and writing for Winston. We are told that his 'greatest pleasure in life' is his work, that 'Winston was good at this kind of thing' (*ibid.*: 42) and that this untroubled relationship with language and texts continues into his private life and – the symbol of that life – his diary. Although he is clearly unused to writing – his writing is 'childish', for example – when he does write it is 'as though by automatic action', his pen slides 'voluptuously over the page' (*ibid.*: 20) as he transcribes his 'interminable restless monologue' (*ibid.*: 12). Thus although the practice of writing might be problematic, Winston's text is already there, awaiting transcription. It is worth noting that Julia (the Party member who becomes Winston's lover; interestingly, we do not learn her full name) is also involved in the production of Party propaganda, having worked, for example, in 'Pornosec', which churns out pornography for the proles. She, however, worked with images rather than words, an example of her 'silencing' which feminist readings of Orwell's text have noted:[1]

> They only have six plots, but they swap them around a bit. Of course I was only on the kaleidoscopes. I was never in the Rewrite Squad. I'm not literary, dear – not even enough for that.
>
> (Orwell 1983: 116)

A relationship between gender and language is thus established: Julia does not *produce* texts or control language, but rather mixes images 'on the kaleidoscopes', and the 'speakwrite' which Winston uses is, by comparison, a sign of relative linguistic empowerment. In this chapter I want to examine feminist fictional and theoretical calls for a specifically gendered, feminine 'speakwrite' or right to speak, to counter cultural silencing or marginalisation of women's voices. These issues are most obviously central to feminist genre fiction which takes as its starting point gender-specific gaps and silences in literary codes and conventions. Whilst my specific focus here will be a feminist dystopian text, questions of gender and its relation to articulation and silence are central to all feminist acts of rewriting. As one of the sibyls in Michèle Roberts' *The Book of Mrs Noah* (1987) suggests, the impulse behind feminist narratives is often to self-consciously 'fill in one of his gaps' (Roberts 1987: 70).[2] The text I will be discussing here, Suzette Haden Elgin's *Native Tongue* (1984), takes this project further to propose and include a women's language, Láadan. Fictional and theoretical claims for such a language are based around a belief in and desire for language shaped by gendered experience and perception: the possibility of a women's language, the 'dream of a common language'.

The mapping out of gender-specific silences has been a crucial concern of feminist critiques and these silences have included women's individual and collective voices, experiences and achievements. Such feminist critiques draw attention to the political nature of such silencing and the means by which this marginalisation of women's voices takes place. Language is thus understood to both reflect and effect the construction of gender difference; to work, as Teresa De Lauretis suggests, as one of a number of 'technologies of gender':

... gender, too, both as representation and as self-representation, is the product of various social technologies, such as cinema, and of institutionalized discourses, epistemologies, and critical practices, as well as practices of daily life.

(De Lauretis 1989: 2)

These 'various social technologies' producing gender are linked by language – they are all at some level linguistically effected – and, obversely, any questioning of these 'technologies' can only come *through* language. Haden Elgin takes up this challenge, proposing in her fiction that if women's relation to language changes, their lived and social experience will change. Whilst the text has been critiqued both for its reliance on a deterministic model of language and for not developing the radical potential of the language suffi-ciently in the space of the novel,[3] I want to suggest that *Native Tongue* be read as immediately *problematising* the possibility of a women's language, rather than as a text which provides some (all too easy) answers to questions concerning the cultural 'silencing' of women. The novel includes within it insistent doubts about trans-lating the 'dream of a common language' into reality.

The novel is set in the twenty-second and twenty-third centuries, when women's legal and civil rights have been revoked to the extent that women are deemed legal minors and are unable to work or hold financial assets without written permission from a male guardian. Those in power are male linguists and their families, The Lines. Language acquisition has become crucial for continuing human intergalactic dominance and thus the linguists have created an environment called an Interface, a space which allows human babies to interact with aliens and thus learn alien languages. Women are allowed to live in linguist households and participate in language work – as translators, negotiators and so on – until menopause, when they are sent to 'Barren Houses', all-women communities. Male linguists have given the women their own lan-guage, Langlish, to develop as a hobby, with the understanding that it is to remain purely a theoretical exercise. In the space of the novel and in the space of the 'Barren Houses' the women secretly begin to construct and speak their own language, Láadan.

Láadan is constructed around the premise that conventional lan-guage does not (and, indeed, cannot) include the possibility of naming women's experience. A woman-centred language would radically transform both means of representation and, subse-quently, reality:

> . . . as more and more little girls acquire Láadan and begin to speak a language that expresses the perceptions of women rather than those of men, reality will begin to change.
>
> (Haden Elgin 1985: 250)

In an article on *Native Tongue*, Elgin attempts to push this radical potential of a women's language even further, stating that if what she calls 'mainstream culture' were to acknowledge women's perceptions, experiences and desires, 'that would result in the culture's self-destruction' (Hadan Elgin 1987: 177). That is to say, patriarchal culture depends upon the silencing of women for its perpetuation.

The bringing into discourse of women's experience is effected in the novel by the process of 'Encoding' which the women use to construct Láadan:

> . . . the making of a name for a chunk of the world that so far we know has never been chosen for naming . . . never before impressed anyone as sufficiently important to deserve its own name.
>
> (Haden Elgin 1985: 22)

This process initially appears to offer a way out of silence and, if we accept Elgin's hypothesis, a way to end oppression in and through language. Within the space of the novel this appears and remains a seductive notion, as these examples from the appendix, 'A First Dictionary and Grammar of Láadan', demonstrate:

> radiidin: non-holiday, a time allegedly a holiday but actually so much a burden because of work and preparations that it is a dreaded occasion; especially when there are too many guests and none of them help.
> rathom: non-pillow, one who lures another to trust and rely on them but has no intention of following through, a 'lean on me so I can step aside and let you fall' person.

However, this utopian possibility is almost immediately undercut when we realise in the narrative where there Encodings come from:

> there is no way at all to search systematically for capital-E Encodings. They come to you out of nowhere and you realize that you have always needed them; but you can't go looking for them, and they don't turn up as concrete entities neatly marked off for you and flashing NAME ME. They are therefore very precious.
>
> (Haden Elgin 1985: 22)

Thus this naming of specifically gendered perceptions seems to emerge from an intuitive 'nowhere' and is based very much on the experience of the individual ('they come to you', 'you have always needed them', 'you can't go looking for them'). Ironically, one of the definitions in the appendix seems to suggest what Láadan might become as a language, through this model of construction:

> raweshalh: . . . a collection of parts with no relationship other than coincidence, a perverse choice of items to call a set; *especially when used as* '*evidence*'.
>
> (Haden Elgin 1985: 303; emphasis mine)

It is indeed the 'evidence' of Láadan within the text – the sampler dictionary and examples of women speaking to each other in Láadan – I want to suggest, which first draws attention to the problems of such a project. Towards the end of *Native Tongue* women in the Barren House begin to converse in the language, although we only get reported speech:

> Susannah chuckled. 'For example . . . when I thought I'd introduce a new word yesterday, for that new way of dancing that we saw on the threedies. You remember, Grace? The one that looks as if the youngsters are all trying to dislocate their shoulders?'
> 'I remember,' Grace said. 'I would swear it had to be painful.'
> 'Well! I thought I had a decent proposal for a word, and I suggested it. And one of the littlebits *corrected* me, I'll have you know!'
> 'Corrected you? How could that be – did you make an error in the morphology? At your age?'
> 'Of course not, it was a perfectly good Láadan word, formed in accordance with every rule. But she did. She said, "Aunt Susannah, it could not be that way. I'm very sorry, but it would have to be *this* way."'
> 'And she was right?'
> 'Goodness, how would I know that?'
>
> (Haden Elgin 1985: 266–7)

Here, we see a prioritising of the instinctive and intuitive – the 'native' – over the 'perfectly good' and linguistically 'correct' and this leads to both exclusion – here, of the old by the young – and confusion ('how would I know?'), an absence of knowledge. Ultimately, then, the women's language threatens to impose a new 'technology of silence' ('it would have to be this way'). As De Lauretis suggests, any new 'technology', any critique of the representation of gender will itself depend upon *another* construction of gender:

Paradoxically, therefore, the construction of gender is also effected by its deconstruction; that is to say, by any discourse, feminist or otherwise, that would discard it as ideological misrepresentation.

(De Lauretis 1989: 3)

This applies equally to Haden Elgin's 'deconstruction' or critique of 'man-made' language. If language is understood to determine reality, then this model will apply equally to Láadan and there is little in the novel to suggest otherwise. Thus the example cited above demonstrates an effacement of difference between women, and, in De Lauretis' terms, another linguistic 'construction of gender' is established.

Whilst there are examples of Láadan countering women's specific 'lack' of language in the text, such instances further problematise the dream of a common language:

> She stopped, because there was no word for it in any language she knew, and she wanted to use the *right* word.
> 'Oh,' she said. 'I know . . . They are *heenahal*.' And she sighed. 'Such a relief, to have a language with the right words in it!'

(Haden Elgin 1985: 267)

It is not only the humour here but also the specific example of 'heenahal' which begins to undermine a prescriptive reading of *Native Tongue*. For such scenes do not provide convincing answers to the question of what a language such as Láadan would offer women. This point is made forcefully by the fact that 'heenahal' does not appear in the sampler dictionary in the appendix and thus the reader is immediately confronted by another kind of exclusion and silence.

Láadan also draws our attention to what the construction of such a language would leave out. Ethnicity is an obvious 'silence' throughout the text, despite the claim that Láadan is deliberately made up of sounds which do not prioritise English-speaking women. This claim is almost immediately undermined by the fact that this same language is based on the experiences, perceptions and desires of a small group of highly-educated linguist women. It is also interesting that within the narrative two women have to be sacrificed in the struggle for a women's language: Michaela, a nurse, who murders a male linguist once he suspects that the women have constructed a real language, and Bella-Anne, who was placed in the Barren House (i.e. not in a linguist household) at twenty for failing to conceive. Thus, those who are in some sense dispensable in the text are not the women linguists. We are told of Michaela:

> She was no linguist and never could be, she couldn't help them with their language and would only be a burden to them if she tried – but she was as skilled at killing as they were at their conjugations and declensions.
>
> (Haden Elgin 1985: 281)

The echoes of Julia in *Nineteen Eighty-Four* are striking here and remind us of the power invested in the construction of Láadan. Its presence in the text serves to problematise rather than advocate the 'dream of a common language', most crucially by reminding us of the issue here: whether this kind of linguistic subversion would disrupt or reinscribe women's marginalisation and silence.

It seems to me that such problems arise if we read *Native Tongue* as, in some sense, a realist and prescriptive text. A more useful and appropriate reading I want to suggest is to foreground the non-realist, science-fiction status of the narrative, and the moments within (and outside of) the text, which immediately deconstruct the possibility of a women's language.

Firstly, the status of the narrative in *Native Tongue* is made emphatically clear in the Preface:

> We believe this book to be the only work of fiction ever written by a member of the Lines . . . *Native Tongue* is not a work of scholarship, or a teaching grammar, or a book of science for the general public; it is a NOVEL.
>
> (Haden Elgin 1985: 5)

Thus the whole text, including the Preface and the Glossary, is a fiction and in this sense, the excerpt from the 'First Dictionary and Grammar of Láadan' becomes not a transcript of what women need in order to change their reality, but a *fantasy* or 'dream' of language. Although Haden Elgin has suggested that her novel be read as 'near future science fiction', I think that the metafictional layers in the text (for example, the excerpts from historical 'documents' as epigraphs to each chapter) problematise, if not prevent, such a reading. One of the last of these epigraphs is a fragment 'alleged' to be from the diary of Nazareth, one of the women most closely involved with the construction of Láadan:

... all joy, all glory, all radiance, had been systematically excluded. And it was from *that* reality, that linguistic construct, that the women of Chornyak Barren House were attempting to extrapolate. It couldn't be done, of course. You cannot weave truth on a loom of lies.

(Haden Elgin 1985: 284)

This seems to be a key moment in a text which is usually read as one which attempts to translate the 'dream' into the 'real'. In this quotation, however, Haden Elgin seems aware both of the complexities of language (a 'loom' from the old English *geloma* meaning 'tool', but a tool only for lies, fictions and, possibly, dreams) and the resulting clash between language and any desire for 'truth'. Thus, the 'dream of a common language' which might 'weave truth' of women's identity and lived experience, is acknowledged to be a fiction in the same way, and in the same place – the chapter epigraphs – as Elgin's text.

The second way in which the claims made in the text for Láadan are simultaneously negated, is through the continued presence of silence, both in and around the language itself. An example of this comes when Nazareth is being humiliated by her father and husband for telling another man that she has fallen in love with him. Láadan offers no solace at this point:

'To have a Chornyak daughter thrust herself upon a Man like a common whore . . . Nazareth it leaves me speachless.'
AND WHY DO YOU GO ON TALKING, THEN? It was a scream but it was silent.

(Haden Elgin 1985: 198)

The women's quarters, the Barren Houses, are the only environment in which the 'native' language has any meaning and any power and this once again draws our attention to its marginality. Outside of this, Láadan serves to constrict movement away from silence. This is most clearly stated by Haden Elgin herself:

In the real world that we are in, I have no such resources available. I have nobody to talk Láadan with. Oh, I have the Láadan group, which is an informal group of people scattered all over the country who correspond, but I haven't time to set up anything like a formal correspondence group where we could write back and forth in Láadan even.

(Haden Elgin 1987: 180)

Láadan is, then, ultimately unworkable in any real sense, a 'limited edition' as the Preface to *Native Tongue* suggests, and any moves towards it leave the speaking subject in what Lucie Armitt calls 'the middle of an absence' – still silenced, still marginalised, like Nazareth's silent scream (Armitt 1991: 134). The 'common language' remains a silence, then, both within and beyond the text (such as, for example, Haden Elgin's attempts to use Láadan with the 'Láadan Group'). One of the chapter epigraphs is an interview with a subject under the influence of LSD, and the interview, itself beyond language as communication, gives us a suggestion of the problems of a feminised language emerging intuitively from beyond discourse:

> A: It's not a thing. It's not a not-thing. It's not an idea. It's not a non-idea. It's not a part of reality. It's not a not-part of reality. It's not a not-part of a not-part of not-reality.
>
> Q: Nils, that's not a hell of a lot of help to us.
> A: (Laughter)
>
> (Haden Elgin 1985: 184)

That Láadan should be framed by a fictional narrative (and not by an article in *Family Circle* or *TV Guide*, which Haden Elgin suggests would have been ideal) which remains shadowed by silences and paradoxes – most obviously, why isn't the text itself in Láadan – disrupts any reading of *Native Tongue* as a 'teaching grammar' or realist text. However, a reading of the text which foregrounds its status as a fantasy, non-realist narrative can incorporate not only fictionality, paradox and silence, but, crucially, the blurring of distinctions between the 'real' and the 'non-real' in the novel, as shown by the closing lines of the book, which give an address for the 'Society for the Furtherance and Study of Fantasy and Science Fiction', who publish the Dictionary and Grammar of Láadan.

Whilst I would want to concur with Donna Haraway's assertion that 'the feminist dream of a common language, like all dreams for a perfectly true language, of a perfectly faithful naming of experience, is a totalising and imperialist one' (Haraway 1990: 215, see Haraway 1985), I would want to suggest that the *dream*, the fantasy of a 'common language' can be retained by marginalised and silenced subjects, as a concept which challenges conventions of representation from the special place of the fantastic narrative. It is only in the translation into the real that such a project becomes potentially 'totalising'. This is not to depoliticise the text but, rather, by foregoing the notion of *Native Tongue* as 'perfectly true' and 'perfectly faithful' as a text, it might be possible to read the text as doubly subversive. This foregrounding of the 'fantasy' element of a women's language – the 'dream' – places Haden Elgin's fiction within a context of theorists who have proposed a feminised language, such as Hélène Cixous and Luce Irigaray.

Cixous advocates looking for a place for women to speak, 'somewhere other than in silence, the place reserved for her in and through the symbolic' (Cixous and Clement 1986: 93), and Irigaray has specified women's linguistic lack:

> We lack, we women with a sex of our own kind, a God in which to share, a word/language to share and to become. Defined as the often obscure, not to say hidden, mother-substance of the word/language of men, we lack our subject, our noun, our verb, our predicates: our elementary sentence, our basic rhythm, our morphological identity, our generic incarnation, our genealogy.
>
> (cited in Whitford 1991: 45)

It seems most useful to read *Native Tongue* in the context of such statements, especially as Haden Elgin comments that before writing the novel she read widely in such theory:

> I read the French feminists. I read Hélène Cixous, I read Irigaray's 'This Sex which is not One', I read Jacques Lacan; I read Adrienne Rich.
>
> (Haden Elgin 1987: 177)

If, as I suggest, *Native Tongue* can be read as a fantasy text which self-consciously offers a utopian vision – but not, ultimately and crucially, the possibility of any translation into the real – it is imperative that this reading remain politicised. All feminist projects remain utopian gestures at some level, as Margaret Whitford's reading of Irigaray convincingly demonstrates (Whitford 1991). She suggests that rather than critiquing Irigaray's texts as depoliticised and anti-materialist, we can read her work as *one* of the many utopian voices within feminism; not as far as we might think from, for example, materialist critiques. Indeed, this can be a productive clash of theories: 'we are standing between two *phantasies*, two versions of the conditions for the future good life between which we cannot and do not need to arbitrate definitively' (*ibid.*: 20; emphasis mine).

Thus we need, we *still* need, to bring women's voices into fictional and theoretical spaces; this remains a contested, political move. As Judith Still has argued recently in an essay on Cixous, 'a theoretical extreme or poetic utopia' can and indeed should inform feminist reading and writing practices, 'even if there is no such thing nor any such place as a feminine economy, there is an ethical, political and theoretical point to retaining that utopic horizon' (Still 1990: 55). My reading of *Native Tongue* has emphasised its status as a 'poetic utopia', that is, a 'fantasy' narrative rather than a 'teaching grammar', and one which can open up (rather than limiting or essentialising) debates around the complex *technologies* – and politics – of language and gender.

NOTES

1. See, for example, B. Campbell (1984); Beddoe (1984) and Patai (1984).
2. For an account of the diversity of feminist genre fiction, see Carr (1989); Gerrard (1989) and Cranny-Francis (1990).
3. See Cameron (1990) and Armitt (1991).

GENDER, LANGUAGE AND EDUCATION

EIGHT

Feminising classroom talk?

Joan Swann and David Graddol

INTRODUCTION

Since the 1970s increasing concern has been expressed about the role of the formal education system in reproducing gender differences and inequalities. This has perhaps been stated most succinctly in Sara Delamont's now classic account of *Sex Roles and the School*:

> schools develop and reinforce sex segregations, stereotypes and even discriminations which exaggerate the negative aspects of sex roles in the outside world, when they could be trying to alleviate them.
>
> (Delamont 1990: 2)

Delamont's concerns derive from (mainly) ethnographic studies of school and classroom life. Classroom talk – the ways teachers talk to girls and boys and the ways girls and boys talk amongst themselves – has also been an important focus of attention. Studies of classroom talk have shown that teachers tend to give more time and attention to boys and that boys themselves tend to monopolise the physical and verbal space. Teachers routinely differentiate between girls and boys; certain forms of behaviour (such as calling out) are acceptable from boys but not from girls; and topics that reflect boys' interests are more frequently selected for discussion. Such evidence comes from both primary and secondary schools and from different areas of the curriculum (see, for instance, Clarricoates 1983; Delamont 1990; French and French 1984; Sadker and Sadker 1985; Spender 1982; Stanworth 1983; Swann and Graddol 1988; Whyte 1986). It is this sort of evidence that has led Katherine Clarricoates to conclude that classroom interaction is 'suffused with gender' (1983: 46).

Concerns about gender differences and inequalities have been primarily social ones, related to girls' and boys' subject and eventual career choices and to their developing gender identities. But there have also been concerns to do more specifically with the notion of talk and learning:

> an enormous amount of research has been undertaken which establishes the primary importance of learners being able to talk about their own experience as a starting point for learning. Yet we have an education system where not only is it extremely difficult for half the population to find an opportunity to talk – particularly to the teacher – but where the experience about which they could talk is seen as inappropriate, as not sufficiently 'interesting' to be talked about.
>
> (Spender 1982: 60)

Dale Spender is suggesting that girls may be educationally disadvantaged by their lack of opportunity to talk in class. But an important point overlooked here is the nature of classroom talk from which girls have traditionally been excluded. Many of the earlier (1970s and 1980s) studies of gender and classroom talk, on which Spender's argument rests, have looked at whole-class or teacher-directed talk such as discussions led by the teacher. Such talk is of a rather public kind – pupils have to speak out in front of the whole class. It may also be competitive, in that pupils obtain speaking turns by raising their hands and being selected by the teacher; by catching the teacher's eye in some way; or sometimes by calling out. It is this kind of talk that seems to favour boys, at least in the sense that those who do most of the talking, and are able to get their points of view across, tend to be boys.

Our own small-scale study of talk in two primary classrooms (Swann and Graddol 1988) suggests that processes favouring the selection of boys as speakers may be subtle; that girls, boys and the teacher all actively participate in these processes; and that the differential between girls and boys may be maintained in a variety of contexts, each requiring different conversational strategies. We found, for instance, that boys more frequently 'chipped in' in a context in which this was allowed, and also raised their hands earlier and more decisively in a context in which this was the usual turn-getting strategy; that, depending on the context, girls' strategies included not chipping in, and raising a hand just after the teacher had begun to direct her gaze towards another pupil; and that, while the teachers occasionally selected a quiet girl to speak, their conversation management strategies systematically favoured boys' participation – e.g. they directed more of their talk towards boys, and they looked more consistently at boys during the formulation of a question. We argued that, through such patterns of interaction, boys might be acquiring the sorts of competitive speaking skills that are necessary for participation in many formal contexts such as meetings and occasions of public speaking.

Clearly, however, such relatively formal teacher-directed talk isn't the only type of talk that takes place in the classroom, and the relationship between talk and learning which underlies Spender's argument has been associated with a different type of talk: talk that is more democratically organised and that is explicitly based on collaboration rather than on competition for the floor. Below we shall explore the view that such talk might actually favour girls rather than boys, but first we need to say something about its educational genesis and its (ideal) characteristics.

THE ORACY MOVEMENT

It was in 1965 that Andrew Wilkinson coined the term 'oracy', by analogy with literacy. Wilkinson, in common with many other educationalists in the 1960s and 1970s, was concerned to emphasise the educational value of talk – as in his now well-known statement that oracy is 'a condition of learning in all subjects' (1965: 58). Educationalists were also interested in the development of spoken language in its own right: it was argued that, in all subjects, pupils should be encouraged to develop a wider repertoire and become familiar with a range of (spoken) registers and styles (see, for instance, Wilkinson 1965; Barnes, Britton and Rosen 1971). The immediate effects of such views upon classroom practice are uncertain, but they rapidly became part of the educational orthodoxy. In 1975 the Bullock report argued:

> Throughout the primary and middle years the change of emphasis from teaching to learning has meant that talk now occupies a position of central importance.
>
> (Department of Education and Science 1975, para. 10.10)

The perceived importance of oracy was maintained through the

1980s: in 1982 the Assessment of Performance Unit began to assess pupils' spoken language as part of their overall monitoring of language development; many public examinations (such as the GCSE, set up in 1986) acquired an oral component; and 1987 saw the advent of the National Oracy Project, funded by the National Curriculum Council to establish and promote good practice in oracy work in the classroom.

The National Oracy Project, and the oracy movement more generally, have encouraged classroom talk of various kinds, including whole-class discussion and talk between teachers and pupils. However, a great deal of emphasis has been given to collaborative talk in small groups, in which pupils learn by discussion – by exploring an issue, or tackling a problem together. Reflecting on 25 years of oracy, Andrew Wilkinson provided a characterisation of what he termed the 'rules' of classroom discussion:

> Take turns; don't interrupt; don't overtalk; share out the talk time; don't allow silence; don't speak at too great a length; listen to others; respect their point of view; find rational reasons for agreeing or dissenting; respond to the merits, not demerits, of others' points; do not be personal; be objective; be positive and constructive; be co-operative; try to arrive at a mutually satisfying conclusion. The consensus may be challenged, but with the intention of arriving at a new consensus by rational argument.
>
> (Wilkinson, Davies and Berrill 1990: 76–7)

Similar values underpin other pronouncements about good or effective talk. The following extract is taken from a list of the characteristics of a good speaker and listener produced by a group of National Oracy Project Coordinators:

> The good speaker and listener:
> - expects the speaker to have something to say to her/him and expects her/his contributions to be valued and sometimes responded to;
> - is open to what the speaker has to say and is able to value others' contributions;
> - brings her/his experience of life and previous talking/listening to an exchange;
> - anticipates what is to come and reflects on what has gone before;
> - relates what is said to what has gone before;
> - can reflect on what the speaker says to correct first impressions and is able to use exploratory talk to consolidate her/his own thinking;
> - is prepared to suspend judgement and modify opinions;
>
> (Johnson 1990: 4)

In both cases there is a concern with conversation management techniques: the need to keep the conversation running smoothly. But there is also a moral requirement: children have to value what others say, and be prepared to modify their opinions. There is an emphasis throughout on collaboration and consensus, the latter made explicit in Wilkinson.

From the late 1980s, with the advent of the national curriculum in England and Wales, such values found their way into curriculum guidelines and associated assessment practices:

> Effective plans provide for a classroom where children feel sufficiently encouraged and secure to be able to express and explore their thoughts, feelings and emotions. It is important that teachers encourage talk which is genuinely tentative and exploratory while at the same time demonstrating to children that speaking and listening are rigorous activities which merit equal attention alongside writing and reading in the classroom. One way of achieving this is to ensure that children are encouraged to reflect upon their own and other people's speaking and listening. This should not be in a negative or fault-finding way, but through appreciating the importance of listening to others and thinking about questions like 'How do I listen?', 'What do I do while I listen?', 'Did I explain my idea?', and about how one speaker differs from another.
>
> (National Curriculum Council 1989: C2)

The National Curriculum Council (NCC), who produced these guidelines, recognised the need for 'equal opportunities' between girls and boys, although they paid scant attention to research findings on gender inequalities such as those referred to above. In line with the prevailing orthodoxy, they focused on the need for 'harmony':

> [In grouping children] the need for equal opportunities for boys and girls should received consideration. Group composition should always be the result of a conscious decision. A guiding principle should be to ensure that over a period of time children learn to work harmoniously and effectively with a range of other children.
>
> (National Curriculum Council 1989: C4)

Such prescriptions about classroom talk, if followed, have implications for girls' and boys' experiences of classroom life. We turn to some of these below. In particular we wish to suggest that the trends in classroom talk we have outlined above can be considered a process of 'feminisation'.

THE FEMINISATION OF CLASSROOM TALK

The set of interactional norms that have emerged from the oracy movement, and that have become enshrined in curriculum guidance, seem to encourage and value features associated with feminine rather than masculine speaking styles. It is in this sense that the trend towards such ways of speaking may be considered a process of feminisation. In suggesting this we are aware of a number of difficulties. First, there is the question of motives. Those who encourage more collaborative talk will have a range of motives (not always made explicit): e.g. to promote more effective learning; to promote greater democracy in the classroom. Such motives are rarely feminist ones – in fact in the early stages of what we have termed the oracy movement there seems to have been little awareness of gender issues. In arguing that there is an association between 'collaborative talk' (we shall use this term as a short-hand for the moment) and 'feminisation' we are not suggesting there is a deliberate policy to feminise classroom talk. Nevertheless it may be that, whatever the motivation, the norms of collaborative talk are consistent with a process of feminisation.

We also need to acknowledge difficulties in defining collaborative talk, at least in any formal sense. We can appeal here to the linguistic truism that formally identified features will have variable meanings: a relatively high use of 'minimal responses', such as *mmh*, may signal 'collaboration' (support for the other speaker) or 'competitiveness' (an up-coming bid for the next turn). Furthermore, the characterisations of collaborative talk, which we cited earlier, have the status of ideals, and may not always be borne out by empirical observations. For instance, Wilkinson's turn-taking rules are premised on a 'one person at a time' model of talk ('take turns; don't interrupt; don't overtalk'). This is probably designed to rule out 'hostile' interruptions or hogging the floor, but in practice informal talk that is interpreted as collaborative would be likely to contain overlapping speech. Coates (1993), for example, suggests that the basic turn-taking mechanism which regulates talk in women's groups does not conform to the 'one person at a time' model, but values and allows overlapping speech. There is a further danger of appealing to stereotypes of female (and male) speech, and of failing to see speech as differentiated and context-dependent. There is not a neat fit between ideals of collaborative talk in the classroom and the ways women and girls actually speak in different contexts.

Despite these caveats, however, some of the (albeit loosely defined and idealised) characteristics of collaborative classroom talk, such as the supportive nature of such talk (speakers should ask questions of others; value others' contributions; listen to others; not interrupt), and its often tentative and exploratory nature, are consistent with the findings of research on women's and girls' talk in the classroom and other contexts (for instance, Coates 1993 (2nd ed.); J. Fisher 1991; Fishman 1978, 1983; Goodwin 1980; Preisler 1986). Research on women's and girls' talk in all-female groups has also explicitly emphasised its collaborative nature (e.g. Coates 1993 (2nd ed.).

There are also widespread beliefs that collaborative interactional norms are beneficial in their own right – particularly to female speakers – in that they promote greater equality between speakers and more democratic procedures in decision making. While there isn't a one-to-one correspondence, some of the ideal characteristics of collaborative classroom talk we've cited are consistent with feminist attempts to encourage collaborative, supportive talk in certain all-female gatherings. Deborah Cameron gives this characterisation of talk in feminist groups:

> When you attend a feminist group or meeting, you soon learn that interruption, talking too much, raising your voice, vehemently disagreeing with others, expressing hostility and so forth are not acceptable behaviour. On the other hand, it is desirable that you express solidarity, give way to other speakers and tolerate long silences if they occur.
>
> (Cameron 1992: 53)

Cameron has argued that collaborative talk in feminist groups is carefully managed in order to give less-confident women space to express their ideas.

Similar collaborative ideals have characterised attempts to ensure greater equality between speakers in mixed-sex contexts, in the classroom and elsewhere. For instance, Hilary Claire describes how she and a fellow teacher tried to reduce the dominance of boys and encourage participation from quiet girls in a class of 6–7 year olds.

Strategies included breaking children up into small groups (initially pairs); making it explicit that they must take it in turns to talk about a topic, and listen to their partner while s/he was speaking; and, in larger groups, imposing time limits on contributions. Claire comments on these strategies: 'What we tried to do was to create situations in which girls and boys needed each other, and gained mutual support' (1986: 45).

A similar strategy was suggested by Janet Holmes (1992) as one of a number of solutions to the problem of gender inequalities in contributions to public seminars: those organising events, she argues, should change some of the contexts for discussion to allow more exploratory talk:

> Provide opportunities for small group discussion as preparation for full session discussion of issues. Exploratory talk will thereby be encouraged and females are more likely to contribute in the full session in the role of reporter on a small group's views.
>
> (Holmes 1992: 145)

So far, we have suggested that trends towards collaborative talk in the classroom, associated with the oracy movement, are consistent with a process of feminisation. The set of norms that underpin notions of collaborative talk emphasises many features associated with female speakers; there are also beliefs that more collaborative talk could be beneficial to girls, both by valuing their speech and by giving them greater access to discussion and opportunities for learning. We would, however, argue that our welcome of such developments should at least be a cautious one. Collaborative talk is generally felt to be a good thing (it is uncommon to find anyone suggesting that talk should *not* be collaborative). But there are dangers associated with talk that suppresses conflict and appeals to a consensus. We shall look first at arguments that the introduction of collaborative talk is not necessarily associated with greater democracy; then at issues relating specifically to girls' use of collaborative features.

Douglas Barnes has pointed out that it is important to consider the motives of those who promote collaborative talk. He observed a close parallel between the curriculum for 'personal and social education' in many secondary schools and that of the oracy curriculum 'as commonly practised':

Both speak for the value of enhancing the individual student's competence to deal with his or her life. Both stress small-group collaboration, including sensitivity to others' perspectives, joint decision-making, persuasion rather than conflict [. . .] In many ways these are admirable values, very like those advocated by liberal-minded English teachers in the 1960s when spoken language came to the forefront as an educational issue. Yet now they are being advocated from quite a different quarter. They are almost identical, for example, with aspects of the pre-vocational programmes which are recommended by government sponsored bodies.

(Barnes 1988: 50)

Barnes suggested that the 'Radical Right' at that time seemed to be replacing the traditional right-wing concerns for 'tighter discipline, conformity to standard English, and more spelling tests' with ones which were thought to service the new and immediate needs of employers. Barnes was interested to note that superficially, the requirements of 'the new vocationalism' were close to those of the oracy movement.

More recently, Norman Fairclough (1993) has also commented on widespread changes in patterns of communication in the workplace, which he describes as a process of 'conversationalisation':

On the one hand, it can be seen as a colonization of the public domain by the practices of the private domain, an opening up of public orders of discourse to discursive practices which we can all attain rather than the elite and exclusive traditional practices of the public domain, and thus a matter of more open access. On the other hand, it can be seen as an appropriation of private domain practices by the public domain: the infusion of practices which are needed in post-traditional public settings for the complex processes of negotiating relationships and identities.

(Fairclough 1993: 140)

Fairclough sees such changes in discourse practices as part of a wider (and ideologically suspicious) trend towards the 'technologization of discourse' – the adoption of specific discourse patterns designed to position participants (workers, customers, managers) in specific (usually exploitative) social relations:

A characteristic of post-Fordist industry is the growing importance of communication on the shop floor. New forms of interaction between shop-floor workers, supervisers, and managers are emerging, such as 'quality circles', groups of five to ten employees who usually work together and meet regularly to discuss ways of improving quality, productivity, and other work-related issues. One unanswered question about quality circles, which may well bear upon trade union suspicions of them and their high failure rate, is whether they really break down old divisions between employees, and give shop-floor workers more power, or whether they are a management tool for using the valuable experience of shop-floor workers, and integrating them into management priorities.

(Fairclough 1992: 228)

We need to ask, then, whether the forms of talk which have been introduced into schools and workplaces really do represent an adoption and valuing of women's patterns of talk, and a mechanism for introducing greater democracy, participation and equality, or whether the progressive and liberal ideals of the oracy movement have been overtaken by other social trends to serve less liberal purposes. The process of feminisation which we have described may have selectively appropriated less powerful styles of communication which can be used to give the appearance of democratic participation whilst being well designed for the manufacture of consensus and consent. There may exist contexts and relations of power in which these styles can serve liberal motives of equal access to debate and learning opportunities. But there are important differences between the relations of power found in most women's groups, or in private conversation, and the contexts of classroom and workplace in which the process of 'conversationalization' has been experienced.

Within the private sphere, participants routinely challenge each other's values and assumptions; they can fall out with each other (sometimes quite violently); and renegotiate their relationships. Within organisations and the workplace such behaviour cannot be allowed: role relations have been largely decided by management and their further negotiability has set limits; individuals must learn to suppress their own feelings and misgivings and support others; it is an arrangement in which everyone may have their say, but not their way – which is often decided according to power relations that are not overtly displayed.

There are specific concerns here in relation to gender and talk in the classroom. We have argued elsewhere that collaboration between pupils in mixed-sex groups may be bound up with unequal power relations: in one instance a re-analysis of an interaction between a girl and a boy, which had been singled out as a positive example of collaborative learning, showed that the collaboration depended upon the girl adopting an 'apprenticeship' role and acquiescing entirely to the boy's suggestions (Swann 1992: 84–90).

The fact that collaborative forms of talk are normally positively evaluated might be thought to bring benefits to girls in terms of assessment – though what limited evidence we have suggests this is not necessarily the case. In an analysis of assessment of girls' and boys' talk at GCSE, Cheshire and Jenkins (1991) (also Jenkins and Cheshire 1990) suggest that whilst boys may be rewarded for using collaborative styles, girls get little special credit. Instead, the conversational support provided by girls in mixed-sex groups serves to boost the grading of the group as a whole.

We would argue that positive evaluations of girls' supportive speech are, at any rate, not unproblematical. In 1992 the School Examinations and Assessment Council (SEAC) issued a video designed to support teacher assessment of young (Key Stage 1) children's language. Part of the video showed a boy, Thomas, working on different tasks and with different pupils. On one occasion he is shown in a 'problem solving' discussion with two girls, Jenny and Michelle. The children have to decide how they might release a cow from a pit in which she has become trapped. A commentary on the interaction criticises Thomas for being over-dominant and compares his performance unfavourably with that of Jenny, who is more supportive:

> Thomas, Jenny and Michelle work together in a group, but Thomas assumes the lead role to an over-dominant extent. He does listen to Jenny's suggestions on occasion ('She might be too heavy to lift up on a rope'), but to meet the requirements of En 1/3c: listen with an increased span of attention to other children and adults, asking and responding to questions and commenting on what has been said he would have to listen more and show greater awareness of others and their contributions. Jenny listens well and is the most supportive member of the group: she shows positive body language and makes eye contact with Thomas. It would not be appropriate to assess Michelle on this occasion as she does not contribute very much to the activity. It is worth noting that assessment of Thomas's work can still be made even though the group interaction is affected by the gender relationship.
> (School Examinations and Assessment Council 1992: 13)

SEAC do not make clear what they mean by 'the gender relationship'.

It would seem, however, that Thomas' contributions are characterised by a 'masculine' speaking style ('assumes the lead role to an
over-dominant extent') and Jenny's contributions are associated
with a 'feminine' speaking style ('supportive'). In this case the
assessors favour Jenny's feminine style.

SEAC's judgement of this interaction was criticised by Roger
Knight in a brief article in the *Guardian* (21.4.1992). Knight is concerned about the negative assessment of Thomas, and some of his
comments are reminiscent of Douglas Barnes' concerns about collaborative talk (Thomas, he says, will need to learn 'to become the
decorous little committee man the system requires'). However, we
were more concerned about the admittedly positive assessment of
Jenny. During the interaction Jenny puts forward several good
ideas for releasing the trapped cow, but all that is commented upon
here is her supportiveness – the fact that she is a good listener. In
focusing on the (stereotypically) feminine aspects of Jenny's speech
the assessors have ignored aspects that are arguably just as important.

CONCLUSION

With any new educational regime it takes time for teachers to
develop teaching strategies which exploit potential and minimise
negative consequences. However, it is not untypical of recent
developments in British education that a new political direction is
ordained before a previous one is fully implemented and understood. In raising questions about the benefits and implications of
collaborative talk in the classroom, we are aware that the progressive approaches to education that have most frequently been
associated with such forms of talk are under attack from other
quarters. Concerns have been expressed from the political right
about what is seen as 'trendy', left-wing practice in education, and
there have been fears that the national curriculum has been
hijacked by progressive educationists.

While Douglas Barnes drew attention to the 'new vocationalism'
espoused by the Radical Right of the late 1980s, more traditional
right-wing concerns have not been jettisoned. The early 1990s have
seen repeated moves towards traditional practices and values
within several areas of education. Revisions proposed to the

English curriculum have included attempts to enforce the teaching of spoken standard English, and to emphasise more structured approaches to the teaching of initial reading (we have argued elsewhere that the way the debate about the content of the English curriculum has been conducted has left progressive educationists with very little room for manoeuvre in articulating a response – Graddol and Swann 1993). There have been calls for greater direction from the teacher, and more whole-class teaching – as in the debate surrounding the commissioning and publication of the 'three wise men' report into primary education (Department of Education and Science 1992) and subsequent government pronouncements. At the time of writing there are renewed demands for schools to give a stronger moral lead as part of a 'back to basics' campaign. In a recent speech to Conservative party activists, the British Prime Minister, John Major, called for an emphasis on 'basic skills': 'being able to read, write and do sums'; and 'discipline': 'orderly classrooms, clear timetables, regular tests, homework, team sport and uniforms' (cited in the *Guardian* 1.1.94: 1).

A full discussion of such trends and their implications is beyond the scope of this chapter. We mention them as an indication that the national curriculum and associated assessment practices, as well as broader questions to do with the overall organisation of school and classroom life, are still, and will probably remain, contested domains – and that the position of progressive approaches within education is by no means secure.

A return to more traditional teacher–pupil relations (with, for instance, a greater emphasis on whole-class teaching, stronger direction from the teacher and less scope for exploratory talk between pupils) would be unlikely to support the interests of female pupils. It was, as we mentioned earlier, such forms of classroom organisation, with their public, competitive forms of discourse, that supplied earlier (1970s and 1980s) evidence of boys' dominance of interaction and of school and classroom life more generally.

We wish to locate our own discussion within a broadly progressive framework. Many valuable developments have taken place within what we have termed the oracy movement, which it is important not to disregard. But we would argue that the social, as well as the educational, implications of collaborative talk in the classroom need to be further documented and debated. The oracy movement is a complex one which contains within it a diversity of ideological positions and potentially conflicting aims. There are a number of tensions surrounding the use of collaborative talk. We have discussed some ways in which such talk, while apparently democratic, may turn out to be exploitative. We have focused particularly on gender issues, arguing that while collaborative talk might be thought to be beneficial to girls, giving them more space to express their ideas and more opportunities for learning than traditionally organised classroom discourse, it is important to be aware of certain dangers: effective collaboration may itself depend upon concealed power relations; it may, in various ways, reproduce inequalities between girls and boys. The implications for learning, and the wider social and political implications of collaborative talk becoming institutionalised within classrooms, is not well investigated. Our discussion in this chapter is thus intended as a contribution to an ongoing educational and political debate.

NINE

Primary school teachers' explanations of boys' disruptiveness in the classroom: a gender-specific aspect of the hidden curriculum

Cleopatra Altani

INTRODUCTION

In this chapter I report selected findings from research on gender construction in the classroom (Altani 1992). I will present findings from a survey of teachers' beliefs carried out in primary schools in Greece aiming to cast light on one aspect of the hidden curriculum[1] which has important implications for children's gender socialisation in school.[2]

As the population was large and widely dispersed, cluster sampling (Cohen and Manion 1985: 99; Oppenheim 1992: 40) was adopted. By cluster sampling, I mean that seventeen schools were randomly selected and questionnaires were distributed to all the teachers working in them. Seventeen was the highest number of schools I could approach in the two and a half months which I had for the data collection.

I visited seventeen schools, the staff of which varied from six to twelve teachers, and distributed a total of 168 questionnaires. The response rate was 67.75% (i.e. 126 questionnaires were returned, 54 from male and 72 from female teachers).

In this chapter I will present an analysis of responses to a pair of questions, one closed and one open-ended. First, the respondents were asked to express their agreement or disagreement with the statement 'boys are more disruptive in the classroom than girls' on a five-point scale. In response to this item two-thirds of the respondents agreed (84: 66.7%), 36 (28.6%) disagreed, while 6 teachers chose 'I do not know'. The distribution of responses is illustrated in Figure 9.1.[3] Then, those who agreed with the above statement were invited to explain why they thought this was the case. Although, on the surface, this question appears to elicit their explanation of only one specific gender difference, it was in fact designed to elicit the respondents' views on the origins of behavioural differences due to gender in general.[4] The crosstabulation of the teachers' responses by age did not indicate a clear correlation. In contrast, teachers' gender clearly correlated with their reported beliefs on this statement. Most teachers agreed with the statement (as shown on the

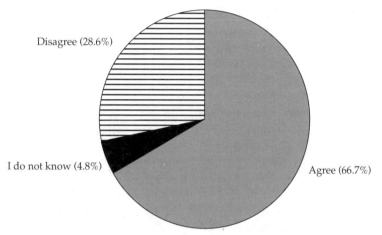

Figure 9.1   Distribution of teachers' responses to the statement 'boys are more disruptive in the classroom than girls'

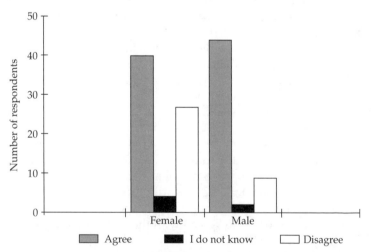

Figure 9.2   Crosstabulation of teachers' responses by gender

first figure) and that, of those who agree, about half were male and about half female. As indicated from these finding, boys' higher level of disruptiveness seems to be a widely accepted classroom 'fact' acknowledged by both female and male teachers.

Boys' disruptiveness and the resulting unfair distribution of teacher attention among male and female pupils has been emphasised by many researchers. For example, Clarricoates (1978: 356), in her paper 'Dinosaurs in the classroom', makes the point that while girls are self-disciplined, the teacher has to constantly try to keep the boys' interest so that they remain quiet.

Undoubtedly, if it is widespread, this practice has very serious implications for girls and the 'lessons' they learn in the classroom. Not only do they have to patiently tolerate the overall domination of teacher time and attention by boys, but more significantly, they are likely to deduce from this that boys are more important since their interests are given priority.

I would however like to draw attention to a further implication of this imbalance for girls' education. This point has been brought out in recent work by Riddell (1989). She carried out classroom observations in two British rural comprehensive schools. Riddell highlighted another way in which patient girls 'lose out' as opposed to disruptive boys. She reported that a female arts teacher told her that 'boys are able but immature, whereas girls can be relied on to work quietly by themselves' (ibid.: 187). Riddell's classroom observations revealed that this belief led this particular teacher, and possibly her colleagues who shared the same opinion, to reward boys' demands for attention with her time while allowing girls to chat quietly by themselves.

TEACHERS' REPORTED EXPLANATIONS OF BOYS' DISRUPTIVENESS

I will now consider the explanations put forward by teachers for boys' higher levels of disruptiveness in the classroom.

In my attempt to categorise the answers provided to the open-ended question, I encountered the scoring difficulties reported by other researchers (for example, Agheysi and Fishman 1970: 148). It is sometimes impossible to decide definitely on the respondent's intended meaning. This point will be made clearer later when I present certain 'ambiguous' answers that could not be assigned to a specific category with certainty.

The main trends that can be abstracted from my analysis of the 68 answers reflect the range of explanations that have been forward for gender differences by many researchers: nature/biology, socialisation or an interaction of nature/biology with socialisation (Kessler and McKenna 1978: 275; O'Leary, Unger and Wallston 1985: 2–3; Swann 1992: 5–11). As many as 15 of the teachers (22.05%) who answered the open-ended question attributed boys' higher degree of disruptiveness in the classroom to *nature/biology*. It is significant that 11 of them actually used the phrase 'by nature' in their responses. The following quotations, which have been translated from Greek, provide examples of these responses. The teachers' gender and age are indicated in parentheses. So, according to a male teacher:

1. Boys are by nature more spirited and less disciplined (M, 46)

Likewise, according to a younger female teacher:

2. Because boys are by nature more aggressive and impatient (F, 28)

The same essentialist view appeared in the responses of 4 teachers, 2 of whom explained boys' disruptiveness as a result of their temperament, whereas the other 2 thought it was due to their age.

At the other end of the continuum of folk beliefs about gender differences was the second major explanation put forward by the teachers in my survey: for 12 teachers (17.6%), disruptiveness was attributed to the boys' *home/early socialisation*. In 8 of these answers, their upbringing was mainly held responsible. In the words of a female respondent, boys are more disruptive because:

3. The Greek family still continues to bring the boy up with more freedom and more rights than the girl (F, 52)

Similarly, a male teacher argued:

4. Using my experience so far I believe it is due to the 'style' of upbringing in the family. While we show tolerance towards boys for such behaviour, the analogous behaviour is criticised in girls (M, 28)

This response also alludes to a double standard operating to the benefit of boys.

Two female teachers alluded to wider gender relations in society as well as to the role of the family in influencing boys' disruptiveness. According to them:

5. In my opinion, this happens because the family and society want to shape the male sex/gender in this way, always pushing boys to display violence and muscular strength (F, 35)

The other respondents referred to early socialisation in addition to stressing the role of the social environment:

6. I believe it is a matter of learning and reinforcement at home and the environment outside the home (F, 24)

Socialisation was also given by itself as an explanation by 2 more teachers. One of them, a male teacher, described it in a more common sense manner as 'what it is that boys have learnt' and implicitly shed light on boys' persistence for teacher attention in class. He wrote:

7. They have learnt to say whatever they want, to be listened to, they have more self-confidence in class (M, 27)

The two main explanations discussed so far, i.e. *nature/biology* and *home/early socialisation* were brought together in the responses of 6 teachers (8.82%). This combination of reasons is described in the following manner:

8. Boys are always more spirited than girls at the fourth grade age. Perhaps the family prejudice that boys are strong and dominant in life plays a role (M, 52)
9. I think it is a matter of heredity but also of influence by family and society (F, 27)

Having presented those answers which could be easily categorised, I now discuss the remaining teachers' opinions. I identified different foci in these although I could not confidently attribute them to the above categories since the teachers could have had either nature/biology, home/early socialisation or both in mind when providing the answers.

The foci which can be abstracted from the remaining teachers' answers are as follows:

(a) *Boys' sex/gender*: first, 2 teachers expressed the view that boys are more disruptive in class than girls because of their sex/gender. Since the Greek language does not have two separate lexical items for sex, i.e. 'a biological distinction', and gender i.e. 'the term used to describe socially constructed categories based on sex' (Coates 1986: 4), the responses could have meant either or both. In the teachers' words, these were the reasons they provided:

10. Because they are boys (M, 55)
11. They are more lively because of their sex/gender (M, 47)

If these teachers saw girls and boys as determined by their biology, their explanations imply that there is little that can be done to promote change in female and male pupils' behaviour and interaction patterns in the classroom.

(b) *Immaturity*: another 2 teachers were of the opinion that boys are more immature than girls and thus more disruptive. To them:

12. They are more immature and have more energy which they cannot control (M, 38)
13. They are more disruptive because they are immature (F, 47)

Once again, these answers are ambiguous as maturity has to do with both biology and experience in the family and society at large.

(c) *Hyperactivity and restlessness*: a further focus in 16 teachers' explanations was boys' hyperactivity and restlessness. Two of these responses are especially worth mentioning. A male teacher provided an interesting answer in the sense that he presented boys' restlessness as one of the ways in which they get teachers' attention. In his words:

14. I think boys are more lively than girls, more restless and more selfish, I would say. As a result, the teachers' attention is focused on them (M, 45)

A female teacher highlighted another interesting aspect of the problem as she implicitly claimed that girls are also restless but try to hide it in order to conform to the Greek feminine stereotype. She wrote:

15. Because boys give vent to their restlessness more easily in contrast to girls, who try to present themselves as more mild and calm (according to the Greek model for a girl and a woman) (F, 30)

Apart from drawing our attention to girls' efforts to abide by the feminine stereotype, this answer is interesting for a further reason: it presents boys' disruptiveness in a positive light since they are presented as being more 'sincere' in expressing their restlessness than girls. Moreover, it is noteworthy that in 14 answers, teachers characterised boys as *lively* or *spirited* rather than using the term *disruptive*, which is actually used in the question they are invited to answer.

Similarly, boys' disruptiveness was valued as 'positive' in the two further foci identified in the respondents' explanations.

(d) *Male superiority*: more specifically, 6 teachers thought that boys are more disruptive because they want to show and prove male superiority. Significantly, there were 5 male and 1 female in this group of respondents. The view of the female teacher is best captured in her own words:

16. I suppose it has to do with the characteristics of the male
    sex/gender. They want to show that they are the strong sex/gender
    and that they must impose themselves in every place. They have
    more physical strength (F, 28)

Moreover, a male teacher gave the following explanation:

17. The sex/gender, i.e. we are boys and we are not interested whether
    you punish us or not and we shall show the girls that we are
    stronger (M, 45)

In my understanding of these statements, the teachers' claim that boys are more disruptive in order to show and/or prove their superiority, entails the assumption that boys are actually superior, an assumption which these teachers seem to have.

(e) *Boys' and girls' typical behaviour*: likewise, 8 teachers attributed disruptiveness to certain characteristics which they claimed are part of boys' and girls' personality and behaviour. Here again, it is surprising but also revealing of their gender-specific assumptions that in spite of the fact that pupils' disruptiveness is usually considered problematic, they manage to present it in a positive light. According to these teachers, boys are disruptive because they are spontaneous, tough, brave, lively, talkative, while girls are just obedient and responsible. The following quotations provide even stronger evidence for this point:

18. Because girls obey more and they make greater efforts to learn (M, 56)
19. They have more courage than girls (F, 24)
20. Because boys do not hide what is happening to them at that moment. Perhaps they are more spontaneous as well (M, 34)[5]

What these views seem to imply is that boys might be restless but at least they are honest about it whereas girls are just trying to keep up appearances. What they do not imply, however, is that social pressures could lead boys and girls to exhibit the reported behaviour.

(f) *Poor academic performance*: finally, I should mention 2 teachers who considered boys' disruptive behaviour to be due to the fact that they were poor students. One of them again provides an 'excuse' for boys, arguing that the teacher might not give the boys enough attention. In his words, the two reasons he provides are:

21. (a) They are negligent and try to attract attention and (b) It is possible that the teacher does not pay as much attention to them as he should (M, 55)

DISCUSSION

Taking the teachers' responses as a whole, there are two points I would like to make. First, it was striking that only 2 teachers attributed some degree of responsibility for boys' disruptiveness to the school and thus to themselves and their colleagues. One of these views has already been mentioned above (example 21) in discussing the answers of the teachers who believed that boys' disruptiveness could be attributed to their not being as good students as girls. Another male teacher was of the opinion that:

22. They are spoilt at home, perhaps they never learnt discipline in the lower grades (M, 60)

Although allusions are made by many teachers to society's influence on boys' behaviour, no direct reference is made to the school's specific role in socialisation. This leads me to the conclusion that the teachers in my study were probably not aware of the school's and thus their own 'contribution' as agents of children's gender socialisation (Arnot 1986; Clifton *et al.* 1986; Delamont 1990; Stanworth 1981; Walkerdine 1981, 1985; Weinrich 1978).

The second point concerns the teachers' reported explanations for boys' disruptiveness. My interpretation here is informed by the critical approach to discourse analysis suggested by Fairclough (1989) since the actual language used by the informants in response to the questionnaire item may be analysed to show up connections between the choice of language they made and their 'hidden' ideology, i.e. their beliefs. Not only is a direct causal relationship established between boys' behaviour and the explanations provided in 28 (41.17%) of the answers but also the reasons provided are presented as categorical truths, that is, the reasons are presented as facts in 45 (66.17%) of the responses, as indicated by the teachers' use of the simple present-tense form (*ibid.*: 129).[6] The fact that some of these answers reflect a common sense essentialist view of gender differences provides support for the argument that teachers' beliefs are stereotypical and have social origins; they are not the idiosyncratic ideas of individuals. They are part of a wider fabric of beliefs which are shared by parents. These beliefs are transmitted to children in the family and are legitimised through school.

More specifically, the family and the school are forms of education which entail primary and secondary 'pedagogic work' (Bourdieu and Passeron 1990: 5, 42–3) respectively. According to Bourdieu and Passeron, pedagogic work is the result of the process of inculcation of dominant cultural beliefs and values. In their book *Reproduction*, they propose a model of social processes which operate 'behind the backs of the agents engaged in the school system' – teachers, students and their parents – and 'often *against their will*' (*ibid.*: ix) to ensure the transmission and valuation of the cultural capital which forms the basis of the social order. According to this model, school plays an important role by legitimating the social order and the cultural beliefs which confirm and support the established order. Bourdieu and Passeron are primarily concerned with class and cultural values. However, their model also provides a means of explaining how patriarchal values are reproduced.

The beliefs that teachers have and convey to their pupils are a set of ideologies about their learning abilities, classroom interaction, the curriculum and gender. They are important because there are implicit assumptions, incidental and probably unintended, which are learned by the pupils without necessarily being referred to explicitly and so form a major part of the hidden curriculum. It should be stressed that because these messages are implicit, the pupils' gender socialisation becomes 'a self-regulating process' (West and Zimmerman 1991: 290) as they gradually 'learn' and probably adhere to stereotypical gender-specific messages.

It is then of primary importance that teachers should be made aware of their gender-specific assumptions about boys' and girls' behaviour in the classroom. Drawing on recent social theory, Fairclough points out that ideology, or in this case, teachers' beliefs, is most effective when we are not aware of it, 'when its workings are least visible' (1989: 85). It is only when teachers become sensitised to common sense assumptions which sustain imbalances in the classroom that these assumptions cease to have such an effect. Then they can react, they can resist and explore ways of changing classroom practices. Teachers need to begin to see gender as a dimension of social identity which is constructed differently in different cultural contexts. This will enable them to question assumptions about 'natural' gender divisions and gender-differentiated expectations in the classroom. Rethinking gender could influence their practices in the classroom and the messages they may be transmitting to their pupils, albeit unconsciously.

NOTES

1. Davies and Mieghan (1975: 171) define the hidden curriculum as 'those aspects of learning in schools that are unofficial or unintentional, or undeclared consequences of the way in which teachers organise and execute teaching and learning'.

2. More specifically, my first research goal was to examine the reported beliefs of Greek primary school teachers about their pupils' gender-specific classroom behaviour. The self-completion questionnaire was chosen as the most effective tool for collecting the necessary evidence.

   Public rather than private schools were chosen because only higher income families have access to private schools, which sometimes have a foreign language as the medium of instruction. I also chose to look at primary schooling because it is a very important phase of a child's education in Greece. It covers two thirds of her/his compulsory education, aiming at the 'multi-faceted intellectual and physical development of pupils' (*Eurydice* 1988: 5). Finally, I chose schools in Athens because among the primary schools there are the Experimental Schools to which a researcher has easier access. The Athens Education Section, however, also covers 'underprivileged' schools where most of the pupils' families belong to the working class.

3. The statistical analysis was carried out using the Statistical Package for Social Sciences. Apart from producing the frequency distributions, I went on to do crosstabulations of the survey data and performed chi-square tests to assess the correlation between the beliefs reported and the two main variables, the respondents' age and gender.

4. Of the 84 teachers who expressed agreement to the above questionnaire item, 16 did not provide any explanation for their answer.

5. This last statement is reminiscent of the view I discussed earlier. It was expressed by a female teacher who thought that girls were also restless but tried to hide it in order to conform to the feminine stereotype (example 15).

6. However, it is also possible that teachers assumed that this was the sort of answer they were expected to provide, given the factual statements used in the questionnaire.

TEN

'We're boys, miss!': finding gendered identities and looking for gendering of identities in the foreign language classroom

Jane Sunderland

Teacher:	two more boys I think boys shh what about Simon and Neil[1] no why not
Girl 1:	we're boys
Girl 2:	we're boys
Girl 3:	we're boys miss
Teacher:	all right we'll have two more girls and then we'll see if the boys have got any courage[2]

This extract is taken from a transcript of classroom discourse made from an audio-recording of a class of eleven- and twelve-year-old girls and boys who are learning German. I was present at this class. The school is a large comprehensive school in the North West of England. The teacher, a woman, has been asking volunteers to 'perform' a German dialogue. The first two volunteers were girls, the second two were boys, and the third two girls. To be 'fair', then, it was the turn of a pair of boys. (The school has its own Equal Opportunities Policy and most teachers are aware that giving male and female students differential attention is something that can easily happen despite good intentions, and is a clear Equal Opportunities issue.) The class is a Year 7 class (first year in secondary school), it is the students' first year of German and so they have not yet been 'setted', and most of the girls and boys are enthusiastic about learning German and keen to answer questions. The girls who called out 'we're boys' did so particularly enthusiastically and their pleas were accompanied by much hand-waving.

In this extract, there is no misunderstanding. Context being a significant determinant of meaning, all classroom participants – the other students, who did not express surprise or incomprehension, and the teacher, who *selected* two girls – recognised the girls' 'we're boys' as a bid for selection by the teacher. It was a predictable piece of classroom behaviour, albeit realised in unpredictable language.

My research topic in this school was (and is) the role of gender, in the sense of gender roles, relations and identities, in the modern foreign language classroom – how gender, though not fixed, can affect language learning opportunities, and how gender is itself shaped by language classroom (as well as other educational) processes. My research approach in this class had been influenced by the literature on classroom ethnography, so I was 'sharing in the life of the classroom': observing and making fieldnotes with the intention of asking the classroom participants (teacher and students) for *their* perspectives on events. Accordingly, I was looking out for anything that might pertain to gender. The 'event' described above seemed to do just that.

'WE'RE BOYS' = 'WE'RE DOGS'?

After transcribing this event, the next step, following ethnographic practice, was to obtain the participants' perceptions of it. I wanted to start with the classroom participants who had actually called out 'we're boys'. The tape suggests that at least three girls did so, quickly getting the idea from each other, but because of where I had been sitting I was aware of two particular girls who said it, Lucy and Diana. (The event had taken place on a Wednesday. I interviewed Lucy and Diana on the following Monday.[3]) The interview (which for the purpose of presentation here has been slightly edited) was as follows:

Jane:	[Plays tape] okay let's can you hear what's happening there . . . you two are talking yes what are you saying she wants to get Simon and Neil and Simon and Neil don't want to do anything	1
Lucy and Diana:	we want we wanted to do it	5
Jane:	so what were you saying [Plays tape again]	
Lucy:	yeah cos she was saying it was just boys and we we were	
Diana:	we were wanting to do it	
Lucy:	we were wanting to do it and were saying we're boys	10
Jane:	yeah so why did you say we're boys	

Lucy:	well we were wanting to do that	
Diana:	we wanted to do it and we always act like boys	
Lucy:	no we don't	15
Jane:	what do you mean you act like boys	
Diana:	well we fight a lot	
Lucy:	I don't you do	
Jane [to Diana]:	is that why you said it	
Diana:	yeah	20
Jane [to Lucy]:	and why do you think you said it	
Lucy:	oh I just said it cos I wanted a go at the thing	
Jane [to Diana]:	do you say that sometimes a lot	
Diana:	yeah a lot	
Lucy:	she always hangs around with the boys	25

One of the interesting things about this is the fact that saying 'we're boys' is *not* a big deal to either Lucy or Diana. Neither is it a big deal to the teacher, who goes along with it and says 'all right we'll have two more girls'. Neither do the other male or female students in the class react to the claims of 'we're boys miss'. Girls saying 'we're boys miss' thus seemed in this context to be a completely unmarked use of language.[4] As Lucy and Diana say, it was a way to get selected – if the teacher wanted boys, they would 'be' boys. They could not see that what I was trying to get at was why they were *happy* to bid for selection by using *those particular words*. For them (and others) it seemed to be purely instrumental: a friend of mine later commented that if the teacher had said 'two more dogs I think', they would have said 'we're dogs!'

My friend may have been correct, but stopping there would be to be perversely gender-blind, and to ignore the *wider* context within which this event took place. Instead, the following analysis of the 'we're boys' event and subsequent interviews draws on insights from poststructuralist theory, especially those of Australian sociologist Bronwyn Davies and of Chris Weedon's 'feminist poststructuralism'. Poststructuralist theory seemed to provide useful ways of looking at this interesting, gendered use of language. I do not propose to discuss poststructuralist theory itself, but rather to allow its insights (with those of more traditional approaches) to inform the data as this chapter progresses.

For poststructuralism, context is not just *co-text*, but also the social and political relations which pertain to an utterance or set of utterances. Further, language does not only reflect social reality but also 'constitutes social reality for us' and is 'the site where meaningful experience is constituted' (Weedon 1987: 27, 86). More fully:

> the common factor in the analysis of social organisation, social
> meanings, power and individual consciousness is language. Language is
> the place where actual and possible forms of social organisation and
> their likely social and political consequences are defined and contested.
> Yet it is also the place where our sense of ourselves, our subjectivity, is
> constructed . . . in ways which are socially specific.
>
> (Weedon 1987: 21)

As well as being gendered, then, in poststructuralist terms the event also seemed like a potentially *gendering* use of language. (I will return to the ideas of 'contestation' and 'subjectivity'.)

Lucy and Diana's comments suggest that they – and presumably the other girls who called out 'we're boys' – are willingly and jokily 'repositioning' themselves as boys, temporarily shifting, for their own instrumental ends, from a feminine gender identity to a masculine. This, as we have seen, is at no apparent cost – on the contrary, two girls (though not at this point Lucy and Diana) end up getting selected.

Lucy and Diana appear to see themselves as autonomous actors and language users. Weedon observes that 'in taking on a subject position, the individual assumes that she is the author of the ideology or discourse which she is speaking' (1987: 31) – and there is no suggestion that Lucy or Diana see themselves as anything other than in complete control when calling out 'we're boys'. Yet the interview suggests that their 'we're boys' is *not* fully explicable in instrumental terms or as a result of 'free choice'. Lucy and Diana have gender identities *as girls*. Those identities seem far from identical: Diana volunteers 'we always act like boys . . . we fight a lot' (ll. 14, 17); Lucy denies this (l. 15), going on to point out that only Diana fights a lot (l. 18) and that Diana 'always hangs around with the boys' (l. 25) (implying that she herself does not). Yet both see boys as people who *are* and *act* differently from them (as girls, they can only act *like* boys). Further, significantly, their 'we're boys' was not idiosyncratic, since several girls took up the call (and the rest of the class accepted it), and what was called out by the different girls was not 'I'm a boy' but 'we're boys', i.e. members of a social group. *Gender* as well as expediency thus appears to have played a large part in both the selection and reception of the words in this event.

BOY AS OK, *GIRL* AS INSULT

The need for an alternative approach to the event using the idea of *gender as a social construct* became still clearer in my next exploration of participants' perceptions – a discussion with the teacher, which took place three weeks later. My supervisor ('D') was also present. Extracts (again slightly edited) from the discussion follow:

[Teacher reads transcript of original event]
J: . . . have they said that before   1
Teacher: no I've never heard I've never had any kids saying it
J: because this was the first time I was aware of having heard
           you say specify a gender at all . . .
Teacher: . . . actually I do do that cos sometimes I'm worried that I   5
           want to keep want to make sure I'm evenly divided
           between the two because they are aware of it because as I
           said as they get older they can be funny 'oh you've asked
           the girls again three sets of girls in a row' and so that's
           why I will do that . . . but one thing you would never ever   10
           get the boys saying 'we're girls' because a term of abuse
           for the boy is to call him a girl in the classroom
J: you mean by another boy or
Teacher: by another boy or by another girl but usually by another
           boy so you can have it that way but you could never ever   15
           have it the other way boys would never do that . . .
[Teacher reads interview with Lucy and Diana]
Teacher: 'and we always act like boys' 'well we fight a lot' [laughs]
           they probably do . . . Diana always hangs around with the
           boys and because she's quite precocious that way and is   20
           very interested in them
D: well that's almost the opposite of identifying with them
Teacher: well yeah yes exactly
D: what was interesting with this 'we're boys we're boys '
           and their interpretation of it in terms of saying but we are   25
           boys in a sense we qualify . . . it wasn't just a game for the
           moment you know we actually see ourselves that way . . .
           one of the underlying issues is how kids get a sense of
           their identity in a class like this and throughout their
           educational history and their home history how do they   30
           get a sense of what gender they belong to and how solidly
           they belong to it . . . you know and these two are saying
           we don't really we belong you know belong to the gender
           ascribed to us and identify across genders

. . .

Teacher: for me it's simply that there is no shame at all in being   35
            attached to being like a boy whereas there is the other way
            round I think they see it as being all right the girls can be
            like boys but boys can't be like girls . . . what's really
            shocked me about school is how often the word girl is used
            for a boy to another boy as a term of abuse . . . it comes up   40
            all the time . . . name-calling related to gender . . . the way
            they use the word slag and things like that . . . I don't mind
            bastard but I really hate slag

The teacher in this discussion illustrates the fact that one word does
not necessarily have only one meaning, as this applies to both *girl*
and *boy*: *girl* can be an insult for a boy, and *boy* can be used by a girl
to refer to herself in a way that is positive. She also illustrates the
potential semantic asymmetry between *boy* and *girl*: *girl* can be a
term of abuse for a boy, but *boy* could not be a term of abuse for a
girl (or boy). Because of this semantic asymmetry, several girls saying 'we're boys' carried no implication of self-deprecation ('there is
no shame at all in being attached to being like a boy' (l. 35)),
whereas the reverse would not be true.

If *boy* can be used of themselves by girls with impunity, what
of the teacher's observations about the use of *girl*? Traditional
feminist linguistics has long recognised the potential for gendered
semantic asymmetry in such 'pairs' as *king–queen, master–mistress,
governor–governess* and *manager–manageress*. In some 'pairs' the
'female' item can be used to sexualise a woman (*mistress*), or can
suggest the inferior status of a woman compared with a man
referred to by the male 'equivalent' (*governess, manageress*) (see
Schulz 1990). The existence of overlexicalisation, that is, an apparent excess of words in one semantic area, in derogatory terms for
women and terms for sexually active women, is also now widely
recognised.

Perhaps most comparable with *girl* as an insult for a boy is *old
woman* as an insult for a man (consider also *queen*). Derogatory use
of both *girl* and *old woman* to insult males, though both are denota-
tively female referents, would seem to be the other side of the same
coin of overlexicalisation: females are gloriously insultable, to insult
a male you simply give him a female label.

To return to Lucy and Diana's use of *boy*, this apparently
unmarked use of a normally male referent by girls to refer to themselves can be compared with girls and women wearing trousers as

unmarked, whereas boys or men wearing a skirt *would* be marked. Relatively powerless social groups can be predicted to emulate more powerful groups and even expected to do so *by* the more powerful groups; the reverse is not true. This is not to say that these girls are powerless *as classroom learners of German* – my observations suggest that in many ways they are not. It *is* to say that gender roles and relations and gendered identities which exist outside the school and classroom can and do find their way into the classroom, where they are continually (though probably not radically) reconstituted.

The means of this continual reconstitution is a range of classroom 'discursive practices', which the classroom participants themselves know, and *use*. Different discursive practices draw on different uses of words, such as those just discussed.

SHIFTING MEANINGS, SHIFTING SUBJECTIVITIES

Importantly, in the case of insults such as *girl* and *old woman*, it is not the terms, or signifiers, themselves that do the oppressing, since the meaning of a term, the signified, cannot be more than temporarily fixed. Any signifier is 'always open to challenge and redefinition with shifts in its discursive context' (Weedon 1987: 24, 25). Weedon cites *woman* as a signifier which can have many conflicting meanings which change over time; the same could be said of the signifiers *girl* and *boy*.

Rather than signifiers such as *old woman* being to 'blame', then, it is the sexist discourses which draw on these terms that, linguistically, do the oppressing. Use of *old woman* and *girl*, when context indicates these refer to males rather than females, is a characteristic of sexist discourse (just as use of *manageress* and *mistress* can also be). In this case, Lucy and Diana by saying 'we're boys' with impunity are drawing on a 'male-as-OK' discourse. In poststructuralist theory, discourse constructs an individual's *subjectivity*, his or her unconscious and conscious self, wants, desires, experiences and ways of understanding the world (Graddol and Swann 1989: 161, 164; Weedon 1987: 32). Like the signified, for poststructuralism, subjectivity is not fixed, but is 'precarious, contradictory and in process, constantly being reconstituted in discourse each time we think or speak' (Weedon 1987: 33). Hence the potential importance for speakers and listeners of even a tiny set of utterances such as those which make up the 'we're boys' event.

Discourses are often conflicting and thus in competition and mutually 'contesting'. *Any* discursive practice may be contested – as it occurs, perhaps through overt challenge; or later, through appropriation of that practice, or through another discursive practice. One contesting strategy may be satirical hyperbole. Of course, a discursive practice may not be contested at all. Whether or not a given word or phrase drawn on by a discourse contests, and is contested, and how, will play a role in reproducing or shifting meaning. 'We're boys', despite drawing on a 'male-as-OK' discourse, may also have been *contesting*, as I shall attempt to show.

The 'male-as-OK' discourse that Lucy and Diana draw on is within this school in conflict with a discourse of sexual equality, as espoused, for example, in 'Personal and Social Education' (PSE) classes, which are about mutual respect, about listening to people, and about equality of status and opportunity. PSE frequently focuses on gender relations. For Lucy and Diana and their peers, these two discourses, with others, offer 'competing ways of giving meaning to the world' (Weedon 1987: 35), and, in poststructuralist theory, 'it is language in the form of conflicting discourses which constitutes us as conscious thinking subjects' (Weedon 1987: 32). Lucy and Diana's use of *boy* can be seen as a site of on-going construction of these children's subjectivity.

GENDER IDENTITIES AND GENDER DIFFERENCES

Subjectivity includes an individual's *gender identity*, over which discourses continually struggle:

> The nature of femininity and masculinity is one of the key sites of discursive struggle for the individual. . . It is a struggle which begins at birth and which is central to upbringing and education. At the centre of the struggle is the common sense assumption that there is a natural way for girls, boys, women and men to be. This gives rise to a battle to fix particular versions of femininity and masculinity as natural. . . For poststructuralism femininity and masculinity are constantly in process, and subjectivity, which most discourses seek to fix, is constantly subject to dispersal.

> (Weedon 1987: 98, 99)

The third investigation of classroom participants' perceptions, this time an interview with two boy volunteers, Harry and Oliver, is an example of how the 'common sense assumption' of gender difference being natural and fixed can be part of children's subjectivity. In focusing on what is *not* said (which may be as important in discourse as what is said), this final interview resonates with the teacher's experience of boys' and girls' asymmetric use of *girl* and *boy*. As before, this is a slightly edited version of the interview.

J:	[Plays tape] . . . so they're saying 'we're boys' why why	1
Oliver:	I think they want to have a go	
J:	. . . what do you think	
Harry:	I think they want to have a go	
J:	yeah so why do you think they're saying 'we're boys'	5
H:	just to get the teacher's attention so that the teacher will pick them to	
J:	yeah any other special reason	
O:	because Dr M . . . asked specified for two boys and the girls were desperately putting their hands up . . .	10
J:	yes okay now if it were the other way round if Dr M . . . had said 'two more girls' and if you wanted to have a go might you say 'we're girls'	
H/O:	no [both laugh]	
J:	no	15
H:	no way	
J:	why why not	
H:	I don't think boys like to (xxx) they're soft or stuff like that so they wouldn't say that they're girls but girls aren't really bothered about being shy and stuff so they just say 'we're boys'	20
J:	okay so you think if you said 'we're girls' it would look as if you were soft	
H:	(xxx) stupid	
J:	yeah why wouldn't you say it	
O:	same reason as Harry everybody would think you were	25
J:	mm hm . . . do you think that's a funny thing the girls will say 'we're boys' but the boys wouldn't say 'we're girls'	
H:	it's something that the boys don't do girls will do anything to get a go at something but boys they have a limit what they can do and if they pass that limit they won't they won't they won't say anything they can't be bothered doing it	30
J:	. . . so what would've happened if you'd said 'we're girls' or if some boys had said 'we're girls'	
O:	the response would've been that everybody laughed their heads off	35

J: . . . everybody would've laughed their heads off so it wouldn't
           have worked right . . . when these girls said 'we're boys'
           nobody laughed
O: it was like sort of normal
J: yeah   40
O: for a girl to sort of like shout out and stuff but like for a boy
           it's just not normal to say that you're a girl

Whereas for the girls it was, if not predictable, unremarkable (literally) that they should attract the teacher's attention with 'we're
boys', there is, according to Harry, 'no way' that he, as a boy,
would have called out 'we're girls' as a way to get what he wanted.
Harry and Oliver agree with the teacher that boys would never say
'we're girls', Harry suggesting that this would amount to saying
they were 'soft or stuff like that', and Oliver claiming that if they
did 'everybody laughed their heads off'. Harry and Oliver's
strength of feeling, mutual agreement and complete *lack of ambivalence* about what girls will do and boys won't, and what is normal
for a girl but not for a boy, are all striking. Weedon observes that
power inheres in difference (1987: 113). The quite extreme difference Harry and Oliver currently accept between the signifieds of
boy and *girl* would suggest an associated idea of the importance of
'difference' in their (unconscious?) views of gender roles and relations as a whole, and of the power associated with this difference.

The clear male–female 'binary opposition' Harry and Oliver (like
Lucy and Diana) perceive has been observed in children's perceptions elsewhere (e.g. Davies 1989). Given current social practices,
however, both of a sexist and non-sexist kind, Davies does not find
this binary opposition surprising:

> Adults interested in liberating children from oppressive sex roles are
> generally not questioning maleness and femaleness as such. They are
> simply rejecting the negative side of femininity for girls . . . and the
> negative side of masculinity for boys. . . Children cannot both be
> required to position themselves as identifiably female or male and at the
> same time be deprived of the means of signifying maleness and
> femaleness . . . Dress, hairstyle, speech patterns and content, choice of
> activity – all become key signifiers that can be used in successfully
> positioning oneself as a girl or a boy.
>
> (Davies 1989: x, 2)

In question here are 'speech patterns and content' – what girls can use, what boys *will not*. This 'absoluteness' of course suggests sex rather than gender – and this is precisely the point. Weedon (1987: 2) observes (and this is not an original insight of poststructuralism!) that one important foundation of patriarchal power is the 'social meanings given to biological sexual difference', and the 'discursive position' Harry and Oliver are adopting is based on this foundation. Presumably they 'see' this discursive position as being in their interest.

THE SOCIAL CONSTRUCTION OF GENDER IN THE FOREIGN LANGUAGE CLASSROOM: GIRLS' 'IDENTIFICATION' WITH BOYS?

Crucial to the notion of the social construction of gender is the question of 'how we acquire gendered subjectivity' (Weedon 1987: 43). This *how* includes the shaping role of a range of out-of-school discoursal practices, the mediated/filtered/specific forms these take in the school and the classroom, and (in this case) the way the *foreign language* classroom potentially reproduces and/or contests (including enabling classroom *participants* to contest) gender roles, identities and relations. As D puts it: how children 'get a sense of what gender they belong to and how solidly they belong to it' and how they 'get a sense of their identity in a class like this and throughout their educational history and their home history'. Weedon describes women as being 'socially constituted as different and subject to social relations and processes *in different ways* to men' (1987: 8) (my emphasis). The 'we're boys' event also suggests that the gendering forces in this classroom, which include notions of both masculinity and femininity, are realised in different *ways* in discourse in relation to girls and boys. We are not here looking at parallel or symmetrical processes.

During the discussion with the teacher, D at one point interprets Lucy's and Diana's use and later explanation of 'we're boys' to mean that they can actually see themselves as boys – a form of *assimilation* of the patriarchal concepts of 'male as norm'/'male as representative of humanity'/'female as other' posited variously by, among others, Dale Spender (1980), and Maria Black and Rosalind Coward (1990). But just because some discourses represent 'male as norm', and although there is linguistic evidence to suggest that

males may have little difficulty in perceiving the world and themselves in this way (e.g. Jeanette Silveira 1980), it does not follow
that females share this perception. It would of course be hard to
establish if and to what extent, at the moment of saying 'we're
boys', these girls *seriously* and *profoundly* 'identi[fied] across genders' (D's phrase). My own reading is that both Lucy and Diana are
sincere in claiming that their words are purely instrumental. Diana
(in ll. 14 and 17) may seem to identify *more* with boys – something
felt also by the teacher who observes that 'Diana always hangs
around with the boys . . . she's quite precocious that way and is
very interested in them' (ll. 18–19) – though as D himself points out,
this is 'almost the opposite of identifying with them'. If the teacher
is right to say that there is no shame in a girl being 'like a boy', this
sheds light on the fact that these girls can apparently say 'we're
boys' and not provoke a reaction, but this is very different from
suggesting that there is the possibility of complete *identification* of
girls with their male peers. Any 'identification' on the part of Lucy
and Diana with the boys seems unlikely to be more than temporary
and jokey. Lucy and Diana do, however, as suggested, recognise a
'male-as-OK' discourse, and may also recognise the 'female-as-
often-NOT-OK' discourse 'identified' by Harry and Oliver.

Girls saying 'we're boys' with impunity and in a spirit of fun and
opportunism can thus be seen not as an identification with boys but
as a form of 'normalisation of masculinity': in this case there are
boys, and girls who can be like boys. Perhaps thinking of *what* Lucy
and Diana were calling out, as well as the calling out itself, Oliver
observes 'it was sort of like normal for a girl to shout out and stuff'.
Lucy and Diana may not have 'been' boys, but to 'play' at being
boys, as we have seen, was in this classroom indeed safe and
'normal'.

Harry and Oliver illustrate how there can be a clear gender differential in attitude to the possibility of even temporary, jokey
cross-sex 'identification': any cross-sex 'identification' in boys,
unlike that of girls, would be highly 'marked'. Oliver concludes by
saying 'for a boy it's just not normal to say that you're a girl'.
Though neither masculinity nor femininity are, nor can be, fixed, if
Oliver is right, and if masculinity has in one sense been 'normalised' inside this classroom, femininity has accordingly been
'pathologised' – and this is in a school with an Equal Opportunities
Policy, in a subject area associated and more popular with girls
than boys, and in a class where girls dominate numerically (if only

slightly), and in which the teacher herself has a strong interest in gender issues and equal opportunities. Gender relations existing outside
the classroom enter and are jointly re-created in the classroom in new
shapes in discourse by all classroom participants. And if masculinity
is 'normalised', femininity 'pathologised', again, girls and boys must
have a very different relation to the processes of normalisation and
pathologisation: it is one thing to 'be' the norm, looking at and in
opposition to the other; quite another to be the 'other'.

Yet 'we're boys' within its wider discoursal context does not just
reflect and create masculine 'norms' and feminine 'others' in ways
which act to the *advantage* of boys, as the next section illustrates.

A BOYS' WORLD?

Harry says that 'girls will do anything to get a go at something' but
that saying 'we're girls' is:

> just something that the boys don't do . . . boys they have a limit what
> they can do and if they pass that limit they won't say anything they can't
> be bothered doing it

Harry's observation reminds us that what we are seeing is girls
having to share their identity as *girls* with what is also a term of
abuse for a boy, whereas the reverse does not apply. In illustrating
also how boys cannot unproblematically reposition themselves as
girls – even jokily, even temporarily, even as a means to an end –
Harry is suggesting that in this sense boys are more restricted and
regulated than girls by certain discursive practices – a 'relative
entrapment in the social order' (Davies 1989: 1).[5]

This 'entrapment' in a sense turns certain 'popular' ideas of masculinity and femininity on their head, since here it results in girls,
far from being 'soft or stuff like that', being bold and uninhibited in
their speech and actions (Lucy and Diana are eventually selected,
with the teacher saying 'right we'll have Lucy and Diana who have
been shrieking in the corner'), boys being inhibited. Simon and Neil
are unwilling to perform the dialogue, and the transcript of this les-
son shows no evidence of other boys being as keen as the girls
to perform it. Masculinity may here be 'normalised', but it leaves
the masculine *stereotype* of boys as bold and uninhibited, as

problematic. In an effort not to associate themselves with 'girlness' in any way, Harry and Oliver's behaviour is restricted and they may even appear shy. When the girls call the shots, the boys retreat.

Harry and Oliver may have a clear 'understanding' of *girl* and *boy* being bipolar opposites, in a 'given' binary opposition. Yet the idea of masculinity and femininity existing as polar opposites even in this one class is clearly problematic. For a start, as we have seen, Lucy and Diana have rather different 'feminine' identities from each other. Secondly, their 'femininities' seem less of a trap than Harry and Oliver's 'masculinities', allowing Lucy and Diana to 'move' from the 'feminine' to the 'masculine' with ease and control, and they can thus be said to be of a different 'shape' from Harry and Oliver's 'masculinities'.[6] Thirdly, the 'we're boys' event is a reminder that gender divisions and relations are, at best, unstable, since events like this, and indeed the participants who are active agents in their creation, are continually 'playing' with gender – reconstituting the divisions and relations, but never exactly in the same way, keeping gender and gender relations in a state of flux.

Harry and Oliver's admittance of limits on what they (but not girls) can say and do and Simon and Neil's reluctance to demonstrate a dialogue illustrate how popular ideas of masculinity are unlikely to apply in all contexts. Yet if the most crucial aspect of masculinity for boys is to be *different* from girls, this behaviour may not be inconsistent with stereotypical and more popular ideas: if the boys feel themselves weak in foreign languages, or simply if the girls are setting the pace in shrieking, the boys will strategically decide silence is manly, seeing this silence as a matter of pride rather than limitation. Masculinity and femininity here lay not only in the words that were called *vis-à-vis* those that would not have been called, but also in the calling out itself. Harry's and Oliver's admittance of limits on their behaviour may be at least in part a reflection of changes in gender roles and identities as they affect *girls*: Angela Phillips notes in *The Trouble with Boys* that

> as women's roles in society have changed, so have the range of possibilities for girls. A girl can now be good at maths without feeling that she will lose status as a female. We have not yet come up with a similarly positive way of suggesting to boys that their definitions of gender could also be expanded.
>
> (Phillips 1993: 216)[8]

To what extent was this event a product of the foreign language classroom? 'Foreign languages' is a particularly gendered subject area: teachers often claim girls are the better language learners and in many countries girls rather than boys opt to continue with languages when they have a choice. Language teachers are frequently female. Girls seem to have advantages over boys *in certain areas* when learning a first language (Maccoby and Jacklin 1974; Coates 1993); some of these advantages or even a possible resultant superiority in L1 use may pertain to learning subsequent languages. Certainly Clare Burstall *et al.*'s 1974 large-scale study of primary school learners of French suggested that in many ways girls were superior to boys. Interestingly, in the German classroom in question, during role play work girls would often make use of the space offered by the whole classroom; I never saw this done by boys, who tended to remain in the area immediately surrounding their own desks. This contrasts with observations made by some teachers about boys' and girls' use of playground space – that boys tend to occupy most of the centre and girls to huddle in pairs or groups around the edge; or use of laboratories and computer labs – that boys tend to colonise the equipment (e.g. Judith Whyte 1984). It may be that mixed-sex language classrooms do have characteristic patterns of discourse and that girls speak more and receive more and better quality attention than in other classrooms. If so, other potentially gendered and gendering discoursal practices of these classrooms would bear further investigation.

SOCIAL CHANGE OR THE *STATUS QUO*?

'Being' a boy, however temporarily and jokily, would appear to put a girl squarely in the 'normalisation of masculinity' trap. At the same time, it allows her to play with and operate within behavioural boundaries which are wider apart than those perceived by boys as open to them (see again Phillips 1993). Girls (and women) are thus in a position to challenge and perhaps change traditional 'meanings' and to confuse – and hence to change – people's thinking. The real and underlying value of this must not be overestimated, however – girls saying 'we're boys', like women wearing trousers or even clothes actually *designed* for men, may be tolerated because it is a joke, or because it is superficial, or because it is seen as nothing more than a temporary aberration, or because, whatever else it may be, it is not threatening. If anything, it is flattering. Women have of course crossed many real, serious boundaries – early this century into higher education, into suffrage – but their doing so may still be hotly contested by significant groups of men (and women), one recent example being the entry of women into the Church of England Ministry.

Weedon notes that 'Social meanings are produced within social institutions and practices in which individuals, who are shaped by these practices, are agents of change . . . change which may either serve hegemonic interests or challenge existing power relations' (1987: 25). Yet identifying whether hegemonic interests are being served or existing power relations challenged is not always a straightforward task. On the one hand, Lucy and Diana, in doing what is acceptable to all classroom participants, seem to be maintaining and re-creating the very discoursal practices which mean there is something 'otherlike' or simply 'wrong' with being a girl, but nothing wrong with being a boy. On the other, although Lucy and Diana are 'only' active agents, rather than what Weedon calls 'sovereign protagonists' in the battle for power on the site of the subjectivity of the individual (1987: 41), they are not passive victims. Though not *overtly* contesting the asymmetry of *boy/girl*, they are, in effect, contesting, for themselves and for others, 'boy-as-OK' discourse. For all participants know – consciously or unconsciously – that boys' use of 'we're girls' would not be possible.

It may be possible to read 'we're boys' as a somewhat problematic example of Michel Foucault's concept of 'reverse discourse' – discourse used by an oppressed group incorporating the same vocabulary and categories as those of the oppressor, but which is used to gain acknowledgement (Weedon 1987: 109). Foucault's example is of homosexuality in the nineteenth century, when the demand by homosexuals was that homosexuality's 'naturality' be acknowledged; Weedon's own example is 'the feminist appropriations of traditionally feminine, devalued subject positions characterised by emotion, intuition and an abandonment of rationality [which] have become the basis of radical-feminist discourse' (Weedon 1987: 110). The difference perhaps is that of intention, since it seems unlikely that Lucy's or Diana's intention was anything like as political as either of these. It is not impossible, however, that whatever else they were trying to do, they were also attempting, consciously or unconsciously, to expose the *boy/girl*

asymmetry and the sexist discourse which employs it – recognising, perhaps, that in many contexts girls do lose out to boys, and
perhaps feeling aggrieved that when girls were clearly willing and
able to perform the dialogue, the teacher's insistence on being 'fair'
was in the wider context not fair at all.

Gendering at school is, of course, about boys and girls as members of social groups. Davies notes:

> Masculinity and femininity are not inherent properties of individuals . . .
> they are inherent or structural properties of our society: that is, they both
> condition and arise from social action.
>
> (Davies 1989: 12–13)

This event (with others) is thus potentially *socially reproductive*. As
Davies puts it: everyone, including children, is 'implicated in the
construction and maintenance of the social world through the very
act of recognising it and through learning its discursive practices'
(Davies 1989: 14–15). It may, however, (also) have a socially *trans-
formative* role to play. To return to an earlier quotation, 'Language is
the place where actual *and possible* forms of social organisation . . .
are defined' (Weedon 1987: 21; my emphasis).

CONCLUSION

The boys and girls in this German class are as concerned to 'get
their gender right' as are any other eleven- and twelve-year-olds.
Though in this class this may involve girls calling out in an 'unfeminine' manner, and boys being unstereotypically more restrained,
what Lucy and Diana call out, and the fact that this is not seen as
curious by anyone else in the class, suggests that though Lucy and
Diana, at least, appear to be learning German successfully, what all
the students have indisputably learned is some of the social world's
dominant discursive practices. If as well as reflecting thought and
practice, language does indeed also *constitute* social reality, construct our subjectivity and is the site where meaningful experience
is constituted, 'we're boys' is a fascinating example of this: socially
specific discourse which would seem to have the potential in its
own small way both to maintain and to transform.

NOTES

1. These and other students' names have been changed.
2. All transcriptions have been kept as 'clean' as possible to avoid suggesting meaning that was not intended by the speakers.
3. The audio-recordings had a supporting role in the research methodology and were made in order to 'preserve real time'.
4. Their agreement may to some extent be a product of the 'collective' nature of this interview, but the fact that they also disagreed with each other suggests that being together was not a large constraint on their individuality.
5. It can be asked whether a boy might wish to say 'we're girls' if this was the only way he could get to speak, but may not do so because of fear of the reactions of his peers. The effect of this can be speculated on. The meaning of *girl* is not fixed; it is potentially a site of struggle, in a different way from the way *boy* is a site of struggle, and it could be transformed through both its use and non-use in specific contexts by both girls and boys.
6. We should not, however, forget the regulative effect on girls of the term of abuse *slag*, as referred to by the teacher, and the double standard its lack of a male equivalent makes obvious. Doing what a boy could do with apparent impunity, what she herself may want to do, or even taking a tiny step in that direction may lead to a girl being labelled a *slag*. The problem is that trying simultaneously to avoid being seen as cold, frigid and/or a lesbian may also lead her to be thus labelled.
7. Interestingly, the psychoanalyst Nancy Chodorow theorises boys' entrapment with reference to early childcare:

> Chodorow argues that mothering involves a woman in a double identification, with her mother and with her child, in which she repeats her own mother–child history. This results in a stronger bond between mother and daughter than between mother and son and a lesser degree of individuation in the case of girls, who consequently develop more flexible ego boundaries...
>
> (Weedon 1987: 58)

This, Chodorow claims, creates the psychological preconditions for the reproduction of women's subordination to men.

ACKNOWLEDGEMENTS

I would like to thank Cindy Mackey, 'Lucy', 'Diana', 'Harry' and 'Oliver' for discussing the original 'We're boys, miss!' extract with me, and to my supervisor Dick Allwright, and Simon Gieve, for their constructive comments on earlier versions of this chapter.

GENDER, LANGUAGE AND CHILDREN

ELEVEN

Dominance and communicative incompetence: the speech habits of a group of 8–11-year-old boys in a Lebanese rural community[1]

Farida Abu-Haidar

1 INTRODUCTION

John Fischer's article 'Social influences on the choice of a linguistic variant' (1958) is one of the earliest works on gender distinction in the speech of children.[2] Since the 1970s interest in this branch of sociolinguistics has grown steadily and we now have a substantial corpus of works on the subject. Investigators have used various methods to find out whether girls and boys speak differently. Some have measured the frequency of interruptions and directives in the speech of both sexes, and found that they occurred more often in the speech of boys (Garvey 1975; Zimmerman and West 1975; Ervin-Tripp 1977; Mitchell-Kernan and Kernan 1977; Andersen 1978; Esposito 1979; Goodwin 1980). Others studying topic control and verbosity in male–female dialogue have come to the conclusion that topics initiated by males tend to dominate conversation (Fishman 1978, 1983; Leet-Pellegrini 1980), and that males generally speak more than females (Eakins and Eakins 1976; Berryman 1980; Swann 1988). However, among young children, girls were found to be on the whole more talkative and more linguistically able than boys (Smith and Connolly 1972; Clarke-Stewart 1973). Haas (1978, cited in Coates 1986), on the other hand, found boys in her sample to be more talkative.

My own observations of the speech of a group of pre-adolescent boys in a Lebanese rural community tallies with the findings of Smith and Connolly (1972) and Clarke-Stewart (1973). I found, moreover, that boys invariably displayed dominance in mixed-sex interaction without having the same communicative competence as girls of similar age. According to Lesley Milroy (1980: 85), communicative competence 'involves knowledge of when to speak or be silent; how to speak on each occasion; how to communicate and interpret meanings of respect, seriousness, humour, politeness or intimacy'. The group of boys whose speech I monitored did not seem to fulfil Milroy's criteria. They often spoke out of turn and did not pay much attention to what was being said, particularly by female interlocutors. They used directives as 'explicit commands rather than as hints or suggestions' (Goodwin 1980: 159). Yet they managed to control the conversation by directing the topic to themselves and their immediate needs, and not to the requirements of the situation at hand.

Dell Hymes (1972), who coined the term 'communicative competence', states that speech can only be explained within the social and cultural contexts in which it occurs, or as Deborah Cameron (1985: 140 2nd ed. 1992) has put it, 'language cannot be sealed off from every other form of social behaviour, nor abstracted from the dimensions of subject'. Because language reflects social values (Graddol and Swann 1989), I shall begin by describing the social structure of the speech community to which the boys in this survey belong, to show that their dominance and seeming lack of communicative competence are not in any way attributable to biological factors, but are in fact the result of long-term conditioning to maintain male hierarchy in the community.

2 THE SPEECH COMMUNITY

I carried out my investigation in a Lebanese mountain village, 50 km north-east of the capital, Beirut, about 1200 metres above sea level. Owing to its remote mountain setting, the village has hardly witnessed any new population settlement throughout the present century. In this way an almost uninterrupted tempo of life has been maintained. The inhabitants are all Christians, the majority being Maronite and the rest Greek Orthodox.[3] The inhabitants' main source of income is from fruit and vegetable farming. There is no stock farming, although a few farmers keep cows, sheep and goats for milk. Goat's cheese is made on some farms and sold locally. Before the outbreak of the civil war in 1975, a growing number of young people were leaving the farms to work in urban areas. But because of the dangerous situation in the cities, and increasing unemployment, many are finding their way back to the village to work on the small family holdings. Some who have kept up contact with relatives in the United States, Canada and Australia are leaving to join their relatives abroad. Emigration from Lebanese villages to America and Australia dates from the last century. It is unusual for a family in a Lebanese mountain village not to have relatives overseas. In the past, money sent by emigrant relatives was another source of income for the villagers.

The community is Arabic-speaking, although some Aramaic is used in Maronite church services. There is no illiteracy, and most people have an adequate command of written Arabic. Those who have completed their secondary education have a good working knowledge of French. State primary education is mixed. But at secondary level girls and boys are taught separately. Apart from segregation at school, males and females mix freely, and arranged marriages are practically non-existent. Young people of both sexes try to follow Western fashions in music and dress. Many unmarried women nowadays are not discouraged from seeking paid employment.

In spite of the fact that social customs in this village are not as taboo-laden as those in some other communities in the Middle East, and the freedom of movement of females is not as restricted, the community is still predominantly patriarchal, promoting 'masculine harmony and solidarity while imposing great strains on women' (Sherzer 1987: 110).[4] Women who earn a living are expected to give up their jobs when they get married, since marriage is seen as a woman's only real 'career' (Jabbra 1980: 466). Girls are brought up from an early age to think of themselves as inferior to their brothers. Parents indulge their sons and rarely discipline them, yet they rebuke their daughters, and even punish them for the slightest misdemeanour. According to Philip Smith (1985: 62), adults in most communities 'have different attitudes towards and expectations of boys and girls from the day the children are born'. In the early 1960s, Edwin Prothro, an American sociologist, published a work entitled *Child rearing in the Lebanon*. Prothro found that in all the Lebanese families he surveyed, regardless of religious or socioeconomic background, boys invariably received preferential treatment. The birth of a girl was not seen as an occasion for rejoicing, like the birth of a boy, and boys were frequently breastfed longer than girls. In fact, popular sayings and oral folk poetry throughout the Lebanon confirm this.

Besides being patriarchal, the community is also patrilocal, patrilineal and patrifocal. Men stay in the family home while women move out when they get married. A woman not only adopts her husband's name, but is also expected to convert to his religion if it is different from hers. In most families the head of the clan, usually the oldest male, has a say in the way younger members run their lives. An overall view would show that the social structure of this community is based on a two-tier hierarchical system, related to age and sex. Community elders are accorded undisputed authority over the rest of the clan, while males of all ages invariably hold sway over their female contemporaries.

3   SOCIAL INTERACTION

The community can best be described as 'a closed social network' (Milroy 1980) where there is more contact with other members of the network than with outsiders. Social interaction between the various members of the network helps to strengthen the bonds of kinship and friendship. Single-sex interaction is usually informal while mixed-sex interaction is often formal.

3.1 Mixed-sex interaction

Formal mixed-sex interaction occurs during evening gatherings when families exchange visits. The guests are usually offered coffee, chocolates and cigarettes. When the visits mark special occasions, such as an engagement or the birth of a child, alcohol is also served. Men and women do not sit separately, but it is usually men, or older women who have acquired status of seniority in the clan, who initiate conversations. On these occasions spontaneous language tends to be polite and guarded. Hosts and their guests also exchange prescribed pleasantries and circumstantial language. During visits following a death, little spontaneous speech occurs and all parties repeat stock phrases coined for the solemn occasion. In mixed-sex gatherings, both sexes refrain from swearing and using words with sexual innuendos which occur frequently in the speech of both men and women in single-sex groups.

3.2 Single-sex interaction

From my observations of this community, I found women to be more prolific conversationalists when communicating in all-women groups. Women also tend to produce more spontaneous language than men, even in mixed-sex interaction. Female interaction occurs throughout the day. There are no fences or walls around houses, and neighbours drift in and out of each other's homes. Women visit each other during the day, usually to lend a hand in some household chore, such as baking bread, or just to have a cup of coffee and a chat. Females in the community form a united, mutually supportive group comprising three or four generations, their daily interaction serving 'the function of joint activity and of consolidating friendship' (Coates 1989a: 120). Girls learn from an early age to interact with older women. From about the age of seven they spend more time at home helping their mothers and grandmothers than in playing with their peers.

Male members of an extended family usually work on adjoining family plots, spending most of the daylight hours in the orchards or vegetable patches. But farmwork in remote mountain areas is often a solitary occupation where men find themselves not near enough to each other to carry on conversation. Married men do not usually mix in single-sex groups after work hours. Some Lebanese mountain men are renowned for improvising oral poetry. In the past, competitions, like eisteddfods, used to take place between representatives from different villages when men challenged each other to improvised verse composition duels. Although these competitions no longer take place, some men still display virtuosity in composing oral poetry, and many of their poems are quoted by other men in the village.[5] In fact most men are proficient at repeating oral poetry, anecdotes and popular sayings, but they produce less spontaneous language than women.

Unlike girls, boys under the age of twelve and thirteen rarely interact with adults. From about the age of seven, when they are allowed out on their own, boys spend most of their leisure time playing with their peers. Adults have little time to spend with them, and there seems to be far less bonding between mothers and young sons than there is between mothers and daughters. The boys' occasional visits home are sometimes dreaded by female members of the family who look on these visits as unwelcome intrusions into their domain.

Communication between boys and their fathers is fairly limited. Men seem to have little time to spend with their sons in the evenings or at weekends, which are taken up by social gatherings. During school holidays some boys work with older male relatives. On these occasions, however, interaction between the two groups tends to be minimal and restricted mainly to directives given to the boys by the older men.

4 THE SAMPLE

For this particular investigation I selected nine boys, aged between eight and eleven. Six of the boys were at the local state school, while the other three went to the fee-paying boys' school run by a Jesuit order. All nine boys were considered to be of above average intelligence, and their school reports confirmed this.

As the boys were either at school or playing outdoors until late in the evening, it was difficult to pin them down for formal recorded interviews. However, two mothers managed to arrange sessions where the boys' speech could be carefully monitored. The boys were recorded singly and in groups of up to five. They were asked to narrate incidents which had struck them as being particularly amusing or disturbing. The present investigation is based on both empirical data and my more general observations.

The following example of the interaction between three boys aged between eight and nine, and two girls aged eight and twelve, took place shortly before I set up my tape-recorder. I had asked the two daughters of the family I was staying with to help me take the tape-recorder from the car to the house. On our way we passed by three boys playing near the house, among whom was the girls' nine-year-old brother. He was the first to notice us.

Boy 1:   [to his younger sister] What's that?
Girl 1:   A tape-recorder.
Boy 1:   What?
Boy 2:   What?
Boy 1:   [to the other two] Come on!

The three boys came rushing towards us.

Boy 1:	Give me!
Girl 1:	No, go away!
Boy 1:	Give me!
Boy 3:	I'll take it . . ./[6]
Boy 1:	No, I want it . . ./
Boy 2:	Let's see, let's see . . ./
Girl 1:	No. I'm taking it into the house . . . we're going to start recording.
Girl 2:	[to her younger sister] Let him take it.
Girl 1:	No, why should I?
Boy 1:	I want it. I'll tell grandmother.
Girl 2:	Oh, do give it to him so we can have some peace.
Girl 1:	[finally giving in] Here you are.
Boy 2:	I want it . . ./
Boy 1:	No!

Eventually the brother of the girls took it in with Boy 2 holding on to it. Boy 3 went away.

The above incident shows how boys can have their own way with female relatives. Even when a girl is determined, she is often told by older girls and women to give in for the sake of family harmony. In this case the younger girl could have insisted on having her own way, but because of advice from her older sister, she knew there was no point in persisting, as her brother would always be allowed to have the upper hand. The other two boys, who were not related to the girls, were not as insistent, knowing that the girls' brother was going to end up with the tape-recorder. One boy, however, stayed to make sure he was holding on to the tape-recorder as well, although there was no need for more than one person to carry it.

The two mothers, whose help I found invaluable, constantly complained that they could not rely on their sons to take messages for them. Mother 1 then proceeded to prove her point by asking her two sons, aged eight and ten, to go to the vegetable plot a few hundred yards away from the house where their father was working, and to call him to lunch. The older boy's reaction was to whisper in his brother's ear and run off. The younger boy, then moved a few steps to where he could see his father and called out without going to him:

'Dad. Dad. Lunch.'

He too ran off to join his brother. In a second house, Mother 2 asked her ten-year-old son to call his grandmother in for a cup of coffee and to meet their visitor. The grandmother was peeling vegetables on the verandah. The boy ran out of the house, and without stopping, shouted:

'Grandma, hey Grandma, Mum wants you. Quick. There's a guest . . .'

Mother 2 then asked her six-year-old daughter to convey the same message. The little girl went up to the verandah and was seen talking to her grandmother. She then helped the older woman up and came back to the house with her.

The mothers of the seven remaining boys agreed to take part in this experiment. Each boy was asked to take a message to a member of the family who happened to be not far away, and to call her/him in. Six of the boys behaved in the same way as the first two. They stood and called out, or just ran past, telling their relatives to come in without stopping to see whether their messages had been understood. Only one ten-year-old went up to the person he was calling, spoke to him and then went away.

The following extract was recorded in the house of one of the boys in the sample. The boy's mother and grandmother, knowing that he would rush in at any moment to ask if he could go to a football match in a nearby village, asked me to set up the tape-recorder. The two women went on talking for about fifteen minutes before the boy came in. He went straight to his mother:

Boy 1:	Georges and Emile are going. Today. to Bikfayya. To see football. I want to go, I want to go . . .
Mother:	Who's taking them?
Boy 1:	They're going.
Mother:	But who're they going with?
Boy 1:	[Silent. Looking vague as if he has not heard.]
G/mother:	Didn't you hear your mother? Who're they going with?
Boy 1:	I want to go . . .
Mother:	I asked you to tell me who they're going with.
Boy 1:	I want to go. I want to . . .

Just then a neighbour walked in.

Neighbour:	Hello, how are you?
Mother:	Hello, come in. Come in.
G/mother:	Welcome. Come and sit down.

The two women then started asking their neighbour about the health of each member of her family. The neighbour's son, another boy in the sample, looked in through the window and tried to attract the attention of his friend.

Boy 2:	Hey, Sami. Hey.
Boy 1:	What?
Boy 2:	Are you coming?
Mother:	Hello, where've you sprung from?
G/mother:	Come in, dear, come and have some peaches.
Boy 2:	I don't want to. Hey, Sami, are you going? To the match?
Boy 1:	Yes.
Mother:	I never said you could go.
Boy 1:	I want to go. Why can't I? They're all going . . .

His mother tried to ignore him and turned to the neighbour. They went on talking, pretending not to hear the boys who were trying to catch their mothers' attention:

Boy 1:	Mum . . .
Boy 2:	Mum . . . Mum . . .
G/mother:	Why don't you boys go out and play and let us hear what we're saying?
Boy 1:	No!
Neighbour:	Be good boys, go and play and let us talk/
Boy 2:	I don't want to . . .

After several more minutes, with the boys continually pestering the three women, the grandmother was the first to give in, exasperated, saying that her grandson could go to the match. The boy's mother said nothing and the neighbour told her son that if he went away to play with his friend she would let him go to the match.

The following conversation took place in the house of another boy in the sample. The boy, aged ten, his eight-year-old sister and parents were explaining how the boy's father and grandfather had levelled a plot of rocky, mountainous land and then turned it into terraces.

Mother:	All this land was hard and stony. What you see now, all level and fertile, is the work of generations of men.
Father:	Yes. There's no doubt about it. We've been working the land for many, many years, my father, his father before him and his father before that. Yes, that's the way it's been in this country.

Mother:	At least in the mountains. Of course it's all different in the cities. Can you imagine anyone in Beirut bending down to do a hard day's work like we do here?
Boy:	When they come here [laughs] they can't walk they keep falling. [more laughter]
Girl:	[laughs]
Father:	They don't know how to walk on rough ground/
Mother:	The women come in their high heels. Of course they can't walk in these mountains. No, they don't know what hard work means.
Girl:	My father leaves the house at four every morning. At four. And he doesn't come home until late/
Mother:	When we were first married I used to get so frustrated, unhappy really, waiting and waiting for him. Counting the hours.
Girl:	Granny says Mummy never let anyone see she was crying. You see she missed Daddy and felt shy with my grandfather and grandmother, Daddy's parents.
Father:	My mother had more to put up with. My father left her when they'd been married two years. He went to Brazil to work with his brother.
Mother:	My mother-in-law was left with her daughter only a few months old.
Girl:	Is Aunty Leila the oldest then?
Mother:	Yes. She . . ./
Father:	But my father came back. He wanted to farm . . ./
Mother:	The business in Brazil went bust . . ./
Father:	He started to dig this thankless land. And now look at it. The Garden of Eden.
Boy:	They took me with them. The big tractor came. So big. Huge. Massive. And it started going bang, bang, bang . . . [laughs] And the soil came tumbling. Whoosh.
Girl:	It got in your eyes and you cried/
Boy:	No, I didn't. [looks at his sister angrily] I didn't! I didn't!
Father:	Of course he didn't. What made you say that?
Girl:	[silent and looking rather abashed]
Mother:	He doesn't cry. You know that.

In the above extract the girl participates in the conversation in a way her brother, who is two years older, seems unable to do. She shows concern that her father works too hard. She is also aware of the difficulties her mother faced when she was newly married. The boy only joins in the conversation when he can talk about himself, and he shifts the topic to the tractor. In spite of the girl's undoubted love for both parents, the couple seem to contradict her in their attempts to support their son's statement, regardless of whether he is telling the truth or not.

I asked six of the boys to tell me in their own words about an incident which had occurred the previous year. A bus carrying more than twenty passengers had been hit by a falling rock. The rock had fallen on the rear end of the bus, which was empty. The passengers had escaped unhurt or with minor injuries. What they reported took less than a minute and a half. They all spoke at once. There was hardly any topic development. The boys kept on interrupting each other to add on different bits of information amid peals of laughter and a fair amount of onomatopoeic utterances, such as 'crash', 'bang'. The three remaining boys were then asked to give an account of the same incident. Their account was also marked by constant interruptions, laughter and onomatopoeic utterances.

Five girls were then asked to relate in their own words what happened when the bus crashed. Their collective testimony lasted more than three minutes. The girls seemed to treat the incident seriously. There was no laughter. The interruptions, which occurred frequently, did not stop the flow of the topic, but added more information, supporting the testimony of the previous speaker.

The following are two short extracts showing the difference in the way boys and girls interrupted each other.

Boys:

Boy 1:   As it, the bus, was coming, turning the corner . . . Crash/
Boy 2:   No, much earlier/
Boy 1:   It was at the corner . . . My uncle was there!
Boy 3:   the rock came down. We heard it. Like thunder . . . /
Boy 4:   Before the corner/
Boy 5:   Whoosh. [Laughs. Laughter all round.]

Girls:

Girl 1:   The rock came rolling down/
Girl 2:   Just as the bus was coming up to the corner/
Girl 3:   You see, they'd been blasting on the other side of the valley . . .
          To build a road/
Girl 1:   Yes, and to widen the road leading to the village/
Girl 4:   They dug too deep . . . /

Girl 2:   They disturbed the soil. That's what my father said . . . /
Girl 5:   Yes, so did my father . . . /
Girl 1:   That's right. Anyway, as I was saying . . .

The two short extracts above show the different attitudes of the two sexes to the incident. Rivalry between the boys can be detected, as they rush to speak out of turn, trying to re-create the noise made by the impact. The girls, on the other hand, appear to talk as a mutually supportive group, their snippets of dialogue providing adequate information on the incident.

5 CONCLUSION

In trying to determine what constitutes a social network, Viv Edwards (1988: 41) isolated the following: 'patterns of work, friendship and leisure'. If one were to apply these determinants to this Lebanese mountain community one would find that the nucleus of the social network is made up of females of all ages, with males on the periphery. Young boys, on the other hand, seem to form a temporary splinter group until the onset of puberty, when they too become part of the large social network. As far as language is concerned, girls and boys learn in early childhood the linguistic behaviour appropriate to their sex (Coates 1986: 161).

Given the different social organisation of boys and girls in this community and the way the two sexes acquire sex-appropriate language, it is hardly surprising that the speech of the nine boys in this survey lacks the fluency and articulate expressions which characterise the speech of girls of the same age. Girls, moreover, seem to produce language which is both 'supportive and co-operative' (see Coates 1989a: 72), while boys' speech, with its constant interruptions and unmitigated directives, appears to display the aggressive and competitive behaviour of males in a society where age-old patriarchal norms go unchallenged.

NOTES

1. I am grateful to Jennifer Coates, who read an earlier version of this chapter. She made some useful suggestions which have been incorporated into the essay.

2. John Fischer measured the frequency of the occurrence of the -ing element in the speech of twenty-four New England primary school children. He found that girls produced the prestigious -ing form more often than boys, who tended towards the less prestigious -in.

3. The Maronites, a Christian community, originally adhering to the Monothelite doctrine, adopted the Roman Catholic faith in the twelfth century.

4. The patriarchal norms of this community seem to have a fair amount of similarity with those of the Araucanian Indians of Chile, as described by Scherzer.

5. There are other communities where men have a gift for oral literature. Webber (1988), for example, found Tunisian men to be prolific story-tellers.

6. A forward slash (/) signifies interrupted dialogue.

TWELVE

Voice and gender in children

Alison Lee, Nigel Hewlett and Moray Nairn

This chapter considers the question of whether the voices of pre-adolescent boys can be distinguished from those of preadolescent girls and examines some of the evidence surrounding this issue.

The chapter is arranged in two sections. The first reviews some experimental evidence concerning listener identification of child gender from voices, certain acoustic characteristics of boys' and girls' voices and the possibility of anatomical differences in their vocal structures. The second section describes a study recently undertaken by one of the authors (Lee), in a UK context, to assess whether a perceptual difference exists between boys' and girls' voices and, if so, its possible basis in speech production.

DOES CHILDREN'S SPEECH DIFFER ACCORDING TO GENDER?

Evidence from listeners' perceptions of gender in children's voices

That gender is identifiable from speech is a foregone conclusion as far as adult voices are concerned (one experiment (Schwartz and Rine 1968) resulted in 100% correct identification based only on samples of isolated whispered utterances of the vowel /a/). In the case of children, on the other hand, it might seem reasonable to predict that the voices of boys and girls would be indistinguishable to listeners until around puberty, when male and female speech become very noticeably different with the 'breaking' of the male voice. However, some convincing evidence exists that the voices of boys and girls are to a large degree distinguishable even prior to puberty.

Several empirical studies have addressed the question of listeners' ability to identify the gender of prepubertal children from their speech (Weinberg and Bennett 1971; Sachs, Lieberman and Erikson 1973; Sachs 1975; Meditch 1975; Bennett and Weinberg 1979a; Gunzburger, Bresser and Ter Keurs 1987). All have involved making tape recordings of samples of children's speech and then asking panels of listeners to identify each subject's gender from the tape-recorded sample. The samples have ranged from extracts of spontaneous speech (with selection criteria designed to minimise potential cues from utterance content) to isolated vowels spoken in a whisper.

Weinberg and Bennett (1971) demonstrated that judges were able to correctly identify the gender of 5- and 6-year-old American children from 30-second samples of spontaneous speech with a success rate of 74%. Meditch (1975) achieved a similar result with the spontaneous speech of a small group of children as young as 3 years Sachs, Lieberman and Erikson (1973) found a success rate of 81% with recorded sentences from a group of children with a rather large age range (4 to 14 years); the success rate dropped to around 66% when the samples consisted of isolated vowels only (Sachs 1975). Gunzburger, Bresser and Ter Keur's (1987) results followed a similar pattern with 7- and 8-year-olds: they found that the average recognition rate of 74% for sentences dropped to 55% when the sample consisted of isolated vowels. In an extensive study, Bennett and Weinberg (1979a) asked listeners to judge the gender of 73 children aged 6 and 7 from various types of speech sample, namely vowels spoken both normally and whispered, and sentences spoken both normally and in a monotonous fashion. Overall, the identification rate was around 68%, with no dramatic differences among the success rates for the different samples. The success rates for the isolated vowels were slightly lower than for the sentences but interestingly enough there was no significant difference between the whispered and the normally spoken vowels. Any advantage for normal intonation over monotonicity appears to have been wiped out by a marked tendency for monotonicity to increase the identification rate for boys. The identification rates of a quarter of the subjects were above 97% for the isolated vowels; however, a significant number of the children were not judged consistently as either male or female. This emphasises the need to consider the distribution of the overall identification score across individual subjects. While the gender of many subjects may be very consistently identified, others may be ambiguous and some may even be consistently identified as having the opposite gender. With regard to possible listener bias in favour of one or the other gender, Meditch (1975) found that listeners made significantly more 'male' guesses (that is, gender judgements in favour of males). However, Bennett and Weinberg (1979a) found no overall bias towards either gender.

The general conclusion that may be drawn from these studies is that perceptible gender differences do exist in the speech of many prepubertal children. Adult listeners are able to correctly identify gender with a success rate of somewhere around 70% from samples of normal speech. Even with samples of isolated vowels, the success rate (at around 66%) is not much reduced. However, the identification rate is by no means as high as it is with adult subjects. Many questions concerning the perception of gender in children's speech remain to be answered: at what age does gender-specific speech start to appear?, are identification rates similar regardless of cultural background?, does rate of identification increase with the age of the subjects?, and so on.

Since (or to the extent that) gender is identifiable from children's speech, there must of course be acoustic features in the speech signal which provide the perceptual cues. We now turn to the question of the identity of these features.

Fundamental frequency of boys' and girls' voices

The fundamental frequency, or 'pitch',[1] of the voice is lower in adult males than in adult females, a feature which has been amply confirmed in all empirical studies which have been carried out into the fundamental frequency characteristics of male and female voices (for a review, see Baken 1987) and which has been demonstrated to be perceptually salient (Lass *et al.* 1976). It is therefore a feature which should obviously be considered in any investigation of gender distinction in children's voices.

There has been a good deal of research over the years to determine the fundamental frequency characteristics of preadolescent children (Eguchi and Hirsh 1969; Cornet, Rilou-Bourret and Louis

1971; Weinberg and Bennett 1971; Sachs, Lieberman and Erikson 1973; Kent 1976; Vuorenkoski 1978; Bennett and Weinberg 1979b; Hasek and Singh 1980; Gunzburger, Bresser and Ter Keurs 1987; Sorenson 1989). Kent (1976), in a review of previous studies up to 1976, concluded that fundamental frequency values are distinguished by sex only after the age of 11 years. Bennett and Weinberg's (1979b) results from their 6- and 7-year-old children (see above) would lend support to this conclusion, as would those of Gunzburger, Bresser and Ter Keurs (1987) from a group of 7–8-year-old subjects. Bennett (1983) carried out a longitudinal study of a group of children from age 8 to age 11 years and reported an average yearly decrease in fundamental frequency of 12 Hz; but she did not find any significant gender-related differences. Sorenson (1989) studied children in different age groups between 6 and 10 years and found no significant overall gender differences in any of the groups but he reported a tendency for male fundamental frequency to drop at age 6–7 years. However, Hasek and Singh (1980), in a study of 5–10-year-old children did find a significant decline with age in the fundamental frequency of the male subjects but none in the female subjects, while Sachs, Lieberman and Erikson (1973) actually found that their male subjects had significantly *higher* fundamental frequency than the female subjects. Despite this latter evidence, the majority of acoustic data fails to support the existence of a sexual dimorphism in average fundamental frequency before adolescence.

There are, however, other aspects of vocal fundamental frequency which might play a role. One is the extent to which fundamental frequency varies over an utterance. Thus Sachs, Lieberman and Erikson (1973) seem to support the idea that 'in general, women seem to have more extremes of low and high intonation than do men' (Sachs, Lieberman and Erikson 1973: 81), and Bennett and Weinberg (1979a, 1979b) found that the tendency towards greater variability in fundamental frequency in girls was a feature which contributed to gender distinction.

Formant frequencies of boys' and girls' voices

In adults another important difference between male and female speech lies in the vocal tract resonances, or 'formants'.[2] Since the male vocal tract tends to be larger than the female vocal tract, male speech tends to have lower formant frequencies. Since formant frequency has been demonstrated to be a major determinant of perceived male–female speech differences in adults (Coleman 1971), formant frequency is the other main candidate which has been considered as the distinguishing feature between girls' and boys' voices.

Bennett and Weinberg (1979) found lower formant frequency values for boys than girls though the differences were not significant. The authors then looked at the best-identified children and the worst-identified children for each sex. For the boys, they found that the correlation between lowness of formants and probability of identifying a voice as that of a boy was significant. In other words, the most boy-like voices had the lowest formants. Conversely, among the girls there was a tendency for the most girl-like voices to have the highest formants, although this correlation was not significant. Sachs, Lieberman and Erikson (1973) obtained a broadly similar result from their study. Bennett (1981) found boys' formants to be lower than girls' in all cases and that vowel quality had an influence on the size of the gender differences.

From the evidence it would seem likely that vocal tract resonance characteristics, unlike fundamental frequency, could play a significant role in the perception of child gender.

Other factors

There are any number of other possible features of speech which might contribute to gender identification: speech rate, phonological factors, loudness, voice quality, to name but a few. Few have yet, to our knowledge, received systematic attention. One study (Robb and Simmons 1990) which examined vocal fold vibration in prepubertal children concluded that differences in the manner in which the vocal folds vibrate do not occur until after puberty.

Anatomical differences or learned behaviour?

Whatever the acoustic cues to gender turn out to be, they are of course produced by the vocal tract gestures of the speakers. The two basic alternatives are (a) that boys and girls have different vocal tract anatomy and thus different acoustic characteristics or (b) that they have the same anatomy but use different gestures in order to produce the acoustic differences. In the case of adults, the acoustic differences are ultimately based on anatomical differences: male vocal folds tend to be longer and thicker and thus vibrate at lower frequencies and male and female vocal tracts tend to have different dimensions and therefore produce different resonant frequencies. However, there is some evidence that the differences due to anatomy are, in many speakers, enhanced by learned patterns of speech production (Mattingly 1966; Bladon, Henton and Pickering 1984; Ohala 1984). Speakers may choose to confine themselves mainly to a higher (or lower) area of their frequency range, for example; or to use habitual lip rounding, or lowering of the larynx, either of which will result in the lowering of formant frequencies. Thus the explanation for the (lesser) gender distinctions in children's voices may either be that there are (less pronounced) anatomical differences or that boys and girls acquire different learned patterns in certain aspects of speech motor production; or any combination of the two.

One obvious approach is to search for gender differences in the anatomical development of the vocal structures. However, Kirchner (1970) found no significant difference in size of the larynx between prepubertal boys and girls, and while Hirano, Kurita and Nakashima (1983) found that the vocal folds continue to grow in length up to the age of 20, they found no length difference between males and females under the age of 10. Walker and Kowalski (1972) found that growth of the lower jaw did not differ according to gender up to about 12 years of age when growth tends to cease in females but not in males. Hunter and Garn's (1972) study of growth of the face reached a similar conclusion. The only claim we have found for gender dimorphism comes from Bennett and Weinberg (1979b), who, on the basis of a reanalysis of some earlier published data, claim that there is evidence for a slightly longer pharynx in male children than in female. Bennett (1980) found a strong correlation between certain measures of body size (such as dimensions of the neck) and formant frequency values, from which she concludes that differences in vocal tract size may underlie the formant differences.

However, the current balance of evidence from anatomical studies would suggest that the vocal organs of prepubertal boys and girls are not significantly different. Sach, Lieberman and Erikson (1973) certainly incline to the view that gender differences in speech are most likely the result of voluntary behaviour and they cite lip configuration as a possible cause for the pattern of formant frequencies they found among their subjects.

Another approach to this question would be the investigation of gender differences in children in different cultures. Most of the studies thus far have been carried out in the United States. If a culture were found in which gender differences did not exist in the speech of prepubertal children this would be strong evidence that gender differences are learned.

The second part of this chapter describes a study undertaken on a group of Scottish children to examine some of the issues raised.

EXPERIMENTAL STUDY OF GENDER AND SPEECH IN A GROUP OF SCOTTISH CHILDREN

The aims of the study were:

1. To investigate whether or not listeners could reliably identify the gender of the children from recordings of their voices.
2. To investigate whether the children involved in this study demonstrated any significant differences in fundamental frequency depending on their gender.
3. To ascertain whether the judges were using fundamental frequency as the basis for judgement of gender.

The subjects were 24 children ranging in age from 5 to 10 years. They comprised 12 boys and 12 girls. The average age of the boys was 7.5 years and that of the girls was 7.2 years. Subjects were asked to read the first two paragraphs of a passage of text ('Arthur the Rat') and to produce the three vowels /a/, /i/ and /u/. High-quality acoustic recordings were made and also recordings of vocal fold vibration were obtained using a Voiscope, a physiological instrument used for monitoring vocal fold activity by means of surface electrodes placed on the neck (Abberton, Howard and Fourcin 1989). The Voiscope recording was used to obtain the mean fundamental frequency and fundamental frequency range for each subject. In order to investigate perceptual judgements of sexual identity, the recordings of every subject were copied onto another tape in random order and 5 of the children (selected at random) were included twice. The recording was played to a panel of judges who were asked to identify each voice as either male or female. A total of 32 adults served as judges, 16 female and 16 male. These two groups each consisted of eight 20–22 year olds and eight people of 45 years and over.

Overall, judges correctly identified the sex of the children 73.5% of the time; for female judges alone the percentage was 73% and for male judges 74%. There was thus little difference in rate of success of identification according to the sex of the judges, and the same was also true of age. Overall there was an 80% test–retest agreement. The judges' responses to each individual subject were also analysed, in terms of percentage of correct judgements. Overall, judges responded 'female' to female speakers 72% of the time; half of the female subjects were identified more than 80% correctly by the judges; the responses to one subject were at chance level; 2 females were identified correctly only 34% of the time, well below chance. These results are illustrated in Figure 12.1, in which the proportion of each bar above the line represents the percentage of correct responses to that subject's speech sample. Judges responded 'male' to male subjects 77% of the time; 7 of the 12 male subjects were identified more than 80% correctly by the judges; 2 were perceived as girls by the majority of the judges, being identified correctly as boys only 13% and 22% of the time, again well below chance. Figure 12.2 illustrates these results, with the proportion of each bar below the line representing the percentage of correct responses to that subject's speech sample.

These results appear to confirm the prominence of gender characteristics in the voices of preadolescent children. At least, they would suggest that Scottish children, like the North American children in the studies reported in the previous section, exhibit such gender differences. It does seem however that the vocal attributes that identify the sex of preadolescent children are present in varying degrees, unlike adults, in which a near total gender identification is reported.

So, having established that the listeners could identify the sex of most subjects successfully, we turn to the results of the fundamental frequency measures. Statistical analysis indicated no significant difference in the fundamental frequency of boys and girls in this study. Further analysis carried out involved comparing the fundamental frequency of those subjects perceived to be girls with those

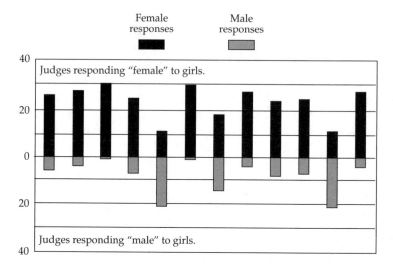

Figure 12.1 Judges' responses to female subjects. The proportion of a bar above the line represents the percentage of correct responses to the relevant subject.

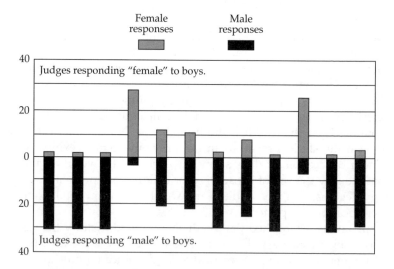

Figure 12.2 Judges' responses to male subjects. The proportion of a bar below the line represents the percentage of correct responses to the relevant subject.

perceived to be boys, irrespective of their actual gender. Statistical analysis again indicated that the fundamental frequency of these two groups was not significantly different. Finally, the fundamental frequency *ranges* of the boys and the girls were compared. Although the girls' mean range was 22 Hz greater than the mean for the boys, the difference was not statistically significant.

In the light of the evidence just described, a search for other cues employed by listeners is obviously required. A limited analysis was therefore carried out to look at the contribution of formant frequency, using the recordings of the isolated vowels. The subjects chosen consisted of the 2 best-identified and the 2 worst-identified for each sex – 8 subjects in all. For each subject, spectrograms were made of the vowel /a/ and the formant frequencies were measured from the spectograms. Results indicated that both the first and second formants of the best-identified girls are higher than those of the worst-identified girls. For the boys, the reverse pattern is observed. Statistical analysis revealed a significant difference between the formant frequencies of the subjects identified as boys and those of the subjects identified as girls. This evidence suggests, therefore, that 'girl-like' voices have higher formant frequencies than 'boy-like' voices.

CONCLUSIONS

It can be asserted with confidence that the gender of many children (at least of those living in the USA or Europe) can be reliably identified from their speech alone well before they reach puberty. However, any explanation which purports to account for this phenomenon must also be able to account for the fact that a significant remainder only acquire appropriate gender-specific speech characteristics after puberty.

The acoustic features responsible for the perceptual difference are far from well established. Formant frequency has emerged as a better predictor of gender identification than fundamental frequency in several studies but it remains likely that a multiplicity of features are involved. The balance of evidence at present suggests that the acoustic features (whatever they turn out to be) are the result of learned behaviour rather than anatomical dimorphism. If this is indeed the case then it would be interesting to discover how extensive the behaviour is across cultures. The children studied thus far have lived in societies in which a great many aspects of the environment of even very young children are divided by gender, including the majority of their clothes and toys and many of their recreational activities. It may be that in a society in which such gender divisions were delayed to an older age, or were less prevalent, gender-specific speech would not be such a widely desired goal for young children.

NOTES

1. Strictly speaking, pitch is a perceptual phenomenon, and fundamental frequency (the rate of repetition of the cycle of a periodic wave) is the physical phenomenon. Fundamental frequency is measured in hertz (abbreviated to Hz), meaning cycles per second.
2. Formants are peaks in the spectrum of a vowel sound. Different vowels are distinguished from each other by the frequencies at which their formants occur.

LANGUAGE, MEDIA/VISUAL ANALYSIS AND GENDER

THIRTEEN

Feminism, language and the rhetoric of television wildlife programmes

Barbara Crowther and Dick Leith

This chapter is concerned with the way gender relates to a range of discursive practices, both verbal and visual, associated with Natural History programmes on television. We'll be looking at the presentation of biological science – its ideology still untouched by feminist challenges and reconceptions – and at the way gender is accommodated in its narratives and discourse; and we'll be considering the implications of the narration (both script and voice) for the gendered construction of its audience. We'll also be addressing the issue of female scientists, and their status in a TV form where almost all the production team are men, and whose appeal, we suggest, is primarily to a male audience.[1]

Our central texts are extracts from three different Natural History films broadcast on television, *Continuing the Line* (the final episode of the BBC's 1990 series *The Trials of Life*), *The Tale of the Pregnant Male* and *Queen of the Beasts*,[2] and the questions we address are: how are they scripted, who narrates them, and how do we, as viewers, interpret the relationship between narration and image? As we progress, more and more tensions are noticeable among these three components – script, narration, audience interpretation.

TELEVISION WILDLIFE, SCIENCE AND NARRATIVE

Natural History programmes on television are probably the most influential source of popular knowledge about wildlife. Though not as high in the ratings as soaps and sport, they consistently rake in audiences large enough to ensure the survival of the genre. They are located at peak family viewing time – between tea and the

9 o'clock watershed – and we suspect that one of their spin-off functions is to allow parents to raise the so-called facts of life with their children, vicariously, through animal examples. Moreover, their reputation for combining state-of-the-art photographic techniques with educational and entertaining television has earned these programmes the much-coveted 'quality' label.

Most wildlife programmes concern themselves at some point, if not centrally, with the gendered behaviour of animals, especially reproduction. Our three examples focus on this aspect of butterflies, seahorses and lions. If programmes like these can be used to allude to sex between humans, it is because of the widespread assumption that we can learn about the social behaviour of humans from our observation of the animal world.

This is, essentially, the premise of sociobiology, a branch of biological science which, although widely contested, is clearly very influential in television Natural History.[3] As a project, sociobiology has earned a reputation as reactionary; although it has generated interesting hypotheses for both traditional and radical scientists to use in research,[4] it tends to set up reductive and determinist patterns of thought that allow for the construction of easy equations between animal and human behaviour, justifying, when taken to its extreme, even the worst excesses of the latter. Unfortunately this makes it a gift to the structures of popular television, offering a version of science that suits television's entertainment brief.

A further, crucial problem with sociobiology is that human descriptions of the animal world are ultimately grounded in human perceptions of what *human* society is like. In short, we can't help describing animal behaviour in terms of our models of the human world. This, of course, is anthropomorphism, and anthropomorphism in turn is heavily inflected with patriarchal assumptions and metaphors, as we shall be illustrating.[5]

The unstable and often ambiguous boundary between the animal world and the human world is reflected in the *address* of wildlife programmes, where what is said about animals sometimes appears to include us, as humans, and sometimes doesn't. Moreover, 'us' is often patriarchal: sometimes it includes females, and sometimes it doesn't. This example comes from David Attenborough, the pre-eminent figure in wildlife broadcasting today:

> It is not surprising that many animals go to great lengths to seize a female at the very moment she becomes sexually available.[6]

Predictably, gender is a fertile area for anthropomorphic play in script and image, and has significant implications. The 'ludic' dimension of such metaphors can be quite appealing, but their ubiquity in wildlife discourse – from Mrs Badger cleaning out the bedding, or the leader of a pack having a 'harem', to the steady undertow of metaphors around mothering and fathering roles, grooming, jilted lovers, jealousy, coyness and so on – suggests that they are more than just gratification for the TV audience. They shape the perception of the researchers themselves, the way they find and tell stories. This recognition that science is embodied in narrative – and is therefore ideologically informed – challenges its claim of objectivity, one of its appeals to rationality.

A restricted range of narrative formats is repeatedly used to present wildlife subjects. One of the most common is the life-cycle story. But this story is almost always told as if reproduction, not death, is the culmination of animal life – an orthodox determinist position that feminists have long been challenging. (Indeed, the whole of the series *The Trials of Life* was couched in this structure: the first episode was *Arriving* – being born – and the concluding one wasn't *Dying* but *Continuing the Line*.) Moreover, the programmes concentrate on the efforts of the *male* to secure genetic survival, a current preoccupation of Natural History. Reproduction is seen as the need to continue the male line: females are assumed to reproduce anyway, and their fitness to survive is not investigated; they do not have to fight for it.

There is also a male focus in another frequently-used narrative format – the quest narrative. Here the naturalist, almost invariably male, acts as hero-seeker, leaving the comforts of civilisation behind to pursue a rare or exotic creature. It's a folk-tale formula, articulated in the natural world. We see David Attenborough taking up this pose as a hero-figure in the first sequence discussed. But he also plays another role – the Scientific Detective – in another common narrative formula, which celebrates the triumph of rational science over the mysteries of nature: Man can explain everything.

The internal demands of entertainment television and the half- or one-hour slot encourage such neat and end-oriented cohesive narrative packages with linear structures, and these reflect, it might be said, the dominant phallocentrism of Western cultural forms. The stress on closure rather than open-endedness, science as progress and discovery rather than an area for debate and contestation, is unfortunately at odds with the more discursive and self-questioning style encouraged by much contemporary feminist science.

The male focus in wildlife narratives and the sexism in the discourse it emanates from may contribute to the fairly widespread sense that these are primarily 'men's programmes'. Recent research indicates that Natural History programmes feature high (third) on the list of programmes that men feel an affiliation towards, but they don't feature in women's preferences – though this may, of course, reflect intended rather than real viewing habits.[7]

ANALYSING THE THREE FILM EXTRACTS: IMAGE, SCRIPT AND NARRATION

In wildlife programmes, more so perhaps than in most television genres, the visual images are in a sense primary. Sequences of images of the natural world are commonly shown without an accompanying commentary, and even at other times the images can be, and probably often are, enjoyed for their own sake, with only casual attention to the verbal script.[8] Wildlife photography offers us a rich source of visual stimuli that feed readily into established categories of the aesthetic. In *The Tale of the Pregnant Male*, for instance, we find a celebration of the diversity of colour and form associated with underwater wildlife. There are lengthy sequences, such as one the script interprets as a seahorse courtship dance, accompanied only by light (waltz-like) music. *Queen of the Beasts* offers us images of animal grandeur and cuddliness, together with some exciting sequences of lions hunting, again not narrated, and accompanied appropriately by African drumming.

Image and script need to be kept conceptually distinct, even though the script sometimes seems to 'caption' the images, helping to shape audience interpretation. However, a sequence of images can in its own right be 'persuasive', creating meanings that may be independent of, even opposed to, the dominant messages encoded in the script, as we shall now show in relation to *Queen of the Beasts*. The script is merely one element in the process of creating meaning, but it is tempting to privilege it in analysing the programmes because its medium is language, which can, so much more easily than the non-linguistic elements, be transcribed and subjected to various well-established systems of textual analysis. On the other hand, the importance of the script needs to be recognised as it does significantly seem to 'frame' our interpretations, partly through *what* is said, and partly through *how* it is said.

First, the *what*. The script will typically offer us an argument, in the form of a story or stories which address a theme. This is openly acknowledged by the programmes themselves, in the title of one, *The Tale of the Pregnant Male*, and in the frequent references to 'the story' of lion family life in *Queen of the Beasts* (see, for instance, the last couple of sentences of note 13). In all three programmes discussed, the overriding theme is reproduction.

Reproduction and the genetic selection process in the animal world is a source of mystery, and the programmes set out to titillate us with the mysteries, and offer possible solutions. *The Tale of the Pregnant Male* invites us to marvel at the wonders of seahorse reproduction, and offers us an accompanying narrative in which scientists-as-heroes patiently and arduously collect evidence and piece it together. In *Queen of the Beasts*, the emphasis is not so much on the mechanics of reproduction as on the social order which governs it: 'Why of all the wild cats in the world, is it only the lion that lives in groups?' The programme seeks to answer this question by narrating the attempts of scientists to offer hypotheses. Two hypotheses are suggested and then rejected; a third, that lions live in family groups to ensure that *lionesses* preserve territory and stability in the face of unwelcome attention from nomadic males looking for an opportunity to further their genes, is then advanced and (apparently) accepted.

From the above account it might appear that the script offers us only referential information, whereas the images contribute aesthetic pleasure.[9] But the script, to use Bakhtin's term, is not monologic.[10] The seriousness with which scientific discovery is presented is tempered frequently by verbal play, often based on an appeal to anthropomorphic thinking. A male seahorse, for instance, filmed in a stream of bubbles in a tank, '*enjoys* a shower of bubbles'. Such 'light relief' forms an important part of the *how* of wildlife narration. But this practice has important implications. The programmes offer us insight into an unknown and perhaps unknowable world, and for this, it is claimed, we need the 'objective' methods of science; but at times, it seems, all animal behaviour can be understood if we only remember what we, as human beings, are like. The message we are given is a paradoxical one: animals are not like us; but they are also just like us. Both propositions may be true, but in certain sensitive areas such as gender, the elasticity of this boundary between nature and culture may cause many problems.

Verbal play of the kind discussed above is, not surprisingly, often marked by the use of certain characteristics of vocal delivery. This brings us to the final aspect of script, the kind of voice used in delivering it (or, to use Goffman's term, animating it).[11] Because of the collective nature of film-making, questions of authorship are complex; but the narrator's voice, with or without an embodied presence, is a voice of authority – and it is almost always male. The light touches are blended in to a compositional style brimming with impressive detail, figures and facts, formulated to express empirical certainty, and this is delivered with appropriate gravitas and the certainty born of empiricism; like a newsreader's, it is not a voice that conveys doubt or expects to be challenged.

Unquestionably the most famous of such voices is that of David Attenborough. Indeed Attenborough could be said to personify the genre. In many of the programmes narrated by him, Attenborough is not only the *animator* but the *principal* as well (see note 11). The values of traditional science are inscribed in his voice; we know him as both scientist and presenter, mediating between the Expert and Everyman. Indeed, some wildlife texts we feel are actually *authored* by him, even though the precise responsibility for the wording of scripts may not be his. This impression is partly created by the fact of his presence on screen in many wildlife films. This physical presence has its own persuasive power: his contorted postures, his enthusiasm and awe, invite us to share his knowledge with him as we share his hands-on experiences. For many viewers, we suspect, watching Attenborough enjoy himself is part of the pleasure of watching his films.

In *The Tale of the Pregnant Male* we hear Attenborough as animator of someone else's (Neil Nightingale's) script. Such is his authority, however, that it is difficult not to feel that the entire programme reflects Attenborough's own values as both scientist and populariser. His narrated script, moreover, keeps all other speaking participants under tight control. Amanda Vincent, the scientist whose research forms the basis of the programme, is granted a voice, but is scripted in a mode entirely in keeping with the script. Bill Macmillan, the man who keeps her tanks supplied with fresh seahorses, is also allowed to speak in voice-over. His words, like Vincent's, are like the direct speech quotations used by newspaper journalists, chosen for the way they illustrate and even repeat the content of the script.

In *Queen of the Beasts* the script is animated by a voice associated with neither science in general nor wildlife in particular, but with drama. Using the voice of an actor rather than a naturalist is a common strategy in television wildlife programmes. In this case, however, the voice is that of a woman, Rula Lenska. Despite the programme's emphasis on the field-research of different teams of scientists, hers is the only voice to be heard. The effects of this choice of narrating voice will be discussed later.

Continuing the Line

In this film, as in all the other episodes of *The Trials of Life*, Attenborough is animator, principal and author, and is often seen on the screen in the guise of the naturalist in the field. The emphasis in the script, as the title implies, is on genetic continuity. But the interest is exclusively on the *male* line. The section transcribed below, which discusses the Helliconius butterfly, is sandwiched between a discussion of crab mating behaviour and that of wolves. The male crab, we are told, 'has already ensured that the eggs [the female crab] will nurture for the next few weeks will carry *his* genes'. And wolves, after coitus, experience a period of 'genital lock', the aftermath of which – and these words are edited on to footage of a male wolf licking his genitals – 'may be slightly painful, but the process has virtually guaranteed him his paternity. And animals that don't take such precautions can't be nearly so certain'.

[*Long shot of Attenborough walking through trees and waving a butterfly net.*]
[Attenborough, voice-over:] A male butterfly has to be just as alert as a crab if he's to secure a mate.
[*Leafy branch with three or four butterflies alighting and flying around it.*]
And this forest in Costa Rica is full of competitors for the females who are appearing from pupae hanging in the bushes.
[*Close shot of Attenborough's head bent sideways, examining pupa and butterfly on the underside of a branch. His gaze throughout alternates between camera and subject.*]

[Attenborough, to camera:] This is a male Helliconius butterfly and he's settled on a pupa which he knows contains a female. He's waiting for that moment when the female will emerge, a virgin, and then in the first few seconds of her adult life he'll mate with her. And so intent is he on achieving that that he won't move even if I touch him with my fingers. But watch what happens if I take this, which is an adult female which is newly mated. What happens if I brush him lightly with her?
[*Male flies off.*]
The reason he left is because this female, when she was mated, was given a particular smell, [*Attenborough lifts female butterfly to his nose and sniffs*] which even I can detect – a smell that all other males find very repugnant. So if I let her fly away that male may return to complete his business.
[*Releases female.*
Close shot, possibly studio-shot, of two butterflies.]
[Attenborough, voice-over:] And even before the newly emerged female's wings have expanded he mates with her, dabbing her with his smell which will repel other males for weeks. No rival will displace *his* sperm.

The script's obsession with patrimony is reinforced by taking the male's perspective, even to the extent of Attenborough detecting the annointed female's scent – 'which all other males find very repugnant'. Even at the level of grammar, the female is presented as sexual object: in two separate instances involving active voice ('he'll mate with her' and 'he mates with her') and by the use of the passive voice in another ('when the female *was mated*'); however, the close-up image of the mating act (accompanying the pen-ultimate sentence) suggests mutual involvement even if the female is still attached to her pupa.[12] Moreover, Attenborough's delivery and his raised eyebrows express some eagerness as he describes her emergence from the pupa, quite redundantly, as '*a virgin*'.

The males, introduced as 'competitors' but not shown in any competitive activity, could, in a different script, be seen as operating a system of squatters rights, and another trope might be developed around entrepreneurial investment, and guarding property.

The Tale of the Pregnant Male

This programme explores an apparent oddity: it is the male sea-horse, not the female, that gets pregnant and gives birth. The script investigates this feature according to the same preoccupation with the behaviour of the males and with patrimony. The film's closing statement reaffirms this obsession:

> Seahorse fathers show that it's possible to be both macho male and a caring parent, though why they in particular have such a tough time remains a bit of a mystery. On the other hand they are probably the only fathers in the world who can be really certain, one hundred percent, of the paternity of all their offspring.

We have selected three sequences early in the film for our analysis.

Extract 1

[*Panning shot across fish tanks to where young woman in yellow short-sleeved shirt has her arm in a tank. Close-up of hand fishing out seahorse.*]
[Attenborough, voice-over:] In this laboratory at Cambridge University there're probably more pregnant males concentrated together than anywhere else in the world. Here Amanda Vincent studies their bizarre breeding behaviour and, as in any maternity ward, she has to keep alert for the unexpected.
[*Low-angled medium shot of Amanda behind tank, lifting out seahorse while talking, occasionally looking direct to camera (her eyebrows express ironic amusement). Shot of hands delivering baby seahorses.*]
[Vincent to camera:] This male seahorse is having problems with a breech birth, so I'm having to act as the midwife. Although it's pregnant I know that it's a male, for, like all other male animals, this seahorse produces sperm. Oh, and female seahorses produce the eggs.
[Attenborough, voice-over:] These babies have got stuck and Amanda is gently teasing them out of their father.
[*Seahorses swimming in tank.*]
In most animals it's the females that care for the young, and males compete with one another to mate with the females. The result is that males tend to be bigger, more aggressive and more macho than females. An exception to the rule might help us understand why.
[*Medium shot of Amanda lowering herself behind tank and talking to camera through tank with seahorse activity in foreground.*]
[Vincent to camera:] By studying the seahorse in which the male invests so heavily in his offspring, I'm trying to understand what really is the foundation of these sex differences.

Extract 2

[*Shot of two seahorses circling round a stem, intercut between (*) and (**) with close-up of Amanda's eyes watching intensely offscreen.*]
[Attenborough, voice-over:] Amanda's real interest is in their courtship and mating and what it can tell us about the roles of the sexes. She regularly pairs seahorses and records their behaviour when they're placed together. Courtship starts almost at once with this slow circling dance.

Amanda has discovered that courtship takes time, about three to four days. (*) She suspects that this is to allow the male to prepare his pouch to accept a brood of eggs. (**) When it's ready he displays by thrusting out his hips in a movement similar to the contractions he'll make when he gives birth.

[*Seahorse continues circling; cut (at ***) to pale motionless seahorse with head bowed. Male joins her and pair swim upwards vertically together, and circle stem.*]
While he has taken considerable time and energy to prepare for pregnancy, his (***) mate has merely watched. It only takes her a few hours to mature her eggs.

Given a choice seahorses establish a bond and usually remate with the same partner. Every day at first light they greet each other with a circular dance not unlike this courtship display.
[*They move away together, bellies and heads touching, their bodies forming a heart shape. As they separate, one egg floats through the water.*]
But the actual mating is unmistakable. Hundreds of eggs transferred from female to male in under five seconds, and only one is spilt.

Extract 3

[*Low angled shot through fish tank of Amanda's body rising behind tank, her yellow shirt reflected by the water surface giving a confused, distorted image. She puts her arm into the water, then withdraws it; again refraction distorts the image.*]
[Attenborough voice-over:] Since males put so much into pregnancy, Amanda wondered whether sexual roles were completely reversed. Perhaps seahorse males are not macho and females are the more aggressive sex. By changing the ratio of males to females she found out which would compete most vigorously for the other.

[*Three seahorses swim around some reeds, one seahorse with bowed head constantly moving away from another's advances, the remark 'No sign of female forwardness here' coinciding with the image of the unresponding seahorse (we might interpret it as 'bashful'). More seahorses swimming, including 'nipping'.*]

If there was only one male to several females they did seem to compete for him, but not very enthusiastically, and he always started the courtship. No sign of female forwardness here. But if two males were let free with a single female the situation was quite different. Even nipping was not ruled out by the two potential fathers as they tried to outmanoeuvre each other for female attention. They may be left holding the babies but seahorse fathers still maintain their more usual male roles. If they put so much effort into pregnancy and are also the aggressive sex, the females must have an unusually easy time.

[*Close-up of Amanda Vincent's head in profile gazing into tank.*]

Amanda is continuing her research to unravel more behind this apparent paradox.

The patriarchal assumptions behind the script and the interpretation it puts on some of the images of seahorses – 'no sign of female forwardness here', 'his mate has merely watched' – are evident. What we want to concentrate on here is the way the work of the female scientist, Amanda Vincent, has been recruited to serve the programme's line, its story of solving the mystery of the 'bizarre breeding behaviour' of seahorses.

Film-makers who are not interested in feminist critiques of patriarchal science and its practices are nevertheless happy to use women to help tell their stories of scientific progress; the presence on screen of such women serves to reflect the reality that observational and experimental research is not a male preserve. Yet the way in which these scientists are represented, and their expertise framed, still draws attention to their sex, their difference.

We have, we argue, a classic example in these extracts. Amanda Vincent is a specialist in seahorse behaviour: her name appears in the credits as the scientific advisor to this BBC film. She is presented as working in the orthodox scientific paradigm, and though focusing on the sex/gender boundary she doesn't appear to be aiming to contest the terms. To the film-makers her work is about gender roles, as though these were universally fixed and not a negotiable/contestable area.

The referencing style used for their academic consultant, calling her Amanda and not Ms Vincent or even Amanda Vincent, tends to

downgrade her status; and the scripting style, where she is introduced in a 'maternity ward', not as, say, an obstetrician but as a
'midwife', reinforces this para-professional status, appropriate to
her sex. She herself feeds this image with her reference to the
'breech birth', but it must be remembered that the script is not her
own: her control is limited, her words embedded in, and authorised
by, the main narration – David Attenborough's. Indeed, there is a
hint of self-mockery in her delivery of 'breech birth'.

There is something in the filming style too that draws attention to
her gender, and it works, we suggest, in two contrasting ways.
Some shots follow the conventions of Western film aesthetics for
filming women, lingering on her face, especially close shots of her
eyes (observing), making her the object of our gaze. But some other
shots counter this 'star' treatment with distorted images, framing
her in a tank, her arm oddly refracted by the water – at one point
she even squats down and continues to speak to us from behind a
tank full of active seahorses. One way or the other, either by glam-
orising her or by distorting her, the authority of her address is, we
feel, undercut. It seems unlikely that a male scientist of equal standing would be filmed in quite this style.

Though she was probably the source of a great deal of the film's
material, Attenborough's contribution as (invisible) narrator is far
more authoritative than hers. The authority and control of the film
is in male hands. To borrow Goffman's terms again, Neil
Nightingale, the scriptwriter, and David Attenborough as the narrator, share the roles of author, principal and animator between
them; Amanda Vincent, for all her scientific status, is brought in for
these few shots as a guest principal

Queen of the Beasts

In this *Survival Special* film, the presenting mystery was why lions
should be the only species of wild cat to live socially, in groups; but
the energy of most of the film went into investigating why these
family groups are so dominated by lionesses, and why males play
so marginal and transitory a role.[13]

By way of an introduction to the part of the programme from
which our extract is taken, the reproductive behaviour of male lions
is described.[14] It has been explained that the resident members of a

pride are all related females, and that young male lions are sent away from the pride at about two years old (when suckling has stopped) by two stronger unrelated males who have been living 'as nomads' for about two years. They move in to the pride, ousting all rival males including the older male(s).

The extract we have chosen is made up of two consecutive sequences, and raises some interesting questions about address, and how we, as audiences, may interpret the relationship between script and image.

[*Shot of single lion raising head and shaking mane – intercut with close shot of head – then he is joined by second male: both sniff ground, raise heads, shake manes, bare teeth.*]
The new masters of the pride have come for the females. One sniffs the spot where a lioness has urinated. Wary of these new and strange males, the females have wisely gone into hiding.

[*Grassy plain, with scattered bushes. Camera focusses in on dark bush in left-hand foreground, until cubs (*) are visible in its shadow.*]
But in this hide-and-seek game of life there is another and more immediate problem for these males. They cannot mate until the lionesses come into season. But the females already have cubs (*) and so will not be ready to mate for another year or more.
[*Cut to close-up of cub's face.*]
The new males simply cannot wait that long for their chance to father some cubs of their own.

[*Tracking shot of lion loping, right to left, across grassland. Cut to cubs in long grass. Cut back to lion, stationary, looking back over his shoulder, then slowly turning head forwards again.*]
They are in their prime now and may only have possession of the females for two years – just two years in which to ensure their genetic patrimony.

[*Cut back to cubs – to lion – to 3 cubs on plain.*]
They cannot afford to look after another male's cubs; they cannot spend their short time at the top protecting another lion's young whilst waiting for their turn to mate.
[*Lion looks left, lowers head and moves off left, gaining speed, then running.*]
They have done their waiting out there on the plains where they wandered for years in search of this opportunity; they can wait no longer. If the females lose their cubs they will come into season within days. The imperative for the new males is overwhelming: they must kill the cubs.

[*He attacks one cub while a second runs off, and picks up and drops its limp body before moving off towards second cub who rears up before being attacked and killed; lion runs on to third, savages it, and picks up body.*

Cut to long shot of lion carrying body of cub as camera zooms out to vista of whole savannah.]

Despite all the years of research into lion behaviour infanticide has rarely been seen and *never* before filmed. For all its apparent ferocity, the killing is only an expression of the urgent demands of the situation. But if the male's behaviour seems harshly pragmatic, perhaps the female's is even more surprising.

[*Male lion, lying beside river, is approached by female and whipped across the head with her tail. She repeats this on two others lying nearby. She settles near them, facing away from them; one male approaches and mounts her. Cut to head-and-shoulder shot of the pair, male licking female and showing his teeth. Cut to male standing quietly; cut to female getting up and walking away followed by male who trots after her licking her rump.*]

Bereft of their cubs the females now have exactly the same drives as the new males. They can expect around two years of stability. If they are to raise cubs they must start immediately. Within as little as 24 hours after losing their cubs the females come into season and start flirting outrageously with the new males. The females are nervous at first, a bit scared of the new males; but the orgies in the first few months after a takeover are a good [*amused tone*] ice-breaker, and soon strong bonds are formed.

For us, the rhetorical interaction of voice and image here poses considerable problems.

We find the infanticide scene incredibly shocking, and part of our discomfort at the sequence may come, we think, from a disparity between our response and the 'preferred reading' suggested by the narration. We have earlier seen shots of a lion with playful cubs (see note 14), and been told 'lions are good fathers'. There is no irony signalled, and we are nowhere warned to expect disturbing images. Throughout the build-up to the unprovoked attack, the same calm, measured voice delivers an explanation of how normal and necessary the lion's (as yet unspecified) behaviour is.

> They cannot afford to look after another male's cubs; they cannot spend their short time at the top protecting another lion's young whilst waiting for their turn to mate . . . they can wait no longer.

The two or three shots of cubs hidden in the grass, cross-cut with the apparently unaggressive lion – a classic suspense technique when co-ordinated with other narrative clues – may give some hint of what is to come; but on the statement 'The imperative is overwhelming: they must kill the cubs', the narration stops and the images on their own carry the narrative. The biological motivation the commentary has offered in exoneration of the lion's behaviour may be satisfactory in scientific terms; but the insistently defensive commentary perhaps acknowledges that the images may also be seen to tell a different story. Far from merely *illustrating* animal behaviour, they are narrating an emotionally powerful drama.

Yet the traumatic effect is never acknowledged. The script makes no allowance for feelings of grief and horror. Our emotional response to the scene seems out of step with the approved response, unauthorised. Rather, the narration foregrounds scientific and technological discourse. As the lion savages the third cub and carries its body across the savannah, the script informs us that '[lion] infanticide has rarely been seen and *never* before filmed'. A technical first for Anglia TV's *Survival* team – an unquestioned privilege for us.[15] This preference for signalling technical and heroic achievement over emotional reaction seems to us to indicate that the masculine (we use the term metaphorically) in the audience is being addressed, a suggestion supported by the script going on to compare the male lion's 'harshly pragmatic' behaviour with the female's 'even *more* surprising' behaviour – described (with only a hint of irony) as 'flirting outrageously'.

It is here that the difference between the narrator and the narration, or, in Goffman's terms again, the animator and the author, is important. The voice and the script seem incongruent. It is unusual for the narrator of a wildlife television film to be female, and here it seems quite significant. We feel that the decision to employ a female narrator in this film, where nominally the lionesses are the focus of the film, is somewhat analogous to employing female commentators for women's tennis. The result is not a change in the substance of the commentary – the *script* – but only in the voice used to narrate it. Rula Lenska's authoritative speaking position accords with the male orientation of both science and prime-time television. This marginalises a 'feminine' response further, and maybe increases one's uneasiness at not sharing the 'preferred reading'.

CONCLUSIONS

We have tried to show that televised Natural History is not an 'innocent' genre, that the benign surface masks some questionable assumptions about sexuality and gender in both human and animal worlds. An immediate and obvious objection to our thesis might be that televised science cannot be taken so seriously; that it is only, after all, entertainment, and that if we want serious scientific knowledge we should go elsewhere. To accept this, however, would be to assume that 'science' and 'television', 'knowledge' and 'entertainment' are as polarised as male and female have come to be in Western thought. As we have argued, television Natural History programmes do seem to mediate the information–entertainment dichotomy, but their hybrid status raises questions not only about how seriously they should be taken as 'science', but indeed about the nature of science itself. How are scientific *meanings* constructed and received in a society that purports to be educated? Does science exist, as it were, outside discourse, or is it necessary to take account (as we suggest) of the rhetorical contexts associated with scientific activity? And how can science win back a non-specialist audience in the late twentieth century, when gender is such a potent political category, without compromising scientific values in the interests of commercial palatability?

NOTES

1. For a complementary exploration of wildlife programmes and gender, see Barbara Crowther (1995); and for a more detailed and programmatic account of the kind of linguistic analysis adopted here, see Dick Leith and George Myerson (1989).
2. *Continuing the Line*, Episode 12 of *The Trials of Life* (BBC Bristol, 1990); *The Tale of the Pregnant Male* (*Wildlife on One*, BBC Bristol, first transmitted 1 March 1988); *Queen of the Beasts* (*Survival Special*, Anglia TV, first transmitted 17 March 1989).
3. David Attenborough's twelve-episode BBC blockbuster, *The Trials of Life*, broadcast in 1990, confirmed sociobiology's status as orthodoxy in the genre. The classic text is E.O. Wilson's *Sociobiology*, published in 1975.
4. Susan Sperling's article, 'Baboons with briefcases' (1991), includes a thorough discussion of how sociobiology has developed. Both this

article, and Donna Haraway's 'Primatology is politics by other means' (1988), offer interesting accounts of the work of Sarah B. Hardy, a feminist sociobiologist.

5. In 'popular' biology on television it is possible for value-laden concepts from the scriptwriter's culture, which are used metaphorically in the interpretation of animal behaviour, to become assimilated into these ostensibly scientific scripts, and then read back as 'natural' in wider human culture. The term 'father', for instance, has connotations in contemporary Western society that stretch beyond the purely biological, yet these may vary considerably from the connotations and role-expectations assigned to it in other cultures. We have noticed that scripts in the television series *The Sexual Imperative* (Channel 4, January 1993) frequently use metaphors from economics (e.g. 'investment', 'pay-off') to explain both human and animal pairing behaviour.

6. This sentence is taken from David Attenborough's book of the series, *The Trials of Life* (1990: 300). It cannot be excused as a mere slip of the tongue in front of the cameras.

7. The following details were available at the 'Spot the Difference' conference on the future of women in British television (March 1991), under the heading 'Programme preference':

	MEN	WOMEN
1.	BBC 9.00 News	Coronation Street
2.	News at Ten	Early evening local news
3.	The Natural World	Antiques Roadshow
4.	Early evening local news	Neighbours
5.	Athletics	Eastenders
6.	A Question of Sport	Inspector Morse
7.	Tomorrow's World	Crimewatch
8.	The Sweeney	The Bill
9.	Snooker	Taggart
10.	The Match	Murder She Wrote

Source: British Market Research Bureau/Target Group Index

8. In this discussion we are using the term 'script' for the verbal component of the film, despite possible objections that films have shooting scripts too.

9. Perhaps the clearest 'referential' function of the script is to 'anchor' a sequence of images by the explicit use of deixis: 'This is a male seahorse, and he's pregnant', where 'this' points to an image we see in front of us. At other times the link is less ostensive but no less clear: 'the' in the minor sentence 'The Serengeti National Park' accompanies shots of land and animals in such a way that we make the connection between script and image without realising it.

10.   See M. Bakhtin (1981), 'Discourse in the novel'.
11.   Erving Goffman (1981). In his terminology, the voice which *animates* a script merely gives voice to it, whereas the voice supposedly upholding the values expressed in the script is the *principal*. Both are distinguished from the *author*, the person who creates the text to be animated.
12.   Interestingly, in his book of the series, Attenborough gives a little space to considering the Darwinist explanation of the Helliconius butterfly's mating habits from the female perspective.

> She herself disperses this chemical message when later courted by other males by exposing her abdominal gland and erecting a pair of plume-like 'stink-clubs' from the end of her abdomen. How he stimulates her to do this and why it should be advantageous for her to have one mate and not several, is still the subject of research. It may be that the boisterous business of being chased and impregnated by rival males carries such a risk of injury that it is advantageous for her to make it clear to potential suitors that she has already been fertilised.
>
> (Attenborough 1990: 302)

The female perspective is rarely explored even this far in the television programmes, which is a marker of the way the discourse of science is popularised for television audiences.
13.   This may be why it was trailered – we seem to remember – as somehow 'feminist'. The pre-title introduction to the film states:

> For centuries lions with their awesome size and power have played a large part in human history, art and folklore. We learn at an early age that the lion is king of the beasts, and that a group of lions is a pride.
>
> For many years scientists have been wondering about those prides. Why, of all the wild cats in the world, is it only the lion that lives in groups?
>
> There do appear to be advantages. There are advantages in sharing family duties; but there are also the tension and conflicts that beset any social grouping.
>
> In unravelling the story one thing has become clear: the males, for all their size and showiness, are more like consorts than kings. If lions can be called the crowned heads of the animal kingdom, then the enduring monarch is not the king – but the queen.

14.   One sequence in the introduction is of particular interest to the

argument of this chapter, in terms of the sociobiological genetic-imperative model, and is reproduced below. Note the male orientation (e.g. 'sire') and the anthropomorphism ('want', 'good fathers'). Over the image of a lion and three or four cubs, where (without the guidance of the commentary) the adult could perhaps be perceived as looking bored and behaving unresponsively to the attention-seeking mauling the cubs are meting out to him, the commentary declares:

> The males themselves are tolerant and affectionate. They are good fathers; but unlike the females they do not stay with the pride all their lives.
>
> The overwhelming driving force in nature is to reproduce. It is not enough just to sire a lot of cubs. The males need to stay with the pride and help to protect their cubs and the mothers against other predators. By staying they increase the chances of their cubs surviving.
>
> The females want the males to stay, and to use their great strength to protect them and their territory. But protect them against what?
>
> Males can only reproduce successfully if they are with a pride. A group of breeding females is a prize worth fighting for, and there are always unattached males wandering the plains in search of mates. Those wanderers are a constant threat to the stability and safety of the lionesses. Perhaps here was a pressure strong enough to have caused the evolution of their social system.

15. The 'technical first', a device claiming to bring to the audience visual phenomena never seen before, or impossible to see with the naked eye, is a common, and self-congratulatory, practice in wildlife programmes.

FOURTEEN

Man in the news: the misrepresentation of women speaking in news-as-narrative-discourse[1]

Carmen Rosa Caldas-Coulthard

1 INTRODUCTION

In this chapter, I examine the ways newspaper reporters 'represent' oral interaction in the discourse of the 'news'. I will explore the concept of 'accessed voice' (Hartley 1982) in the representation of speech, in other words, who is given voice and how this voice is reported in the press. Since, much of the time, 'news is what is said', the values and words of a privileged body of people who have special roles in society are generally put forward. Women in general are part of the unaccessed voice group and the small quantity of female speech reported in the press, as I point out below, is sufficient to demonstrate that their social role has a special or deviant status. Unequal access is evident in what is reported and who speaks, and, as a consequence, the linguistic code imposes and reinforces attitudes and values on what it represents.

The discourse of the media in general is an instrument of cultural reproduction, highly implicated within power structures and reflecting values about the world. One of them is male supremacy. Writers in quality papers seem to abide by and to be dominated by this ideology. News 'is not a value-free reflection of fact' (Fowler 1991: 4) but a construction and representation of the world through language. Newspapers in general, both quality and the tabloids, are basically oriented to a male audience and exclude women from the speaking position.

Although women constitute 52% of the population, they are misrepresented in the news. They are also described differently; in other words, women are a separate category, generally dissociated from power structures. Men, in general, are represented speaking in their public or professional roles, while women, when they speak, are identified with the private sphere. They are the mothers, the daughters, the wives, the widows, the page three girls, the stars. The private/public distinction is a very important feature of social organisation. If women are represented mostly speaking in their personal roles, they are marginalised in terms of public or ritual speech.

Newspapers, as I show here, handle men and women in terms of different sets of categories or different stereotypes. 'News' in the quality papers, one of the institutional gatekeepers of linguistic production, reinforces sexism – a system in which women and men are not simply different, but unequal.

If, in the media, women are less heard than men, and their contributions less reported, newspapers continue to encode bias and legitimate assumptions about linguistic behaviour and social asymmetries.

2 QUALITY PAPERS AS DATA

The sample for my analysis consists of 200 narratives from quality papers (the *Guardian*, the *Independent* and *The Times*) collected during a period of ten consecutive days (January 1992). From the three broad categories of printed media content – news, service information and opinion – the genre 'news' was chosen (130 Home and 70 International) since this is the most prominent genre read by many people (Bell 1991). I concentrated on what is called by journalists the core news product or 'hard news' – reports of accidents, political events, conflicts, crimes, discoveries.

My choice was motivated by the following assumptions:

1. Quality newspapers, because targeted at an educated audience, were likely to have a 'serious' insight of what is considered 'important'.
2. News in quality papers would be addressed to a non-gender-marked population since both women and men read (and watch on TV) the news on a daily basis.

These texts, therefore, should not in principle, favour one of the sexes. However, as I quickly realised by examining the sample, this was not the case.

In order to back up and confirm my findings, I also made use of concordance lists of verbs of 'saying' from a 5,000,000 word corpus of *The Times* and frequency counts of some significant lexical items from *The Times* corpus and from a 20,000,000-word corpus of the BBC World Service.[2]

3 THE STRUCTURE OF HARD NEWS

Hard news is a subgenre of narrative discourse. Like any other narrative text, hard news is centrally concerned with past events, which develop to some kind of conclusion. In contrast with commentary/opinion and political evaluation, hard news focuses on event orientation and causality. The structural components of 'news' are headlines, lead (the first paragraph that summarises the whole story – a micro story), source attributions, actors, time and place. In fact, according to Bell (1991: 175), journalists have a short list of what should go in a story, the five Ws and an H – who, when, where, what, why and how.

As in other narrative texts, speech representation is a pervasive feature of the news. In fact, most news is what 'people say more than what people do' (Bell 1991: 53).

4 SHE SAID, HE SAID

Linguistically, 'quote' is the last layer in a hierarchy of narrative levels, since it is the introduction of one text into another. Halliday (1985) refers to the notion of projection – 'the logical-semantic relationship whereby a clause comes to function not as a direct representation of (non-linguistic) experience, but as a representation of a (linguistic) representation' (1985: 287–8). The projecting clause – 'he said . . .' – is a verbal process of saying, while the projected clause – 'he said: "..."' or 'he said that . . . .' – represents what is said; they have the status of a wording which, for Halliday, is the representation of a lexico-grammatical phenomenon. 'The main function of the projecting clause is simply to show that the other one is projected: someone said it' (*ibid.*).

Although quoted material *represents* interaction, it is an intra-textual game because the words are either borrowed from another interactive situation, or created by an author. In either case, represented speech is always a mediated and indirect discourse, since it is always produced by a recounter who interprets the speech acts represented according to her/his point of view.

Writers, when representing oral interaction, make use of their assumptions about real interactive strategies in order to create their intra-textual interactions. Represented conversations, however, are nothing but tidied-up versions of real talk. The representation of speech is a simplification and a reduction of the organisational characteristics of real interaction.

According to Bell (1991), most information journalists use is second hand and the process of news-making is a case of language produced by multiple parties. The final 'copy', or the actual written news story, is handled by a number of people and follows a complex route. The news source can be a written document or a face-to-face interview, submitted to a chief reporter, who passes it on to a writer who writes up the events into narrative. The chief reporter then checks the text for changes and passes it on to a sub-editor and editor who edit the final copy.

Although we could arrive at an outside source who produced some 'saying' in the real world, since the 'averral' (Sinclair 1986) or the verbal assertion of a fact depends on a saying outside the text, the above complicating situation of authorship makes the process of reporting factual speech very problematic. In some cases two explicit layers of narration could be arrived at – the primary source and the reporter – but both of them could be submitted to questions of truthfulness. However, because of the linguistic property of 'recursiveness' – 'He said that she said that Mary said that . . .' – the quoted saying can be presented through many different voices and the 'real' words become as fictionalised as any dialogue created by a fictional narrator. An example from *The Times* (20 January 1992, p. 10) illustrates this point:

> BBC Television quoted Mr Nazarbayev as saying of his republic's nuclear weapons: 'We are prepared. We are ready to sign all of the treaties . . .'.

In this case, the reporter from *The Times*, Susan Viets, quotes the institutionalised voice (the BBC) as quoting Mr Nazarbayev! The multi-layering of saying makes the direct quote very doubtful.

Who is then ultimately responsible for selecting and organising the representation of a 'saying' in a factual situation? The problem is that the words of a real person, already interpreted and represented according to the point of view of a first reporter, are reinterpreted (and probably changed) by a chain of people. In most cases, a direct attribution to characters in a direct mode:

Mary said: "I will not go there".

or the averral by the teller in an indirect mode

Mary refused to go there.

have nothing to do with people speaking in the real world. The direct mode is a textual strategy which dramatises the narrative, legitimates or evaluates the story being told. The indirect mode marks the explicit interference of the reporter in her/his report. In this mode, there is 'integration' of the secondary discourse into the discourse of the narrator: the primary discourse absorbs the secondary one. The author, therefore, is in complete control of the character's supposed talk, since a speech act verb generally introduces reported utterances that are averred by the author. There is not even the pretence that the voice of the character is heard. In both cases, however, the recounter is always in control of what is being reported, and faithfulness to the words originally produced can always be challenged.

What we have to realise, therefore, is that like rituals, art, games and other symbolic configurations, the representation of people talking in hard news texts is a cultural construct that encodes values. The same supposed words uttered by a real person, for example, can be interpreted and therefore retold differently in different newspapers, according to different points of view and according to different social conventions and roles. The choice of who is given voice depends on the importance given to some people instead of others. But the selection of the speakers, like the representation of people, reflects cultural belief systems and power structures.

5 PAGE TWO MAN

It is not insignificant that *The Times* of 21 January 1992 presents a section on page 2 headed 'Man in the news'.

After examining 35 pages of Home News and 22 pages of International News, it became evident that most texts were about men and written by men. Of the 200 total stories, 149 were written by male writers, 29 by female writers and 22 were press releases. A frequency count of some reference items (see Table 14.1 below), illustrates the differential presence of women and men in the Cobuild *Times* and BBC World Service corpora. It is interesting to note that the words *chairperson* and *spokesperson* generally refer to a woman and not to a man. In one of the examples, *chairperson* was glossed, as if necessary:

Frances D'Souza, female chairperson of the Rushdie Committee . . .
(BBC World Service)

I also looked at frequency counts of other significant lexical items. These items (shown in Table 14.2) demonstrate again the under-representation of women in the written press. The pairs *wife/husband* and *widow/widower* are very important. Although these words do not have a high frequency in the overall corpora, they signal world views. Women are more frequently labelled in their roles as wives and widows than men are as husbands and widowers. I also counted the adverts published in two sections of all the newspapers examined. Not surprisingly, cars, banks, building societies, photocopying machines, business links and hotels for the business men were there. There was only one advert for fitted bedrooms and one clothes shop, which, even then, was advertising

Table 14.1

	The Times	BBC World Service
Miss	1078	2271
Mrs	2462	8505
Ms	165	207
Mr	15586	94951
spokeswoman	60	477
spokesperson	6	20
spokesman	643	7747
chairwoman	6	23
chairperson	2	5
chairman	1817	3255

Table 14.2

	The Times	BBC World Service
she	5417	11103
he	27255	97389
woman	1523	2115
man	1949	7555
wife	637	1218
husband	337	581
widow	89	250
widower	1	3

shirts for men!!! Again, the adverts significantly tell us to whom the discourse is addressed.

If we consider the topics explored in 'hard' news (politics, economy, foreign affairs, relations between governments, report of wars, tragedies or accidents, crime and court reports), we can see that they basically cover the public sphere. 'Soft' news, as the name implies, is often defined by the journalistic profession (Hartley 1982: 38) as having a 'woman's angle', in other words, the sphere of the private life. However, there is an overwhelming bias towards the public as opposed to the private life. Decisions about the economy, politics and working relations are given priority while topics such as personal relations, sexuality, family and working conditions are invisible in the news. Hartley asks the relevant question:

> Are the events that get so much coverage there because they already 'affect our lives', or do they affect our lives largely because they are constantly reported in the news?
>
> (Hartley 1982: 39)

6 WOMEN AS PART OF THE UNACCESSED VOICE GROUP – SOME FIGURES

Since most news is about public issues, it is normal that voice is given to representative personalities. Typically, therefore, the exploitation of a topic includes the opinions and 'arguments' of a privileged body of powerful members of the society. As Fowler suggests, access is a reciprocal relationship between the powerful and the media:

> the media conventionally expect and receive the right of access to the statements of these individuals, because the individuals have roles in the public domain; and reciprocally, these people receive access to the columns of the papers when they wish to air their views.
>
> (Fowler 1991: 22)

This political difference between the accessed and the unaccessed provokes

> an imbalance between the representation of the already privileged, on the one hand, and the already unprivileged, on the other, with the views of the official, the powerful and the rich being constantly invoked to legitimate the status quo.
>
> (Fowler 1991: 22)

Women, in general, are part of the unaccessed voice. To demonstrate this point, I selected from the Cobuild *Times* corpus one example (the most frequent one) of the subcategories of a general taxonomy of verbs of saying (Caldas-Coulthard 1987, 1988). I classified the verbs of saying according to their function in relation to the reported clause.

Neutral and structuring 'glossing' verbs are the ones that introduce a 'saying' without explicitly evaluating it. So, verbs such as *say, tell, ask, inquire* simply signal the illocutionary act – the saying. By using these verbs, the author only gives the reader the 'literal meaning' ('sense' and 'reference' in Austin's terms) of the speech. The intended meaning ('illocutionary force') has to be derived from the saying itself.

The illocutionary glossing verbs are the ones that convey the presence of the author in the text, and are highly interpretative. They name a supposed speech situation, they clarify and make explicit the illocutionary force of the quotation they refer to. These verbs are not only metalinguistic, they are also metapropositional, since they label and categorise the contribution of a speaker. Verbs such as *urge, declare* or *grumble* mark, for example, a directive, an assertive or an expressive proposition. Other verbs are descriptive in relation to the represented interaction. Verbs such as *yell, shout, scream* or *whisper, murmur* mark manner and attitude of speaker in relation to what is being said. Finally, discourse-signalling verbs such as *repeat, add, pause, continue, go on* are not speech-reporting verbs, but very often they accompany direct speech. They mark the relationship of the quote to other parts of the discourse or they mark the development of the discourse. Table 14.3 summarises this taxonomy.

The neutral verb *say* in its past tense from *said* is the most frequent verb in the corpus, with a total occurrence of 14,154 instances. The present-tense form *says* occurs 3634 times. The verb *tell* also in its past form is the next more frequent neutral verb,

Table 14.3

SPEECH-REPORTING VERBS		
NEUTRAL		say, tell
STRUCTURING		ask, inquire
		reply, answer
METAPROPOSITIONAL	assertives	remark, explain
		agree, assent, accept
		correct, counter
	directives	urge, instruct, order
	expressives	accuse, grumble, lament
		confess, complain, swear
METALINGUISTIC		narrate, quote, recount
STAGE-DIRECTION VERBS		
PROSODIC		cry, intone, shout, yell, scream
PARALINGUISTIC	voice qualifier (manner)	whisper, murmur, mutter
	voice qualification (attitude)	laugh, giggle
		sigh, gasp, groan
TRANSCRIPT VERBS		
DISCOURSE	relation to other	repeat, echo, add,
SIGNALLING	parts of discourse	amend
	discourse progress	pause, go on, hesitate, continue

occurring 1445 times. The structuring verb *ask*, in its past form, appears 1050 times. By contrast, all the other reporting verbs occur less than 500 times. The discourse-signalling verb *add* (*added*) occurs 1023 times and the metapropositional *agree* (*agreed*), 794.

I examined 250 occurrences of the more frequent verbs and 150 of the less frequent ones. I also looked at 100 occurrences of those verbs that appear between 100 and 200 times. These were the metapropositional *suggest* (*suggested*) and the discourse-signalling *continue* (*continued*). All the other verbs that occur in the corpus less than 100 times were disregarded.

The main thrust of this research was to verify whether the sayer was a woman or a man. The results are indicative: men are quoted 497 times, women, 62 times.

As expected, the frequency of the descriptive verbs (stage-direction verbs) is very low. However, these verbs point to a crucial linguistic assumption about gender relations. Men 'shout' and 'groan' while women (and children) 'scream' and 'yell'. Other verbs such as *nag, gossip, chatter*, etc are also associated with beliefs which are accepted as common sense within a society and mark stereotypes of particular groups. There is a vocabulary, according to Cameron (1985: 31), which denigrates the talk of women who do not conform to the male ideas of femininity. 'Screaming', 'yelling', 'nagging' mark the negative image of the 'housewife', the 'mother-in-law', the 'mother'. The quotation below exemplifies these assumptions:

> The Labour party is like a wife . . . who is always complaining about her husband to the neighbours and nagging him at home . . .
>
> (Alan Watkins, the *Observer*, 9 February 1992)

Returning to my own corpus of texts, I isolated 451 instances where men were given voice as compared with 76 times for the females.

The piecharts in Figure 14.1 summarise the findings. They show that there is a rhetoric of silencing and alienation at work in the way women are excluded from speaking the news. The figures confirm the theoretical model proposed by the anthropologists S. and E. Ardener of the 'dominant' and 'muted' groups (Ardener 1975). They suggest that in every society the communicative channels are under the control of a dominant group. Women are the 'muted group'. Although they generate a reality of their own, they do not

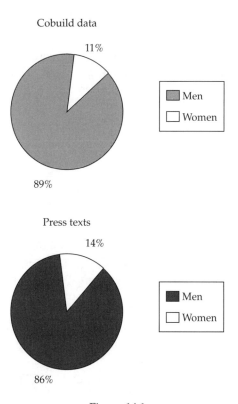

Figure 14.1

have access to ways of expressing this reality linguistically. Cameron (1985: 103), discussing the Ardeners' theories, suggests that for them, silence is not the defining characteristic of a muted group, since women can speak a lot. The question is whether they are able to say what they want to say, in the appropriate place and time.

In the context of the news, women are in statistical terms under-represented linguistically. When given voice, they are not given the same speaking space. Sara Dunn, writing for the women's page of the *Guardian* (20 February 1992, p. 36), states, for example, that women make up 10 per cent of Britain's four million anglers and hold the most coveted salmon fishing record, and she asks the question: 'So why do they get so little coverage in publishing and the press?'

7 HOW WOMEN ARE DESCRIBED IN THE PRESS

The other question I want to discuss here is the differential manner in which women are described when given voice. As I suggested earlier, access is given to representatives of some kind of power – the more powerful or established a person is in an institution, the more attributes she/he will have when introduced as a speaker. I found a cline of modification ranging from the personal name of the speaker through the simple term of address (Mr, Mrs, Miss) or a title (Dr, Lord) to highly complex nominal groups. The categorisation of the speakers depends on his/her role in the power structures.

Generally, male speakers are glossed by their professional designations or position in the government or in some kind of public institution. The following examples (in a cline from simple to complex nominal groups) illustrate the point:

Mr Maxwell
Dr Bartell
Lord Deborough
Jades Camel, the broker
Keith Wafter, medical director of Cilag
Mr Paul Davie, economist
Mr name + surname, the chairman of Warner
Mr name + surname, the Australian syndicate chairman
Mr name + surname, chief opposition spokesman on employment
Mr name + surname, Northern Ireland Education Minister
Prof. Patrick Minford, of the University of Liverpool, a monetarist and supply side economist
Denis Giffod, the founder of ACE the Association for Comics Enthusiast and owner
Dr Jan Pentreath, chief scientist of the government authority
Sir Charles Tidbury, former chairman of Whitbread brewers
The prominent Conservative activist, Paul Weyrich
Clinton, front runner for the Democratic presidential nomination, the Arkansas Governor

Women, on the other hand, are described differently:

Jane Grigson
Mrs Reagan

Miss Hilary Campbell, of Edinburgh
23-year-old Nicole Stewart
His grandmother, Mrs Barbara Wilkinson
Mrs Frances McDaid, his mother
Ursula Vaughan Williams, widow of the composer
Richard's cousin Anne, chain-smoking behind the bar
Tricia Howard, 48, the woman with whom the Liberal democrat
    leader dallied in 1986
Mrs Clasper, a mother of two and part time charity worker
Hilary, Mr Clinton's politically attuned wife
The wife of the front-running Democratic presidential contender,
    Bill Clinton
The 18-year-old Miss Black America beauty pageant contestant
Miss Asia Chorley, of Sotheby's
Lyz Stayce, policy director of Mind
Miss Ann Widdecombe, Conservative MP for . . .
Sara Keays, the colonel's daughter who once hoped to marry the
    then Conservative Party chairman Cecil Parkinson and become
    an MP
Miss Keays, aged 44, left with an epileptic eight-year-old
    daughter

Although we could say that unimportant people, both male and female, are described similarly, either by full name or by a simple term of address, the striking difference between the two columns is that women are, in the main, characterised in terms of marital or family relations, especially in their relationship with a man, and also in terms of age. I could not find any examples where a professional male is presented in relation to a female.

The following made-up examples are unlikely to occur:

Lord MacGregor of Durris, husband of the chairwoman of Blogg,
    Dr Mary Smith
Mr Ted Hughes, widower of the famous poet Sylvia Plath

However, I found this counter-example:

The wife of Dr Wyatt, Dr Vall Hall, said that

Even when women are described in their professional status, the nominal groups qualifying them tend to be shorter, as we can see from the list and examples above.

8 CONCLUDING REMARKS

Quality newspapers, as I indicated, see women as a minority group that is marginalised by being denied the role of speakers. The linguistic differences in the way women are represented in hard news are a reflection of women's lack of access to power, since language is located in a power structure which is, in its turn, reflected in the linguistic production. The male representatives of powerful institutions, frequently accessed, 'provide newspapers with the modes of discourse which already encode the attitudes of a powerful elite' (Fowler 1991: 23). And women, according to the research documented in this chapter, are far from being in powerful positions. The striking disproportion in the way men and women are represented in the news makes clear a more general disproportion which most people do not reflect upon.

By pointing out the differences between the amount of talk given to men in relation to what is given to women, I have tried to make visible these differences, showing that quality newspapers handle women and men as different categories. There is no doubt that language simply reflects 'facts' and the ways society in general treats the genders, but by ignoring the asymmetries we tend to reinforce the stereotypes. As Fowler (*ibid.*: 105) says, 'it would be complacent to accept that the relationship between language and society is merely reflective'. By pointing out the asymmetrical reproduction of power relations between the genders, I hope to make readers aware of the discrimination in practice to which we are exposed daily.

NOTES

1. This is a version of the paper 'From discourse analysis to critical discourse analysis: the differential representation of women and men speaking in the written press', in J. Sinclair, M. Hoey and G. Fox (eds.), *Techniques of Description – Spoken and Written Discourse*, Routledge, London, 1993, 196–208.
2. Both corpora are part of the Bank of English at COBUILD, Collins Birmingham University International Language Database.

FIFTEEN

Commonplaces: the woman in the street: text and image in the work of Jenny Holzer and Barbara Kruger

Helen Hills

The starting point for this chapter is a question raised by Frederic Jameson about the relationship between postmodernism and consumer capitalism:

> There is some agreement that the older modernism functioned against its society in ways which are variously described as critical, negative, contestatory, subversive, oppositional and the like. Can anything of the sort be affirmed about postmodernism and its social moment? We have seen that there is a way in which postmodernism replicates or reproduces – reinforces – the logic of consumer capitalism; the more significant question is whether there is also a way in which it resists that logic.
>
> (Jameson 1984: 73)

The use of the designation 'postmodern' can be seen as part of a strategy to classify and contain diverse and complex practices and to cover over difficulties and differences.[1] The term 'postmodern' has been applied (usually in description rather than definition) in many different, often contradictory ways, suggesting that the usefulness of the term is often greater for critics' careers than conceptually. Certainly it is revealing that already the most prominent names associated with postmodern art and literature tend to be those of men.

However, Jameson's question can be rephrased and is still a demanding one. To criticise consumer culture, do you have to step outside its popular media, to books, oil paints and canvases? Or can you criticise it from within? If it was the modernist strategy to step back from popular culture, perhaps the postmodern strategy may be to engage with it?

I have decided to use the work of Barbara Kruger (b. 1945) and

Jenny Holzer (b. 1950), two contemporary North American female artists, to address Jameson's question.[2] Both of them try to stay within the cultural forms of consumerism in order to criticise it. Are they successful? Do either or both of them manage to resist the logic? Are they successful in their guerilla tactics of undermining closed and hegemonic systems of thought?

My theoretical orientation is derived from the work of Walter Benjamin. His work provides a useful paradoxical approach of involvement in and detachment from, fascination in and critique of, new cultural forms (Benjamin 1973, 1979). This chapter first analyses the work of Barbara Kruger, an artist who uses both texts (usually clichés) and images to explore cultural constructions of gender stereotypes. Next I turn to the work of Jenny Holzer, an artist who uses texts only. In both cases I seek to illuminate the limitations to critical interventions by female artists using words.

Barbara Kruger has described her own work as 'a series of attempts to ruin certain representations and to welcome the female spectator into the audience of men' (Kruger 1984). To do this she uses montages of photographic images with texts. For instance, in an untitled piece of 1983, mannerist large type, stamped over a photograph of the head of a woman, prone, with two leaves over her closed eyes, reads, 'We won't play nature to your culture' (Figure 15.1). Here she attempts to expose the subjugation contained in the binary oppositions of culture/nature and man/woman present in both the elision of eyes and leaves and the angle of the photograph. Meanwhile, her choice of the verb 'play' hints at the element of female complicity. In her work she follows Kristeva (and Foucault and Derrida) in indicating that an effective feminism can only be a negative feminism, deconstructing everything and refusing to construct anything. In Kristeva's words,

A woman cannot be; it is something which does not even belong in the order of being. It follows that a feminist practice can only be negative, at odds with what already exists so that we may say 'that's not it' and 'that's still not it'.

(Kristeva 1981: 137)

In this way Kruger neatly sidesteps one of the central problems of feminist politics: if gender is simply a social construct, the need and even the possibility of a feminist politics becomes immediately problematic. What can we demand in the name of women if

Figure 15.1 Barbara Kruger: Untitled (1983)
('We won't play nature to your culture')
(Courtesy Ydessa Hendeles Collection)

'women' do not exist and demands in their name simply reinforce the myth that they do?[3]

Kruger makes no demands in the name of 'women'. Instead she attempts to reveal aspects of the construction of women. In 1987 she made this statement about her work:

> When I show my work, people ask questions. Whenever they ask what a work means, I say that the construction of meaning shifts. And it shifts according to each spectator.
>
> (Squiers 1987: 79)

Clearly the personal pronouns 'I', 'we', 'you', which Kruger has used in her work since 1980, help to shift meaning.[4] In this she adopts a device of the mass media. Indeed, the colours and forms of Kruger's art works place them somewhere between billboard and old movie; she uses other strategies common to advertising: manipulating letter size, the angle of the text, the relationship of captions to images. Barthes has argued how the mass media personalises all information, makes every utterance a direct challenge, not directed at the entire mass of readers, but at each reader in particular (Barthes 1983: 266). Again, politics have followed: Reagan and Bush, Thatcher and Major appear to deny the existence of social groups between the individual or the family and the great new world. However, Kruger is trying to elbow enough space for the consumer to feel alienated. Her captions are intended to prevent the audience from taking up the position of subject, object or objectifier. The address of Kruger's work is almost always gender specific. Her point however is not that masculinity and femininity are fixed positions assigned in advance by the representational

Figure 15.2 Barbara Kruger: Untitled (1983) ('You are not yourself')
In the collection of Edward R. Downe, Jr., New York. Courtesy of Mary
Boone Gallery, New York.

Figure 15.3 Barbara Kruger: Untitled (1983) ('We have received orders not to move'). Private collection. Courtesy of Mary Boone Gallery, New York.

apparatus. Rather, Kruger uses a term with no fixed content 'I'/'you' in order to demonstrate that masculine and feminine are not stable identities.

Just as Kruger uses 'found' images, so she adopts clichéd phrases. Commonplace phrases are at the heart of Kruger's work: 'Surveillance is your busywork' (1983), 'Captive audience' (1983), 'Fact is stranger than fiction' (1983), 'You are not yourself' (1983) (Figure 15.2). In particular, she incorporates bold phrases adopted from stereotypically male speech patterns to point up the results of the wielding of power that those phrases signify. For instance, in a work of 1983, 'We have received orders not to move', a clichéd phrase from military command, is stamped across the bent-over sil-houetted profile of a woman who is pinned to the surface (Figure 15.3). She cannot move without pain and she is imprisoned behind the text. Here she seeks to show that far from witnessing the death of the author, we have not yet heard her speak.

Figure 15.4 Barbara Kruger: Untitled (1981) ('Your gaze hits the side of my face'). In the collection of Vijak Mahdavi and Bernardo Nadal-Ginard, Boston. Courtesy of Mary Boone Gallery, New York.

Many contemporary artists work within the regime of the stereo-type, manipulating mass-cultural imagery so that hidden ideological agendas are supposedly exposed. But unlike most of these artists, Kruger does not treat the stereotype as something easy to depose. Usually images in magazines or on advertisement hoardings eliminate the need to decode power; Kruger's work has the opposite intention. Increasingly her work uses not stereotypical photographs but images which are emblematical of situations.[5] In Kruger's more recent work neither photo nor text is privileged as truth; what truths come out are a result of the dialectical revision of one by the other. It is the *juxtaposition* of text and image which make this possible. In common with other artists, such as Cindy Sherman, Mary Kelly and Sherrie Levine, Barbara Kruger works with a theoretically informed interrogation of representation to destabilise the image.

In a piece made in 1981 the words 'Your gaze hits the side of my face' are displayed beside a female sculpted head (Figure 15.4). She alludes here to the gaze which objectifies and masters. Foucault has argued that the exercise of power aims at the effective immobilisation of the social body (Foucault 1977: 25); here the exercise of male power immobilises the female body, freezing her as 'art'. An equation is made between aesthetic reflection, the alienation of the gaze, and disempowerment. 'Against the immobility of the pose, Kruger proposes the mobilization of the spectator', claims Craig Owens (Owens 1984: 104). She is striving to show up the position of women within patriarchal capitalism. Her ruptures of conventional stereotypes do not create a new speech; rather, they point to the need for a female voice whose lack they convey.

'Rather than abstracting or repressing daily life into busywork, I became a reporter', she explained in an interview in 1987, '[b]ecause I felt that daily life and the social relations around it are what is repressed in art' (Squiers 1987: 83). A particularly good example of this is an image which shows a giant baby bottle, seen head on, a drop of milk about to drip from its nipple, with these words spilling from it: 'you are getting what you paid for'. At once a comment on consumer dependency and a comment on the consumerism of contemporary politics, this work also addresses the infantilisation that these processes entail.

Kruger's work reminds me of Walter Benjamin's declaration that the ethical task of the modern writer is to be not a creator, but a destroyer – a 'destroyer' of shallow inwardness, of the consoling notion of the universally human, dilettantish creativity, and empty phrases (Benjamin 1979: 157–9).

There is much about Kruger's work which follows Benjamin's direction of the ethical path for a modern artist. Kruger is a destroyer. She uses intertextuality to subvert the patriarchal ideology of our society by engaging directly with its representations, and to subvert them in ways which are ineluctable. Her work focuses on the complex intersections of a schema which contains a vertical class of women crossing the horizontal classes of capitalism and dominated by the vertical and horizontal classes of patriarchy.

The strength of Kruger's work is precisely that she realises that she and her work are inevitably caught up in the web of that nexus. In answer to criticisms about the fact that she was selling her work in commercial galleries rather than printing posters, she replied:

These are *objects* . . . I wanted them to enter the marketplace because I

Figure 15.5 Jenny Holzer: Untitled with selections from Truism. 1984
Electronic LED. Courtesy of Barbara Gladstone Gallery, 99 Greene Street,
New York.

began to understand that outside the market there is nothing – not a
piece of lint, a cardigan, a coffee table, a human being. That's what the
frames were about: how to commodify them.

(Squiers 1987: 84)

Kruger engages with the dominant culture itself. She does not
abandon it in despair to engage in an alternative, because there is
no alternative while these forms are active and untouched, while
their consumers are dormant.

At first sight, the work of Jenny Holzer appears to be more radical, more challenging and subversive than Kruger's deliberately
concentrated, carefully focused work. Physically, it is certainly
more ambitious. Holzer has, by and large, eschewed galleries, the
conquest of high modernism, in order to make art do more than
make money for its producer and the gallery owners. Further, she
has attempted to do what it is not safe for women to do: to feature
alone at night in the street in the big urban centres – London, New
York, Toronto. The anonymity of her work attempts to avoid the
tendency to focus on the person rather than the ideas. Moreover,
she takes advantage of the latest developments in technology to
introduce an anti-elitist and potentially democratic and accessible
cultural form, to erode the old boundary between high culture and
mass or popular culture. This is a brave attempt to engage directly
with the dominant culture itself and an even braver attempt to
engage the man in the street.

The works themselves adopt forms like those Walter Benjamin
seems to be proposing in *One Way Street*:

Significant literary work can only come into being in a strict alternation
between action and writing; it must nurture the inconspicuous forms

Figure 15.6 Jenny Holzer: Truisms, 1982. Installation view, Dokumenta 7, Kassel, Germany. Courtesy of Barbara Gladstone Gallery, 99 Greene Street, New York.

that better fit its influence in active communities than does the pretentious, universal gesture of the book – in leaflets, brochures, articles and placards. Only this prompt language shows itself actively equal to the moment.

(Benjamin 1979: 45)

Holzer's 'prompt language' first appeared in the Truisms (1977–80), a series initially parodying the ideas contained in the Whitney's extensive reading list (Figure 15.5). These mock clichés were intended to make 'the big issues in culture intelligible as public art' (Waldman 1989). Listed alphabetically, they comprise 'Children are the cruellest of all', 'Children are the hope of the future', 'Murder has its sexual side', 'Nothing upsets the balance of good and evil' and 'Your oldest fears are the worst ones'. Contradiction is an important component in all her work. This contradictory approach

Figure 15.7 Jenny Holzer; Selections from Truisms: Spectacolor sign, Times Square, New York, 1982. Courtesy of Barbara Gladstone Gallery, 99 Greene Street, New York.

reveals beliefs and biases, rather than truths:

> 'For the truisms to be operational,' Holzer has explained, 'I have to make them believable – construct them in such a way that if you personally didn't believe them in your heart of hearts, you could certainly see when someone else might.
>
> (Town 1983: 52)

Hal Foster has read as an important grounding for her work the idea that language is true and false; truths are arbitrary. Surprisingly, Holzer hoped her work would make for not simply sharper criticism but greater tolerance, as she explained in an interview in 1985:

> I also wanted to show that truths as experienced by individuals are valid. I wanted to give each assertion equal weight in the hope that the whole series would instill some sense of tolerance in the onlooker or the reader.
>
> (Siegel 1985: 65)

In seeking to understand the implications of Holzer's work, the context in which it appears is crucial. The Truisms were first seen as posters and photocopies on Lower Manhattan walls. Since then

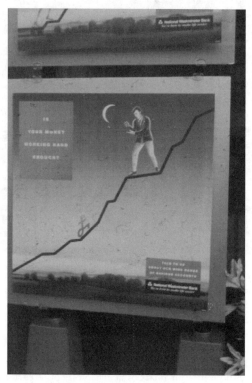

Figure 15.8 Advertisement in Stoke-on-Trent, April 1992
(© Helen Hills)

they have been painted mural size on a building for Dokumenta
(Figure 15.6); they have been displayed on the Spectacolor sign in
Times Square (Siegel 1985: 64); they have hung in the Chase
Manhattan Bank and been removed from that bank because the
statement 'it's not good to operate on credit' ran contrary to the
bank's *modus operandi* (Town 1983: 52). Most recently they have
appeared on T-shirts; on trains; on styrofoam cups, in the same way
that a company tries to encourage its employees by printing incen-
tives on canteen coffee cups. Again, Benjamin may be useful here.
He distinguishes between two ways of seeing art: in concentration
and in distraction. He suggests that it is in distraction that we
wander round cities and experience their architecture. While
Kruger demands our concentration to follow her deconstructive art,
perhaps Holzer's texts are an attempt to allow subversive messages

Figure 15.9 Advertisement in Stoke-on-Trent, April 1992
(© Helen Hills)

to reach us, even while we are in distraction. Certainly Holzer recognises that most of her audience has a very limited attention span:

> I realise that people's attention span, especially if they are on their way to lunch, might be 2.3 seconds and so I try to make each statement have a lot of impact and stand on its own.
> (Siegel 1985: 68)

Tellingly, however, in Toronto her posters were displayed along Queen Street West. They took their place among printed ephemera announcing concerts, events and garage sales. Wealthier up-town areas of Toronto were not postered. There Holzer's posters might be viewed as a 'defacement of private property'. As Elke Town has commented:

> the Queen Street West area also happens to have the highest

Figure 15.10   Advertisement in Stoke-on-Trent, April 1992
(© Helen Hills)

> concentration of artists, galleries, the art-viewing public. This gave
> assurance that Holzer's work might be recognized as art as well as
> noticed by the casual passers-by.
> (Town 1983: 51)

So here is the aestheticisation of the street – or, rather, of particular
streets; and it is doubtful that the works were perceived significantly differently as a result of appearing in such streets rather than
in the galleries that line them. Sometimes, however, the context of
Holzer's work is more challenging. In 1982, for example, nine
Truisms were beamed in 40-second sequences from the Spectacolor
sign above Times Square in central New York (Figure 15.7). They
included 'Money creates taste' and 'Private property created crime'.
These texts were linked by their site and form to
the advertisements all around, while apparently challenging the

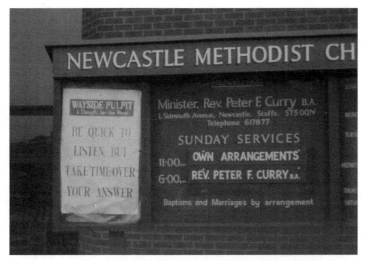

Figure 15.11 Methodist Church noticeboard, Newcastle-under-Lyme,
Stoke-on-Trent, April 1992 (© Helen Hills)

property structures on which capitalist advertising rests.

Are they sincere? Are they ironic? How are we to know what they are? We cannot know and this ambiguity leads to our ambivalence. Is that all she is trying to do? to unsettle our response by removing the apparent clarity of the speaking voice? It's clearly not Vladivar urging us to try some Vodka, but who is it? And that irony and ambiguity cross the fragile line between communication and obfuscation. Afterwards does she want us to carry forward that ambivalence to the next advertisement for Vladivar Vodka? This is certainly the reading of her work offered by Hal Foster. Her signs are subversive he argues:

> for the Truisms expose the false homogeneity of signs of the street among which they are often placed.

> (Foster 1982: 108)

He goes on:

> The Truisms read like a dictionary of [coercive] languages, with the effect that they are depleted, robbed of the fascist power to compel . . . The experience of Truistic entrapment cedes to a feeling of anarchic release. For Truism exposes the coercion that is usually hidden in language, and once exposed, appears ridiculous.

> (Foster 1982: 109)

Foster is arguing that Holzer deconstructs society's circulation of signs, which presents itself as a unified system; that is, that Holzer produces a revelatory moment. This reading rests on the presupposition of a monolithic code, perceived by the subject and open to subversion.[6]

But is the language simply coercive? The problem seems to be that skilful advertising of consumer products already blurs the distinction between communication and obfuscation and – simultaneously – leaves it clearly open. Advertising works through a series of suspensions followed by partial resolutions: 'Is your money working hard enough?' (Figure 15.8); 'How far will your cat go?' (Figure 15.9); 'There is no such thing as a born lover' (Figure 15.10). These suspensions are partially resolved by the answers provided by the posters: 'ask the Natwest Bank'; 'as far as Go-Cat'; 'you have to learn how to be a lover'. But the full resolution comes only with the acquisition of the bank account, the cat food and the book. To that extent the advertiser wants to leave no ambiguity in his or her audience's mind.

It is the absence of explicit resolution in Holzer's work which distinguishes it from the advertisements which usually surround it. Even the most authoritarian and Holzer-like poster that I have come across in Stoke-on-Trent, where I live, leaves a space for the resolution. 'Be quick to listen but take time over your answer' is splashed across the Methodist Church noticeboard, with the dates and times of meetings underneath (Figure 15.11). Advertisements provide the question and the answer. Jenny Holzer gives us answers without the questions. But her answers – unlike the answers of the advertisements – are not products. And, in turn, this points out and by implication questions the activity of advertising: the giving of moral weight to products.

David Burrows and Andrew Williamson have usefully suggested replacing Hal Foster's idea of coercion (culled from Barthes' idea that language is legislation, speech its code; 'to utter a discourse is not, as too often repeated, to communicate; it is to subjugate') with consumption.[7] That is, after all, how capitalism works in the international first world. If this is a condition that is not lived entirely in alienation, then Holzer fails. Again I am reminded of Benjamin:

> fascism sees its salvation in giving [the] masses not their right, but instead a chance to express themselves. The masses have a right to change relations; fascism seeks to give them all expression while

preserving property. The logical result of fascism is the introduction of aesthetics into political life.

(Benjamin 1973: 241)

The forms of expression offered by capitalism may be an ecstatic experience of consumption, rather than one of alienation; one in which property is carefully preserved.

At one level, Holzer is a success. She is internationally known. Her work has appeared in many countries of the world. But the very elasticity of capitalism allows the cannibalisation of her work, a reappropriation against which her work is ill-equipped to guard. As T.J. Clark has argued, perhaps late capitalism *wants* subversive imagery, and prepares for and subsidises it.[8] The rapid consumption of sign values and surface effects may neutralise Holzer's strategies. In spite of a superficially radical stance, her work can be easily rendered the servant of the multinational corporate Big Brother she purports to attack. Ironically, Kruger, by striving to illuminate the very limited possibilities of articulation within cultural representation, manages to go further. And she does so pincering the viewer between text and image. Text alone thus appears insufficient to subvert the texts it attempts to critique; texts and images together can go considerably further by exposing the contradictory mechanisms of cultural constructions. This serves as a reminder of how cultural constructions are extremely complex, composed not just of images or of words, but of the relationships between the two. It is, therefore, with their inter-relationship that feminist scholars should be concerned.

NOTES

1. This is illuminatingly discussed by Janet Wolff (Wolff 1990: 88–90).
2. For biographical information on these artists, see Chadwick (1990) and R. Rosen and C. Brawer (1990: 139–41, 195, 197, 215).
3. This problem is well articulated by L. Alcoff (Alcoff 1988: 415–22).
4. This is discussed by Hal Foster (Foster 1982: 90) and by Craig Owens, drawing on the work of Emile Benveniste (Owens 1984: 98).
5. In this she has shifted from the more simplistic approach of her earlier work. A piece made in 1980, for example, presents a photograph of the torso of a primly dressed woman, her hands clasped neatly together, with the word 'Perfect' emblazoned across it. As Hal Foster has pointed

out, the verbal assault seems too easy here; the stereotype seems set up only to be condemned, with the problematic implication that the artist is free of ideology and that stereotypes are more absolute (and therefore more easily contradicted) than they are (Foster 1982: 89).

6. This assumption is also made by Susan Dyer (Dyer 1992: 18).

7. D. Burrows and A. Williamson, 'The search for Canetti's vanishing point', paper delivered at the Association of Art Historians Annual Conference, Leeds, 1992.

8. T.J. Clark, 'The very idea of the subversive history of art', paper delivered at the Association of Art Historians Annual Conference, 1992. In relation to Holzer, one needs to know the details of the financing of the public display of her work. This central question is – revealingly – ignored in all the interviews and articles about her work I have found.

Conclusions

Sara Mills

This collection of diverse essays on the theme of language and gender has aimed to encourage dialogue across disciplinary boundaries. Rather than simply discussing language and gender so that colleagues and fellow researchers can learn about our work, it is an important part of feminist praxis that we should write in an accessible way so that we make our work available to other researchers from other fields. In this way, we will be able to gain insights from reading about 'our' subject from other perspectives and we will also see our focus and methodology defamiliarised in the process. A further benefit from this interdisciplinary work is that we can accord other perspectives on language and gender the same seriousness that we accord our own discipline's perspective.

This collection of essays has indicated some of the directions which future research might follow. One trend that several of the essays seem to be pursuing is that of studying the language of women or men in very specific contexts, rather than making generalisations about sex-specific language as a whole. When women's language is considered, it is necessary now to specify which type of women's language, in which context, at which historical moment, and so on. A further concern which many of these essays display is to consider sex difference in relational terms: in order to define women's language we need to set that language use in relation to feminine norms, masculine norms and also the actual language use of various groupings of women and men. Certainly, for example, in attempting to define lesbian language, we would need to consider the perceived institutional constraints that heterosexism imposes on language; we would then define the parameters of lesbian language in relation to other uses of language, for example heterosexual female use and the elided male, institutionalised language use. This 'male' usage might be something which lesbian writers would react against or play with in their writing. A similar process may be seen to be at work in heterosexual women's speech and writing, in that, within this developing model of language use, it is not assumed that any grouping of women or men can unproblematically adopt a simple language role. Thus a more fluid notion of what men's and women's language use might be is necessary. Rather than focussing on particular language items which women or men are supposed to use, it might be useful to consider strategies which are used by specific communities of women or men.

It is also clear that the context of occurrence of utterances is becoming increasingly important in the analysis of language and gender. Rather than theoretical statements being made about disembodied pieces of discourse, now the focus of attention is on genre distinctions, differences of register, the differences between literary and non-literary writing, the visual and the textual. This collection of essays has shown that focussing on very specific contexts is particularly productive; focussing on Lebanese boys' language use in mixed-sex conversation or British girls' language use in the foreign-language classroom can tell us a great deal about the way that gender is enacted, rather than seeing gender identity as a static position or role which individual subjects adopt. We can see that the value attributed to male speech or female speech, for example, is not something inherent in particular utterances or speech styles, but rather a factor which is specific to certain contexts. Furthermore, we can then see gender as something which indi-viduals *do*, and about which individuals have some measure of choice. Dorothy Smith's work has been very useful in this context in allowing us to see that gender is something which is constantly worked at; it is a process rather than something which is ever achieved (D. Smith 1990). Many of the essays in this collection, particularly Deborah Cameron's essay, have examined the way that gender identity is negotiated rather than simply being imposed, and this focus is clearly one which will be engaged with in future research.

A further area which many of these essays have addressed is the intersection of variables, for example sexual orientation, class and race. Whilst many theorists have gestured in the direction of analysing the gendered aspects of language in relation to other variables, few theorists have gone on to demonstrate the ways in which this more complex form of research can be undertaken.

These essays have attempted to consider the way that other variables might be considered, for example Black lesbian writing, children's gendered language. Future research will need to map out strategies for researchers to analyse data in complex ways. For example, it is now becoming clear that sexual orientation is not simply a concern which homosexual women and men need to consider but something which needs to be addressed specifically by heterosexuals (see Kitzinger *et al* 1993). Racial identity is a concern which white women and men need to consider and not just Black women and men (Frankenberg 1994).

All of these essays have demonstrated an unease with current research in language and gender, a suspicion of the very terms that we use when we describe both language and gender identity. It is a healthy suspicion of certainties which has moved research in this field away from a concern with concrete items which indicate male or female language to a concern with the problems of interpretation, the difficulty of knowing exactly what a particular item means. This concern has led to several of the essays, (for example Alison Lee *et al*.'s analysis of the difficult process of assigning gender identity to children's voices, and Helen Hills' analysis of the difficulty of fixing an interpretation on language strategies in women artists' work), considering the different ways that language items can be interpreted. This lack of fixity does not lead to theoretical impasse as many theorists have predicted, but rather this sceptical concern with interpretation and the resultant attempt to map out the parameters of interpretation is a trend which will lead to productive future research.

The diversity of approach of these essays signals a lively area of research where there is still much work to be done and more arguments to be engaged in. It has been one of the pleasures of working on this collection that the essays have not focussed exclusively on the constraining elements which oppress and restrict women's language choices. Instead, at the same time as recognising that different groups of women are constrained by the language choices and roles available to them, it is clear that many of these essays suggest that women and men can intervene in language to negotiate their own positions and to question the way that hierarchies are currently organised. It is this type of work which can be genuinely empowering to women, which can lead us to consider the ways in which we can change those structures which constrain us.

Bibliography

Abberton, E., Howard, D. and Fourcin, A. (1989) Laryngographic assessment of normal voice; a tutorial, *Clinical Linguistics and Phonetics*, 89, 281–96.

Agheysi, R. and Fishman, D. (1970) Language attitude surveys: a brief survey of methological approaches, *Anthropological Linguistics*, 12, 137–57.

Alcroff, L. (1988) Cultural feminism versus postructuralism: the identity crisis in feminist theory, *Signs*, 13, part 3, 405–36

Altani, C. (1992) Gender construction in classroom interaction, unpublished PhD thesis, Dept of Linguistics, University of Lancaster.

Andersen, E. S. (1978) Will you don't snore, please? Directives in young children's role-play speech *Papers and Reports on Child Language Development*, 15, 140–50.

Ardener, S. (ed.) (1965) *Perceiving Women*, Malaby Press, London.

Ardill S. and O'Sullivan, S. (1990) Butch femme obsessions, *Feminist Review*, 34: 79–85.

Aries, E. (1976) Interaction patterns and themes of male, female and mixed groups, *Small Group behaviour* 7 (1), 7–18

Armitt, L. (ed.) (1991) *Where no Man has Gone Before: Women and Science Fiction*, Routledge, London.

Arnot, M. (1986) State education policies and girls' educational experience, pp. 136–65 in v. Beechey and E. Whitelegg (eds) *Women in Britain Today*, Open University Press, Milton Keynes.

Atkinson, K. (in press) *Elderly Talk*, Longman, London.

Attenborough, D. (1990) *The Trials of Life*, Collins/BBC, London.

Austin, J. (1962) *How to Do Things with Words*, Clarendon, Oxford.

Baken, R. (1987) *Clinical Measurement of Speech and Voice*, Taylor and Francis, London.

Bakhtin, M. (1981) *The Dialogic Imagination: Four Essays* (ed. Holquist, M.), University of Texas Press, Austin.

Balmer, J. (trans 1992) *Sappho: Poems and Fragments*, Bloodaxe Books, Newcastle.

Barker, D. (1988) Saving money and the world, *Guardian*, 11 November.

Barnes, D. Britton, J. and Rosen, H. (1971) *Language, the Learner and the School*, Penguin, Harmondsworth.

Barnes, D. (1928a) Introduction to the selected letters of Elsa von Freytag Loringhoven, *transition*, 11, 19–20.

Barnes, D. (1928b) *The Ladies Almanack*, Darrantière, Dijon.

Barnes, D. (1936) *Nightwood*, Faber and Faber, London.

Barnes, D. (1971) Language in the secondary classroom, pp. 11–77 in Barnes, Britton and Rosen 1971.

Barnes, D. (1981) *Creatures in an Alphabet*, Dial, New York.

Barnes, D. (1988) The politics of oracy, pp. 45–54 in M. Maclure, T. Phillips and A. Wilkinson (eds) *Oracy Matters*, Open University Press, Milton Keynes.

Barr, M. S. (1981) (ed.) *Future Females: A Critical Anthology*, Bowling Green University Popular Press, Bowling Green, OH.

Barthes, R. (1977) Structural analysis of narratives, pp. 79–124 in S. Heath (ed.) *Image, Music Text*, London, Collins.

Barthes, R. (1983) *The Fashion System*, (trans M. Ward and R. Howard), New York.

Beckman, H. B. and Frankel, R. M. (1984) The effect of physician behaviour on the collection of data, *Annals of Internal Medecine*, 101, 692–6

Beddoe, D. (1984) Hindrance or help-meets: women in the writings of George Orwell, pp. 139–54 in C. Norris (ed.) *Inside the Myth*, Lawrence and Wishart, London.

Belenky, M., Clinchy, B., Goldberger, N. and Tarule, J. (1988) *Women's Ways of Knowing*, Basic Books, New York.

Bell, A. (1991) *The Language of the News Media*, Blackwell, Oxford.

Benjamin, W. (1973) The work of art in the age of mechanical reproduction, pp. 209–44 in *Illuminations*, New Left Books, London.

Benjamin, W. (1979) *One Way Street and Other Writings*, New Left Books, London.

Bennett, S. (1981) Vowel formant frequency characteristics of preadolescent males and females. *Journal of the Acoustical Society of America*, 69: 231–8

Bennett, S. (1983) A 3 year longitudinal study of school-aged children's fundamental frequencies. *Journal of Speech and Hearing Research*, 26: 137–42.

Bennett, S. and Weinberg, B. (1979a) Sexual characteristics of pre-adolescent children's voices, *Journal of Acoustical Society of America*, 65: 179–89.

Bennett, S. and Weinberg, B.(1979b) Acoustic correlates of perceived sexual identity in pre-adolescent children's voices, *Journal of the Acoustical Society of America*, 66: 989–100

Benton, J. R. (1992) *The Medieval Menagerie: Animals in Art in the Middle Ages*, Abbeville, New York.

Bergk, T. (1982) *Poetae Lyrici Graeci*, Vol 3, Leipzig, Teubner.

Bergen, A. (1983) Language and the female in early Greek thought, *Arethusa*, 16, 69–95.

Berryman, C. (1980) Attitudes towards male and female sex-appropriate and sex-inappropriate language, in C. Berryman and C. Eman (eds) *Communication, Language and Sex*, Newbury House, Rowley, MA.

Birke, L. (1991) Science, feminism and animal natures I: extending the boundaries, and II: Feminist critiques and the places of animals in science, pp. 443–5 and 451–8 in *Women's Studies International Forum*, XIV, 5.

Black, M. and Coward, R. (1990) Linguistic, social and sexual relations: a review of Dale Spender's *Man Made Language*, pp. 111–33 in Deborah Cameron (ed.) *The Feminist Critique of Language: A Reader*, Routledge, London.

Blackman, I. and Perry, K. (1990) Skirting the issue: lesbian fashion for the 1990s, *Feminist Review*, 34: 67–78.

Bladon, R. Henton, C. and Pickering, J. (1984) Outline of an auditory theory of speaker normalisation, in M. van den Broecke and A. Cohen (eds) *Proceedings of the Xth International Congress of Phonetic Sciences*, Foris, Dordrecht.

Bleier, R. (1984) *Science and Gender*, Pergamon, London.

Bleier, R. (1988) (ed.) *Feminist Approaches to Science*, Pergamon, London.

Bourdieu, R. and Passeron, J. (1990) *Reproduction in Education, Society and Culture*, Sage, London (2nd edition).

Braxton, J. M. and McLaughlin, A. N. (eds) (1990) *Wild Women in the Whirlwind: Afra-American Culture and the Contemporary Literary Renaissance*, Serpent's Tail, London.

Broe, M. L. (1991) (ed.) *Silence and Power: Djuna Barnes, a Re-evaluation*, Southern Illinois University Press, Carbondale.

Bulkin, E. and Larkin, Joan (1981) *Lesbian Poetry: An Anthology*, Persephone Press, MA.

Burstall, C., Jamieson, M., Cohen, S. and Hargreaves, M. (1974) *Primary French in the Balance*, National Foundation for Educational Research, Windsor.

Butler, J. (1990) *Gender Trouble: Feminism and the Subversion of Identity*, Routledge, London and New York.

Butler, O. (1977) *Mind of my Mind*, Doubleday, New York.

Butler, O. (1988) *Dawn*, VGSF, London.

Butler, O. (1989) *Adulthood Rites*, VGSF, London.

Butler, O. (1990) *Imago*, VGSF, London.

Cadigan, P. (1991) *Synners*, Bantam, New York.

Calame, C. (1986) Le récrit en Grèce ancienne: énonciations et représentations des poètes, Paris, Meridiens-Klincksieck.

Caldas-Coulthard, C. (1987) Reporting speech in narrative written texts, in R. Coulthard (ed.) *Discussing Discourse*, Discourse Analysis Monographs, no. 14, ELR, University of Birmingham.

Caldas-Coulthard, C. (1988) Reported interaction in narrative: a study of speech representation in written discourse, unpublished PhD thesis, University of Birmingham.

Cameron, D. (1992) *Feminism and Linguistic Theory*, Macmillan, London (first published 1985).

Cameron, D., McAlinden, F. and O'Leary, K. (1988) Lakoff in context: the social and linguistic functions of tag questions, pp. 13–26 in J. Coates and D. Cameron (eds) *Women in their Speech Communities*, Longman, Harlow.

Cameron, D. (ed.) (1990) *The Feminist Critique of Language: A Reader*, Routledge, London.

Campbell, B. (1984) Orwell-paterfamilias or Big Brother, pp. 126–38 in C. Norris (ed.) *Inside the Myth*, Lawrence and Wishart, London.

Campbell, B. (1988) Master class, *Guardian*, 5 October, p. 16.

Campbell, D. A. (ed.) (1982) *Greek Lyric I and II*, Heineman, Cambridge, MA, and London.

Campbell, K. and Jerry, C. (1988) Woman and speaker: a conflict in roles, in S. S. Brehm (ed.) *Seeing Female: Social Roles and Personal Lives*, Greenwood Press, New York.

Cantarella, E. (1992) *Bisexuality in the Ancient World*, Yale University Press, New Haven and London.

Carr, H. (ed.) (1989) *From My Guy to Sci-Fi: Genre and Women's Writing in the Postmodern World*, Pandora, London.

Chadwick, W. (1990) *Women, Art and Society*, Thames and Hudson, London.

Cheshire, J. and Jenkins, N. (1991) Gender issues in the GCSE oral English examination, Part II, pp. 19–40, *Language and Education*, 5, 1

Chibnall, S. (1977) *Law and Order News*, Tavistock, London.

Chodorow, N. (1978) *The Reproduction of Mothering*, University of California Press, Berkeley.

Cixous, H. and Clement, C. (1986) *The Newly Born Women*, trans Betsey Wing, Manchester University Press, Manchester.

Claire, H. (1986) Collaborative work as an anti-sexist process, pp. 43–5 in Inner London Education Authority *Primary Matters: Some Approaches to Equal Opportunities in the Primary School*, ILEA, London.

Clark-Stewart, K. (1973) Interactions between mothers and their young children: characteristics and consequences, *Monographs of the Society for Research in Child Development*, 38 (153), 1–109.

Clarricoates, K. (1978) Dinosaurs in the classroom – a re-examination of some aspects of the hidden curriculum in primary schools, *Women's Studies International Quarterly*, 1, 353–64.

Clarricoates, K. (1983) Classroom interaction, pp. 46–61 in J. Whyld (ed.) *Sexism in the Secondary Curriculum*, Harper and Row, London.

Clifton, R., Perry, R., Parsonson, K., Hyrniuk, S. (1986) Effects of ethnicity and sex on teachers' expectations of junior high school students, *Sociology of Education*, 59, 58–67.

Coates, J. (1986) *Women, Men and Language*, Longman, London (2nd edition 1993).

Coates, J. (1989a) Gossip revisited: language in all-female groups, pp. 94–121 in J. Coates and D. Cameron (eds) *Women in their Speech Communities*, Longman, London.

Coates, J. (1989b) Women's speech, women's strength?, *York Papers in Linguistics*, 13, 65–76.

Coates, J. (1991) Women's cooperative talk: a new kind of conversational duet?, pp. 296–311 in Claud Uhlig and Rudiger Zimmerman (eds) *Proceedings of the Anglistentag 1990 Marburg*, Max Niermeyer Verlag, Tubingen.

Coates, J. (1994) No gaps, lots of overlap: turn-taking in the talk of women friends, pp. 177–92 in D. Graddoll, J. Maybin and B. Stierer (eds) *Researching Language and Literacy in Social Context*, Clevedon Avon, Multilingual Matters / Open University.

Coates, J. (forthcoming) *Women Talking to Women*, Blackwell, Oxford.

Cohen, L. and Manion, L. (1985) *Research Methods in Education*, Croom Helm, London.

Coleman, R. (1971) Male and female voice quality and its relationship to vowel formant frequencies, *Journal of Speech and Hearing Research*, 14: 565–71.

Collecott, D. (1990) What is not said: a study in textual inversion, *Textual Practice*, vol. 4, no. 2, pp. 236–58.

Cornet, G., Rilou-Bourret, V. and Louis, M. (1971) Contribution à l'enfant normal de 5 à 9 ans, *Folia Phoniatrica*, 23: 381–9.

Coulthard, R. (1977) *Introduction to Discourse Analysis*, Longman, London.

Coward, R. (1998) The sex life of stick-insects, pp. 207–15 in *Female Desire*, Paladin, London.

Cranny-Francis, A. (1990) *Feminist Fiction*, Basil Blackwell/Polity, Cambridge.

Crowther, B. (forthcoming) Towards a feminist critique of television natural history programmes, in P. Florence and D. Reynolds (eds) *Feminist Subjects: Multi-Media*, Manchester University Press, Manchester.

Daley, J. (1990) Some women confine themselves to the nursery pool of life, *Independent* 20 December, p. 16.

Davies, B. (1989) *Frogs and Snails and Feminist Tales*, Allen and Unwin, Sydney.

Davies, L, Meighan, R. (1975) A review of schooling and sex roles, *Educational Review*, 27 (3) 165–78.

DeFrancisco, V. (1991) The sounds of silence: how men silence women in marital relations, *Discourse and Society*, 2 (4), 413–24.

Delamont, S. (1990) *Sex Roles and the School*, Methuen, London (first published 1980).

De Lauretis, R. (1989) *Technologies of Gender*, Macmillan, London.

Department of Education and Science (1975) *A Language for Life*, London, HMSO, The Bullock Report.

Department of Education and Science (1992) *Curriculum Education and Practice in Primary Schools: Discussion Document*, London, HMSO.

Derrida, J. (1973) *Speech and Phenomena and Other Essays on Husserl's Phenomenology of Signs*, Northwestern University Press, Evanston, ILL.

DeShazer, M. K. (1986) *Inspiring Women: Reimagining the Muse*, Pergamon Press, New York.

Dover, K. J. (1978) *Greek Homosexuality*, Duckworth, London.

DuBois, P. (1984) Sappho and Helen, pp. 95–105 in J. Perradotto and J. P. Sullivan (eds) *Women in the Ancient World*, SUNY Press, Albany NY.

Duplessis, R. B. (1985) *Writing beyond the Ending: Narrative Strategies of Twentieth Century Women Writers*, Indiana University Press, Bloomington.

Duplessis, R. B. (1986) *H.D. the Career of that Struggle*, Harvester Press, Brighton.

Dyer, S. (1992) The sybil's cave revisited: Jenny Holzer, *Women's Art Magazine*, no. 46, 17–18.

Eakins, N. and Eakins, G. (1976) Verbal turntaking and exchanges in faculty dialogue, in M. Dubois and I. Crouch (eds) *The Sociology of the Language of American Women*, Papers in Southwest English IV, Trinity University, San Antonio.

Edelsky, C. (1981) Who's got the floor? *Language in Society*, 10, 383–421.

Edwards, V. (1988) The speech of British Black women in Dudley, West Midlands, pp. 35–50 in J. Coates and D. Cameron (eds) *Women in their Speech Communities*, Longman, Harlow.

Eguchi, S. and Hirch, I. (1969) Development of speech sounds, *Acta Otalyrngologica Supplementum*, 257: 5–48.

Ervin-Tripp, S. (1977) Wait for me, roller-skate! pp. 165–88 in S. Ervin-Tripp and C. Mitchell-Kernan (eds) *Child Discourse*, Academic Press, New York.

Esposito, A. (1979) Sex differences in children's conversation, *Language and Speech*, 22: 213–30.

EURIDYCE (1988) The Greek Education System (revd edn), Commission of the European Community's Task Force.

Eveleyn, J. and M. (1690) *Mundus Muliebris*, London.

Faderman, L. (1985) *Surpassing the Love of Men*, Women's Press, London.

Fairclough, N. (1989) Discourse representation in media discourse *Sociolinguistics*, 17: 125: 39.

Fairclough, N. (1992) *Discourse and Social Change*, Polity Press, Cambridge.

Fairclough, N. (1993) Critical discourse analysis and the marketisation of public discourse: the universities, *Discourse and Society*, 4 (2), 138–68.

Falk, J. (1980) The conversational duet, *Proceedings of the 6th Annual Meeting of the Berkeley Linguistics Society*, 6, 506–14.

Field, A. (1985) *Djuna: The Formidable Miss Barnes*, Texas University Press, TX.

Fischer, J. L. (1958) Social influences on the choice of linguistic variant, *Word*, 14, 47–56.

Fisher, J. (1991) Unequal voices: gender and assessment, pp. A106–A111 in Open University *Talk and Learning*, 5–16, The Open University, Milton Keynes.

Fisher, S. (1991) A discourse of the social: medical talk / power talk / oppositional talk, *Discourse and Society*, 2 (2), 157–82.

Fishman, P. (1978) What do couples talk about when they're alone? pp. 11–22 in D. Butturf and E. L. Epstein (eds) *Women's Language and Style*, Department of English, University of Akron.

Fishman, P. (1980) Interactional shitwork, *Heresies*, 2, 99–101.

Fishman, P. (1983) Interaction: the work women do, pp. 89–101 in B. Thorne and N. Henley (eds) *Language, Gender and Society*, Newbury House, Rowley, MA.

Fishman, P. (1990) Conversational insecurity, pp. 234–41 in D. Cameron (ed.) *The Feminist Critique of Language*, Routledge, London.

Foley, H. P. (ed.) (1981) *Reflections of Women in Antiquity*, Gordon and Breach, New York.

Foster, H. (1982) Subversive signs, *Art in America*, Vol. 70, Part II, 88–92.

Foucault, M. (1987) *The History of Sexuality*, vol. 2, Penguin, London.

Fowler, R. (1991) *Language in the News*, Routledge, London.

Frankel, R. (1983) The laying on of hands: aspects of the organisation of gaze, touch and talk in a medical encounter, pp. 19–54 in Sue Fisher and Alexandra Dundas Todd (eds) *The Social Organisation of Doctor–Patient Communication*, Centre for Applied Linguistics, Washington, DC.

Frankel, R. (in press) Talking in interviews: a dispreference for patient initiated questions, in G. Psathas (ed.) *Interactional Competence*, Irvington, New York.

Frankenberg, R. (1994) *White Women, Race Matters: The Social Construction of Whiteness*, Routledge, London.

French, J. and French, P. (1984) Gender imbalance in the primary classroom: an interactional account, pp. 127–36 in *Educational Research*, 26, 2.

Fuss, D. (1989) *Essentially Speaking: Feminism, Nature and Difference*, Routledge, London.

Gallop, J. (1982) *Feminism and Psychoanalysis: The Daughter's Seduction* Macmillan, London.

Garvey, C. (1975) Requests and responses in children's speech, *Journal of Child Language*, 2: 41–63.

Gerrard, N. (1989) *Into the Mainstream: How Feminism has Changed Women's Writing*, Pandora, London.

Gibson, W. (1986) *Neuromancer*, Grafton, London.

Gilligan, C. (1982) *In a Different Voice*, Harvard University Press, Cambridge, MA.

Gilligan, C., Ward, J. and Taylor, J. M. (eds) (1988) *Mapping the Moral Domain*, Harvard University Press, Cambridge, MA.

Goffman, E. (1981) *Forms of Talk*, Blackwell, Oxford.

Goodwin, M. (1980) Directive-response speech sequences in girls' and boys' task activities, pp. 157–73 in Sally McConnell-Ginet *et al.* (eds) *Women and Language in Literature and Society*, Praeger, New York.

Goodwin, M. (1982) Processes of dispute management among urban black children, *American Ethnologist*, 9, 799–819.

Goodwin, M. (1988) Co-operation and competition across girls' play activities, pp. 55–94 in Alexandra Dundas Todd and Sue Fisher (eds) *Gender and Discourse: The Power of Talk*, Ablex, NJ.

Goodwin, M. (1992) *He-said, She-said* Indiana University Press, Bloomington and Indianapolis.

Graddol, D. and Swann, J. (1989) *Gender Voices*, Blackwell, Oxford.

Graddol, D. and Swann, J. (1993) The English debate in British education: defining a professional response, paper presented to the Vth Convention on Language in Education, University of East Anglia, March.

Grice, H. P. (1975) Logic and conversation, pp. 41–58 in P. Cole and J. L. Morgan (eds) *Syntax and Semantics vol. 3: Speech Acts*, Academic Press, New York.

Gross, A. (1990) *The Rhetoric of Science*, Harvard University Press, Cambridge, MA.

Gubar, S. (1984) Sapphistries, *Signs: Journal of Women in Culture and Society*, 10 (1), 43–62.

Gunzburger, D., Bresser, A. and Ter Keurs, M. (1987) Voice identification of prepubertal boys and girls by normally sighted and visually handicapped subjects, *Language and Speech*, 30: 47–58.

Haden Elgin, S. (1985) *Native Tongue*, Women's Press, London.

Haden Elgin, S. (1987) Women's language and near future science fiction: a reply, *Women's Studies*, 14, 175–81.

Hall, C. (1985) Private persons versus public someones: class, gender and politics in England 1780–1850, pp. 10–33 in Carolyn Steedman, Cathy Urwin and Valerie Walkerdine (eds) *Language, Gender and Childhood*, Routledge, London.

Hall, R. (1928) *The Well of Loneliness*, Cape, London.

Halliday, M. (1985) *An Introduction to Functional Grammar*, Arnold, London.

Halperin, D. M. (1990) *One Hundred Years of Homosexuality and Other Essays on Greek Love*, Routledge, New York and London..

Haraway, D. (1985) A manifesto for cyborgs: science, technology and socialist feminism in the 1980s, *Socialist Review*, 80, Part 80, 65–107, and also in L. Nicholson (ed.) *Feminism/Postmodernism*, Routledge, London, 1990.

Haraway, D. (1988) Primatology is politics by other means. pp. 77–118 in R. Bleier (ed.) *Feminist Approaches to Science*, Pergamon, London.

Haraway, D. (1992) *Primate Visions*, Verso, London.

Harding, S. (1986) *The Science Question in Feminism*, Open University Press, Milton Keynes.

Harding, S. (1991) Feminism and theories of scientific knowledge, *Women: A Cultural Review*, 1, 1, 87–98.

Harris, S. (1984) Questions as a mode of control in magistrates' courts, *International Journal of the Sociology of Language*, 49, 5–27.

Hartley, J. (1982) *Understanding News*, Methuen, London.

Hasek, C. and Singh, S. (1980) Acoustic attributes of preadolescent voices, *Journal of the Acoustical Society of America*, 68: 1262–5.

Hertz, N. (1985) A reading of Longinus, pp. 1–20 in *The End of the Line: Essays on Psychoanalysis and the Sublime*, Columbia University Press, New York.

H.D. (1984) *Collected Poems 1912–1944*, Manchester University Press, Manchester.

Hirano, M., Kurita, S. and Nakashima, T. (1983) The structure of vocal folds, pp. 33–41 in K. Stevens and M. Hirano (eds) *Vocal Fold Physiology*, University of Tokyo Press, Tokyo.

Hobby, E. (1988) *Virtue of Necessity*, Virago, London.

Holmes, J. (1987) Hedging, fencing and other conversational gambits: an analysis of gender differences in New Zealand speech, pp. 59–79 in Anne Pauwels (ed.) *Women and Language in Australian and New Zealand Society*, Australian Professional Publication, Sydney.

Holmes, J. (1992) Women's voices in public contexts, *Discourse and Society*, 3, 2, 131–50.

Humm, M. (1991) *Border Traffic: Strategies of Contemporary Women Writers*, Manchester University Press, Manchester.

Hunter, W. and Garn, S. (1972) Disproportionate sexual dimorphism in the human face, *American Journal of Psychical Anthropology*, 36: 133–8.

Huyssen, A. (1986) *After the Great Divide: Modernism, Mass Culture, Postmodernism*, Indiana University Press, Bloomington.

Hymes, D. H. On communicative competence, in J. Pride and J. Holmes (eds), *Sociolinguistics*, Penguin, Harmondsworth.

I.D. (1992) The Technology issue, no. 102, March.

Irigaray, L. (1980) When our lips speak together, pp. 35–72, trans Carolyn Burke, *Signs: Journal of Women in Culture and Society* 6, (1).

Irigaray, L. (1985a) *Speculum of the Other Woman*, trans G. C. Gill, Cornell University Press, Ithaca, New York.

Irigaray, L. (1985b) 'This sex which is not one' in *This Sex which is not One*, trans C. Porter with C. Burke, Cornell University Press, Ithaca, New York.

Irigaray, L. (1986) *Divine Women*, trans C. Mueke, Local Consumption Occasional Papers 8, Sydney.

Jabbra, N. (1980) Sex roles and language in Lebanon, *Ethnology*, 19–4, 459–74.

Jameson, F. (1984) Postmodernism or the cultural logic of late capitalism, *New Left Review*, 146, 53–92.

Jameson, F. (1985) Postmodernism and consumer society, pp. 111–25 in H. Foster (ed.) *Postmodern Culture*, Pluto, London and Sydney.

Jameson, F. (1991) *Postmodernism or the Cultural Logic of Late Capitalism*, Verso, London and New York.

Jay, K. (1988) *The Amazon and the Page: Natalie Clifford-Barney and Renee Vivien*, Indiana University Press, Bloomington.

Jay, K. (1991) The outsider among the expatriates: Djuna Barnes and the ladies of the Almanac, in L. Broe (ed.) *Silence and Power: Djuna Barnes, a Re-evaluation*, Southern Illinois University Press, Carbondale.

Jefferson, A. (1989) Bodymatters, pp. 152–77 in K. Hirschkop and D. Shepherd (eds) *Bakhtin and Cultural Theory*, Manchester University Press, Manchester.

Jenkins, N. and Cheshire, J. (1990) Gender issues in the GCSE oral English examination Part I, *Language and Education*, 4, 4, 261–92.

Johnson, J. (1990) What is the project saying about assessment?, *Oracy Issues* no. 5, Autumn, 1–4.

Jones, D. (1980) Gossip: notes on women's oral culture, pp. 193–8 in C. Kramarae (ed.) *The Voices and Words of Women and Men*, Pergamon, Oxford.

Kalcik, S. (1975) . . . like Ann's gynaecologist or the time I was almost raped – personal narratives in women's rap groups, *Journal of American Folklore*, 88, 3–11.

Kent, R. (1976) Anatomical and neuromuscular maturation of the speech mechanism: evidence from acoustic studies, *Journal of Speech and Hearing Research*, 19: 421–47.

Kessler, S. and McKenna, W. (1978) *Gender: An Ethnomethodological Approach*, University of Chicago, Chicago and London.

Kirchner, J. (1970) *Physiology of the Larynx*, Rochester, MN.

Kitzinger, C. *et al.* (eds) (1993) *Heterosexuality*, Sage Publications, London.

Korg, J. (1979) *Language in Modern Literature: Innovation and Experiment*, Harvester Press, Brighton.

Kristeva, J. (1981) Woman can never be defined, pp. 137–41 in E. Marks and I. DeCourtivron (eds) *New French Feminisms*, University of Massachusetts Press, New York.

Kruger, B. (1984) *Press Release*, Annina Nosei Gallery, New York.

Labov, W. (1972) The transformation of experience in narrative syntax, in *Language in the Inner City*, University of Pennsylvania Press, Philadelphia.

Lakoff, R. (1975) *Language and Woman's Place*, Harper and Row, New York.

Landon, B. (1991) Bet on it: Cyber/video/punk/performance, pp. 239–44 in L. McCaffery *Storming the Reality Studio*, Duke University, Durham, NC.

Lanser, S. S. (1991) 'Speaking in tongues': Ladies Almanack and the discourse of desire, pp. 156–69 in Broe 1991.

Lass, N., Hughes, K., Bowyer, M., Waters, L. and Bourne, V. (1976) Speaker sex identification from voiced, whispered and filtered isolated vowels, *Journal of the Acoustical Society of America*, 59: 675–8.

Leary, T. (1991) The cyberpunk: the individual as reality pilot, pp. 245–58 in L. McCaffery (ed.) *Storming the Reality Studio*, Duke University, Durham, NC.

Leet-Pellegrini, H. M. (1980) Conversational dominance as a function of gender and expertise, pp. 97–104 in H. Giles, W. Robinson and P. Smith (eds) *Language: Social Psychological Perspectives*, Pergamon, Oxford.

Lefanu, S. (1988) *In the Chinks of the World Machine*, The Women's Press, London.

Leith, D. and Myerson, G. (1989) *The Power of Address*, Routledge, London.

Lesbian History Group (1989) *Not a Passing Phase: Lesbians in History 1840–1985*, Women's Press, London.

Levi-Strauss, C. (1968) *Structural Anthropology*, Penguin, Harmondsworth.

Lewis, G. (1990) Audre Lorde: Vignettes and mental conversations, *Feminist Review*, 34, 100–15.

Lorde, A. (1978) *The Black Unicorn: Poems*, W. W. Norton, New York.

Lorde, A. (1982a) *Chosen Poems – Old and New*, W. W. Norton, New York.

Lorde, A. (1982b) *Zami: A New Spelling of My Name*, Sheba, London.

Lorde, A. (1986) *Our Dead Behind Us*, Sheba, London.

Lorde, A. (1984) *Sister Outsider: Essays and Speeches by Audrey Lorde*, Crossing Press, New York.

Lorde, A. (1988a) *A Burst of Light: Essays by Audre Lorde*, Sheba, London.

Lorde, A. (1988b) Age, race, class and sex, pp. 269–76 in McEwen and O'Sullivan 1988.

Lovenduski, J. (1989) Euro resolve, *Guardian*, 6 June, p. 17.

Maccoby, E. and Jacklin, C. (1974) *The Psychology of Sex Differences*, Stanford University Press, Stanford.

Maltz, D. and Borker, R. (1982) A cultural approach to male female miscommunication, pp. 195–216 in John Gumperz (ed.) *Language and Social Identity*, Cambridge University Press, Cambridge.

Manning, M. with Haddock, P. (1989) *Leadership Skills for Women: Achieving Impact as a Manager*, Crisp Publication, California.

Martin, E. (1991) The egg and the sperm: how science has constructed a romance based on stereotypical male and female roles, *Signs*, 16, 3, 485–501.

Mattingly, I. (1966) Speaker variation and vocal tract size, *Journal of the Acoustical Society of America*, 39: 1219 (abstract).

McCaffery, L. (ed.) (1991) *Storming the Reality Studio*, Duke University, Durham, NC.

McConnell-Ginet, S. *et al.* (eds) (1982) *Women and Language in Literature and Society*, Praeger, New York.

McEwan, C. and O'Sullivan, S. (eds) (1988) *Out the Other Side: Contemporary Lesbian Writing*, Virago, London.

McHale, B. (1987) *Postmodern Fiction*, Methuen, New York and London.

McHale, B. (1991) POSTcyberMODERNpunkISM, pp. 308–23 in McCaffery 1991.

McIntyre, V. (1984) *Superluminal*, Pocket, New York.

McNeil, M. and Franklin, S. (1991) Science and technology: questions for cultural studies and feminism, pp. 129–46 in Franklin *et al. Off-centre: Feminism and Cultural Studies*, Harper Collins, London.

Meditch, A. (1975) The development of sex-specific speech patterns in young children, *Anthopological Linguistics*, 17: 421–33.

Mehan, H. (1979) *Learning Lessons: Social Organisation in the Classroom*, Harvard University Press, New York.

Michel, F. (1991) All women are not women all: Ladies Almanack and women's writing, in Broe 1991.

Miller, J. B. (1976) *Towards a New Psychology of Women*, Beacon Press, Boston.

Milroy, L. (1980) *Language and Social Networks*, Basil Blackwell, Oxford.

Mishler, E. G. (1984) *The Discourse of Medecine: Dialectics of Medical Interviews*, Ablex, Norwood, NJ.

Mitchell-Kernan, C. and Kernan, K. (1977) Pragmatics of directive-choice among children, pp. 189–208 in Ervin-Tripp, S. and Mitchell-Kernan (eds) *Child Discourse*, Academic Press, New York.

Modleski, T. (1991) *Feminism without Women: Culture and Criticism in a 'Post-feminist' Age*, Routledge, London.

Murray, O. M. (1983a) The Greek symposium in history, pp. 257–72 in *Tria Corda: Studies in Honour of A Momigliano*, Edizione New Press, Como.

Murray, O. M. (1983b) The symposium as social organisation, pp. 195–9 in R. Hagg (ed.) *The Greek Renaissance of the Eighth Century BC*, Svenska Institut i Athen, Stockholm.

Murray, O. M. (ed.) (1990) *Sympotica*, Clarendon, Oxford.

Murray, O. M. (1993) *Early Greece*, Harper Collins, London.

National Curriculum Council (1989) *English Key Stage 1: Non Statutory Guidance*, York NCC.

Nelson, M. (1988) Women's ways: interactive patterns in predominantly female research teams, pp. 199–232 in Barbara Bate and Anita Taylor (eds) *Women Communicating: Studies of Women's Talk*, Ablex, New Jersey.

Newton, E. (1984) The mythic, mannish lesbian: Radclyffe Hall and the New Woman, *Signs*, 9, 557–75.

Ohala, J. (1984) The phonological end justifies any means, in S. Hattori and K. Inoue (eds) *Proceedings of the XIIIth International Congress of Linguistics*, Tokyo.

O'Leary, V., Unger, R. and Wallston, B. (eds) (1985) *Women, Gender and Social Psychology*, Lawrence Erlbaum, New Jersey.

Oppenheim, A. N. (1992) *Questionnaire Design*, Printe Publishers, London.

Orwell, G. (1983) *Nineteen Eighty-Four*, Penguin, Harmondsworth (first published 1949).

Owens, C. (1984) The medusa effect or the specular ruse, *Art in America*, 72, 97–105.

Page, D. L. (1995) *Sappho and Alcaeus*, Oxford University Press, Oxford.

Page, D. L. (1981) *Further Greek Epigrams*, Cambridge University Press, Cambridge.

Patai, D. (1984) *The Orwell Mystique: A Study in Male Ideology*, University of Massachusetts Press, Amherst.

Phillips, A. (1993) *The Trouble with Boys*, Pandora, London.

Preisler, B. (1986) *Linguistic Sex Roles in Conversation: Social Variation in the Expression of Tentativeness in English*, Mouton de Gruyter, Berlin.

Prothro, E. T. (1961) Childrearing in the Lebanon, Harvard Middle Eastern Monograph Series, Cambridge, MA.

Rich, A. (1975) *Poems: Selected and New 1950–74*, W. W. Norton, New York.

Rich, A. (1976) Is it the lesbian in us .. ? in *On Lies, Secrets and Silences: Selected Prose 1966–78*, Virago, London.

Riddell, S. (1989) Pupils, resistance and gender codes: a study of classroom encounters, *Gender and Education*, 1 (2), 183–97.

Robb, M. and Simmons, J. (1990) Gender comparisons of children's vocal fold contact behaviour, *Journal of the Acoustical Society of America*, 88 (3), 1318–22.

Roberts, M. (1987) *The Book of Mrs Noah*, Methuen, London.

Rosen, R. and Brawer, C. (eds) (1990) *Making their Mark: Women Artists Move into the Mainstream*, Abbeville Press, New York.

Rossi, L. (1983) Il simposio greco arcaico come spectacolo e se stesso, pp. 41–50 in *Atti del VII convegno di Studi: Spettacoli Conviviali*, Centro di studi sul teatro medioevale a rinascinamentale, Viterbo, Maggio.

Rukeyser, M. (1982) *Collected Poems of Muriel Rukeyser*, McGraw-Hill, New York.

Russ, J. (1985) *The Female Man*, The Women's Press, London.

Sachs, J. (1975) Cues to the identification of sex in children's speech, pp. 152–71 in Thorne and Henley 1975.

Sachs, J., Lieberman, P. and Erikson, D. (1973) Anatomical and cultural determinants of male and female speech, pp. 74–84 in R. Shuy and R. Fasold (eds) *Language Attitudes: Current Trends and Prospects*, Georgetown University Press, Washington DC.

Sacks, H., Schegloff, E. and Jefferson, G. (1974) A simplest systematics for the organisation of turn taking in conversation, *Language*, 50, 696–735.

Sadker, M. and Sadker, D. (1985) Sexism in the schoolroom of the 80s, *Psychology Today*, March, 54–7.

Salgado G. (ed.) (1972) *Coney Catchers and Bawdy Baskets*, Penguin, Harmondsworth.

School Examinations and Assessment Council (1992) *Children's Work Assessed, Key Stage 1*, London, The Schools Examinations and Assessment Council (SEAC).

Schultz, M. (1990) The semantic derogation of women, pp. 134–47 in Cameron 1990.

Schwartz, M. and Rine, H. (1968) Identification of speaker sex from isolated whispered vowels, *Journal of the Acoustical Society of America*, 44: 1736–7.

Scott, B. K. (ed.) (1990) *The Gender of Modernism*, Indiana University Press, Bloomington.

Secrest, M. (1974) *Between Me and Life: A Biography of Romaine Brooks*, Macdonald and Janes, New York.

Sheldon, A. (1990) Pickle fights: gendered talk in pre-school disputes, *Discourse Processes*, 13 (1), 5–31.

Sheldon, A. (1992) Conflict talk: sociolinguistic challenges to self-assertion and how young girls meet them, *Merrill-Palmer Quarterly*, 38 (1), 95–117.

Sherzer, J. (1987) A diversity of voices: men's and women's speech in ethnographic perspective, in S. V. Phillips, S. Steele and C. Tanz (eds) *Language, Gender and Sex in Comparative Perspective*, Cambridge University Press, Cambridge.

Showalter, E. (ed.) (1985) *The New Feminist Criticism*, Virago, London.

Showalter, E. (ed.) (1989) *Speaking of Gender*, Routledge, London.

Siegel, J. (1985) Jenny Holzer's language games, *Arts Magazine*, pp. 64–8.

Silveira, J. (1980) Generic masculine words and thinking, *Women's Studies International Quarterly*, 3, 165–78.

Sinclair, J. (1986) Fictional worlds, pp. 43–60 in R. Coulthard (ed.) *Talking about Text*, Discourse Analysis monographs no. 13, ELR, University of Birmingham.

Skinner, M. (1993) Women and Language in Archaic Greece or Why is Sappho a woman?, pp. 125–44 in M. S. Rabinowitz and A. Richlin (eds) *Feminist Theory and the Classics*, Routledge, New York and London.

Slings, S. R. (1990) The I in personal archaic lyric, in S. R. Slings (ed.) *The Poet's 'I' in Archaic Greek Lyric*, VU University Press, Amsterdam.

Slusser, G. (1991) Literary MTV, pp. 334–42 in McCaffery 1991.

Smith, D. (1990) *Texts, Facts and Femininity: Exploring the Relations of Ruling*, Routledge, London.

Smith, P. M. (1985) *Language, the Sexes and Society*, Basil Blackwell, Oxford.

Smith, R. K. and Connolly, K. (1972) Patterns of play and social interaction in pre-school children, in N. B. Jones (ed.) *Ethnological Studies of Child Behaviour*, Cambridge University Press, Cambridge.

Snyder, J. (1989) *The Woman and the Lyre: Women Writers in Classical Greece*, Bristol Classical Press, Bristol.

Sorenson, D. (1989) A fundamental frequency investigation of children aged 6–10 years old, *Journal of Communication Disorders*, 22: 115–23.

Spender, D. (1980) *Man Made Language*, Routledge and Kegan Paul, London.

Spender, D. (1982) *Invisible Women: The Schooling Scandal*, Writers and Readers Publishing Cooperative, London.

Sperling, S. (1991) Baboons with briefcases: feminism, functionalism and sociobiology in the evolution of primate gender, *Signs*, XVII, 1, 1–27.

Squiers, C. (1987) Diversionary syn/tactics: Barbara Kruger has a way with words, *Art News* 85, 77–85.

Stanworth, M. (1981) *Gender and Schooling: A Study of Sexual Divisions in the Classroom*, Hutchinson, London (2nd edition 1983).

Stehle, E. (1990) Sappho's gaze: fantasies of a goddess and young man, in *differences*, 2, 1, 88–125.

Sterling, B. (ed.) (1988) *Mirrorshades*, Paladin, London.

Stigers, E. (1981) Sappho's private world in Foley (ed.), *Reflections of Women in Antiquity*, Gordon and Breach, New York, pp. 219–245.

Still, J. (1990) A feminine economy: some preliminary thoughts, pp. 49–60 in H. Wilcox, K. McWatters, A. Thompson and L. Williams (eds) *The Body and the Test: Hélène Cixous Reading and Teaching*, Harvester Wheatsheaf, Hemel Hempstead.

Stubbs, M. (1983) *Discourse Analysis*, Blackwell, Oxford.

Swann, J. (1988) Gender inequalities in classroom talk, *English in Education*, 22 (1), 48–65.

Swann, J. (1989) Talk control: an illustration from the classroom of problems in analysing male dominance in education, pp. 122–40 in Jennifer Coates and D. Cameron (eds) *Women in their Speech Communities*, Longman, London.

Swann, J. (1992) *Girls, Boys and Language*, Blackwell, Oxford.

Swann, J. and Graddol, D. (1988) Gender inequalities in classroom talk, *English in Education*, 22 (1), 48–65.

Tannen, D. (1990a) Gender differences in topical coherence: creating involvement in best friends' talk, *Discourse Processes*, 13, (1), 73–90.

Tannen, D. (1990b) *You Just Don't Understand*, William Morrow, New York.

Tannen, D. (1992) Response to Senta Troemel-Ploetz's 'Selling the apolitical', *Discourse and Society*, 3 (2), 249–54.

Tatsumi, T. (1988) Some real mothers: an interview with Samuel R. Delaney, *Science Fiction*, 1, 5–11.

Thorne, B. and Henley, N. (eds) (1975) *Language and Sex: Difference and Dominance*, Newbury House, Rowley, MA.

Todd, A. D. and Fisher, S. (1988) *Gender and Discourse: The Power of Talk*, Ablex, New Jersey.

Todd, J. (1989) *The Sign of Angellica: Women, Writing and Fiction 1660–1800*, Women's Press, London.

Town, E. (1983) Jenny Holzer, *Parachute*, Summer, 51–2.

Troemel-Ploetz, S. (1985) Women's conversational culture: rupturing patriarchal discourse, ROLIG-papier 36, Roskilde Universitetcenter, Denmark.

Troemel-Ploetz, S. (1991) Selling the apolitical, *Discourse and Society*, 2 (4), 489–92.

Vetta, M. (1983) (ed.) *Poesia e symposio nella Grecia antica: puida storica e critica*, Rome-Laterza, Bari.

Voigt, E. M. (1971) *Sappho et Alcaeus*, Polak and Van Genep, Amsterdam.

Volosinov, V. (1973) *Marxism and the Philosophy of Language*, Seminar Press, New York.

Vuorenkoski, V. (1978) Fundamental voice frequency during abnormal growth and after androgen treatment, *Archives of Disease of Childhood*, 53: 201–9.

Waldman, D. (1989) *Jenny Holzer: Solomon R. Guggenheim Exhibition Catalogue*, New York.

Walker, G. and Kowalski, C. (1972) On the growth of the mandible, American Journal of Physical Anthropology, 36: 111–17.

Walkerdine, V. (1981) Sex, power and pedagogy, *Screen Education*, 38, 14–24.

Walkderdine, V. (1985) On the regulation of speaking and silence: subjectivity, class and gender in contemporary schooling, pp. 203–37 in C. Steedman, C. Urwin and V. Walkerdine (eds) *Language, Gender and Childhood*, Routledge, London.

Warnock, M. (1987) Why women are their own worst enemies, *Daily Telegraph*, 19 January, p. 10.

Webber, S. (1988) Living proof: a structure for male storytelling events in a Tunisian Mediterranean town, *Edebiyat*, vol II, nos 1–2, 41–76.

Weedon, C. (1987) *Feminist Practice and Poststructuralist Theory*, Basil Blackwell, Oxford.

Weinberg, B. and Bennett, S. (1971) Speaker recognition of 5- and 6-year old children's voices, *Journal of the Acoustical Society of America*, 50: 1210–13.

Weinrich, H. (1978) Sex role socialisation, pp. 18–27 in J. Chetwyns and O. Hartnett (eds) *The Sex Role System: Psychological and Sociological Perspectives*, Routledge, London.

West, C. (1984a) When the doctor is a 'lady': power, status and gender in physician patient encounters, *Symbolic Interaction*, 7, 87–106.

West, C. (1984b) *Routine Complications: Troubles with Talk between Doctors and Patients*, Indiana University Press, Bloomington.

West, C. (1990) Not just 'doctor's ordered': directive–response sequences in patients' visits to women and men physicians, *Discourse and Society*, 1(1), 85–112.

West, C. and Frankel, R. (1991) Miscommunication in medecine, pp. 166–94 in Nikolas Coupland, Howard Giles and John Wiemann (eds) *Miscommunication and Problematic Talk*, Sage Publications, London.

West, C. and Zimmerman, D. (1977) Woman's place in everyday talk: reflections on parent–child interaction, Social Problems 24, 521–9.

West, C. and Zimmerman, D. (1983) Small insults: a study of interruptions in cross-sex conversations between unacquainted persons, in B. Thorne, C. Kramarae and N. Henley (eds) *Language, Gender and Society*, Newbury House, Rowley, MA.

West, C. and Zimmerman, D. (1991) Doing gender, pp. 281–97 in J. Lorber and S. Farrell (eds) *The Social Construction of Gender*, Sage, London.

West, M. L. (1993) *Greek Lyric Poetry*, Clarendon, Oxford.

Whitford, M. (1991) *Luce Irigaray: Philosophy in the Feminine*, Routledge, London.

Whyte, J. (1984) Observing sex stereotypes and interactions in the school lab and workshop, *Educational Review*, 36/1, 75–86.

Whyte, J. (1986) *Girls into Science and Technology: The Story of a Project*, Routledge, London.

Wilkinson, A. with Davies, A. and Atkinson, D. (1965) *Spoken English: University of Birmingham Educational Review*, Occasional Papers 2.

Wilkinson, A, Davies, A. and Berrill, D. (1990) *Spoken English Illuminated*, Open University, Milton Keynes.

Wilson, E. (1975) *Sociobiology*, Harvard University Press, Cambridge, MA.

Winkler, J. J. (1990) Double consciousness in Sappho's Lyrics, pp. 162–87 in *The Constraints of Desire*, Routledge, New York and London.

Wolff, J. (1990) *Feminine Sentences*, Polity Press / Blackwell, Cambridge.

Wolmark, J. (1993) *Aliens and Others, Science Fiction, Feminism and Postmodernism*, Harvester Wheatsheaf, Hemel Hempstead.

Woods, N. (1989) Talking shop: sex and status as determinants of floor apportionment in a work setting, pp. 141–57 in J. Coates and D. Cameron (eds) *Women in their Speech Communities* Longman, London.

Yorke, L. (1991) *Impertinent Voices: Subversive Strategies in Contemporary Women's Poetry*, Routledge, London.

Zimmerman, D. and West, C. (1975) Sex roles, interruptions and silences in conversation, pp. 105–29 in Thorne and Henley 1975.

Index

straight, 4
subject/object, 80–5, 87
Swann, 145, 152, 181
Swann & Graddol, 135, 136
symposia, 79–80
syntax, 108

tag-questions, 38
Tannen, 5, 31-44
Tatsumi, 115
technologies of gender, 122–3
technologisation of discourse, 143
technology, 118, 119
technology of silence, 125
tentative language, 38
Thorne & Henley, 13
Todd, 102
Tongue, 15
topic control, 181
Town, 252
Troemel-Ploetz, 29, 30, 31, 32
turn-taking, 19–21, 23–4, 140

utopia, 131

Vetta, 93
Vincent, 212, 217
visual analysis, 1, 9, 99, 205–56, 258
vocal fold, 198, 200
voice, 38, 115, 194–204, 207, 213, 220
Voigt, 91
Voiscope, 200
Von Freytag, 95–6

Vuoronkovsky, 197

Waldman, 248
Walker & Kowalski, 199
Walkerdine, 157
Warnock, 14
Webber, 193
Weedon, 162, 163, 166, 167, 169, 170, 176
Weinberg & Bennett, 195, 197
Weinrich, 157
West, C., 24, 30, 33
West, M., 92
West & Zimmerman, 158
white, 4
Whitford, 94, 130
Whyte, 135, 174
wildlife programmes, 207–25
Wilkinson, 137, 138–9
Wilson, 222
Winkler, 77, 92, 93
Wolff, 111
Wolmark, 120
woman-centred language, 123
women's discourse, 21–4
women's language, 122, 257
women's public speech, 24–9
women's studies, 2, 3
Woods, 30

Yorke, 74

Zimmerman & West, 20, 33, 181